Robert Morris
The Financier
and
The Finances
of the
American Revolution

Robert Morris The Financier and The Finances of the American Revolution

By

William Graham Sumner

Volume II

BeardBooks
Washington, D.C.

Reprinted 2000 by Beard Books, Washington, D.C.

ISBN 1-893122-98-0

(Vol. II)

Printed in the United States of America

CONTENTS TO VOLUME II.

CHAPTER XVI.

PAGE

ↄAN BY SPAIN; ATTEMPT TO GET SPECIE FROM HAVANA; REMONSTRANCES OF FRANCE AGAINST UNDUE DEPENDENCE ON HER; JAY'S DISTRESS; GILLON AND THE SUPPLIES FROM HOLLAND; THE END OF 1781 . . 1

CHAPTER XVII.

HE BANK OF PENNSYLVANIA AND THE BANK OF NORTH AMERICA 21

CHAPTER XVIII.

XCHANGE, MINT, AND COINAGE 36

CHAPTER XIX.

'82: PEREMPTORY REFUSAL OF AID BY FRANCE: MORRIS'S DISCONTENT; CHARGES AGAINST HIM; ARTHUR LEE'S ACCOUNTS; MORRIS EXPECTED TO DEFAULT; THE LOAN OF 1782 IN HOLLAND; STATE BORROWING; CONTRACTS 48

CHAPTER XX.

HE IMPOST; TAXATION UNTIL 1789 64

CHAPTER XXI.

PAGE

Morris's Unpopularity in the Southern States; More Heterogeneous Tasks; the Memorial of the Army Officers; the Overdraft of January, 1783; More Appeals to France 81

CHAPTER XXII.

Morris Resigns; Consents to continue in order to pay off the Army; Issues Notes for that Purpose; Fault-finding with him; Last Vain Appeals to France; the Loan in Holland; the Overdraft of 1784; Morris quits Office; the Subsequent Organization of the Treasury 94

CHAPTER XXIII.

Review and Summary of Morris's Administration; the Cost of the War 125

CHAPTER XXIV.

The Burden of the War upon the People 135

CHAPTER XXV.

The Notes of Robert Morris 149

CHAPTER XXVI.

Morris's Business Enterprises and Lawsuits, 1783-1793 162

CHAPTER XXVII.

The Bank War of 1785-1786 178

CHAPTER XXVIII.

The Commercial Convention and the Constitutional Convention 193

CHAPTER XXIX.

PAGE

The Accounts of Robert Morris as Agent of the State of Pennsylvania, as Superintendent of Finance, and with the Old Committee of Commerce 205

CHAPTER XXX.

Morris's Social Position and Relations 221

CHAPTER XXXI.

Morris in the Senate of the United States 230

CHAPTER XXXII.

The Federal Capital 235

CHAPTER XXXIII.

Morris's Land Speculations 251

CHAPTER XXXIV.

Was Robert Morris ever Rich? 271

CHAPTER XXXV.

"Confidence has furled her banners, which no longer wave over the heads of M. and N." 279

CHAPTER XXXVI.

Morris's Account of his Property; his Wife's Pension; his Death; his Family; his Estate 293

List of Authorities 307

Index 319

THE FINANCIER

AND THE

FINANCES OF THE AMERICAN REVOLUTION

THE FINANCIER

AND THE

FINANCES OF THE AMERICAN REVOLUTION.

CHAPTER XVI.

LOAN BY SPAIN; ATTEMPT TO GET SPECIE FROM HAVANA; REMONSTRANCES OF FRANCE AGAINST UNDUE DEPENDENCE ON HER; JAY'S DISTRESS; GILLON AND THE SUPPLIES FROM HOLLAND; THE END OF 1781.

WHEN Morris took office, he had eager hopes of loans from Spain. In July, 1781, he wrote a long letter to Jay to stimulate him to apply for such loan, and to provide him with arguments by which he might persuade the Spanish Minister.[1] He proposed that the United States should help Spain to conquer Florida, the Bahamas, and perhaps Jamaica. Then he suggested that Nova Scotia might be conquered, thus depriving Great Britain of ship timber, and obtaining a cheap supply of it for Spain. This would destroy the fisheries of Great Britain, on which she relied as a "nursery for seamen." England could be driven out of the Gulf of Mexico, and Spain could open a port in East Florida for trade with the United States. He wanted a loan of five million dollars. If more could be got, more could be done. The United States "do not mean to beg gratuities, but to make rational requests."

[1] Dip. Corr. Rev. vii. 423.

In a republic, time is sure to be lost before a revenue can be established. He cannot even reform the expenditure without money, because he cannot make contracts, and the people resent taxes while they see the administration loose and wasteful. Paper money has been used too much; hence loans are necessary. He was trying to provide Jay with answers to the reproach that the Americans would not pay taxes, and to the question why they did not tax rather than borrow.

In his eagerness to get resources, Morris even suggested that a loan might be obtained of Portugal. "No chance ought to be neglected."[1]

Jay thought Morris's despatch so good a plea that he had it translated and submitted in full to the Spanish Minister. The latter thought that Morris's requests were very serious, and called for mature consideration. In fact, the despatch contained American arguments and American ideas of what motives ought to influence Spain; but it did not contain any offer to Spain which could really act as an inducement to her. General arguments about the advancement of the purposes of the alliance and about weakening England, although not foreign to her interests and wishes, did not call out her zeal. She wanted Gibraltar, she wanted to close the Mississippi, and she wanted to secure the Gulf of Mexico as a Spanish sea. She wanted to hear some proposition which would bear upon these definite desires.[2]

One of Morris's enterprises, on which he entered with great zeal as soon as he had taken office, was the importation of specie from Havana. The scheme was that this specie should be paid for by bills on Paris drawn against the French loan.

In May, 1781, John Laurens wrote from Paris that the

[1] Dip. Corr. Rev. vii. 442. [2] Cf. vol. i. pp. 249, 256.

Spanish agent was at first very willing to send specie from Mexico to the United States and give it for bills on Paris; but when he heard that the specie had been safely transported to Havana, he refused to furnish the United States with money which would have to be charged against the Spanish loan otherwise than by a bill on the treasury of Spain at six months' sight.[1] This accorded with the resolution of the Spanish government, which they had stated at that time, to pay the subsidy to the United States in six months.[2] Before Laurens's letter reached Morris, however, the latter had entered upon his plan. We have seen above that he wanted five million dollars or more in a loan from Spain. He wanted it sent from Havana in kegs.[3] July 11, he asked Congress to give him control of the frigate "Trumbull."[4] On the 13th he wrote to Franklin about this plan, and argued earnestly to show how much strength would be given to America as a member of the alliance, if this specie could be obtained.[5] On the 17th he applied to the Governor of Havana for $400,000 in silver, and stated his reasons for wanting it, which show what he hoped to gain by this importation of specie when specie was abundant and was coming in by way of commerce.[6] He wanted to deposit the dollars in the bank which he proposed to found, thereby doubling its capital and adding to its power. He goes on to say that Robert Smith has been appointed agent of the United States at Havana. To him a bill on France has been sent that he may negotiate it and ship the money to Morris. Bills on Jay for $120,381 are also sent to Smith to be deposited with the Governor, in the hope that he will advance that sum, in confidence that the court of Spain will give a subsidy of that amount;

[1] Dip. Corr. Rev. ix. 231.
[2] See vol. i. p. 225.
[3] Dip. Corr. Rev. vii. 434.
[4] State Dep. MSS. 137, i. 177.
[5] Dip. Corr. Rev. xi. 379.
[6] See vol. i. p, 98. fg.

if not, Smith is to contract to repay the Governor in flour. All this is sent in one of the continental frigates, which also carries flour to be sold for dollars; Morris also begs that the usual duties on the exportation of specie may be remitted in this case.[1] On the same day he wrote to Robert Smith, who had, it appears, been appointed without his own knowledge or consent, and without salary, — because, as Morris says, the United States cannot afford to pay any, and are engaged in reducing salaries, not in making new ones. He asks him to undertake the negotiation. He adds a warning with respect to the frigate itself. He has forbidden the captain to cruise; but if he should fall in with a good prize on the way, half of it belongs to the continent, and must be remitted in dollars. Finally, he gives Smith an earnest and anxious warning: "Whatever supplies the frigate is absolutely in need of, you must let her have; but I entreat that the expenses may be as moderate as possible, and the best way to secure this is to despatch her quickly, for the moment they get clear of the salt water air and feel their land tacks on board, every soul of them will try to get his hands into your pockets."[2]

All this project, so eagerly planned, came to naught. In August there was reason to fear that the "Trumbull" had been captured, but Morris hoped that the bills had been thrown overboard in time. He wrote to Paris and Madrid to stop payment of them.[3] This letter was captured by the English and published by Rivington. Thereupon several Congressmen called upon Morris to ask why he had stopped payment of bills drawn by order of Congress,[4] and this was the chief result of his enterprise.

In November another effort was made to import specie from Havana on the same plan, and in 1782 still another.[5]

[1] Dip. Corr. Rev. vii. 387. [2] Ibid. 395. [3] Ibid. 436.
[4] Ibid. 468. [5] Ibid. vii. 510: xii. 261.

Morris desisted from his effort in 1781, on account of the arrival of specie obtained by Laurens.[1]

In the Report of 1785, Morris, referring to his attempts to sell bills in Havana, says: "At that time there was a loss of ten per cent on bills sold here; whereas the demand for money in Cadiz was such, and such the desire to remit it thither from Havana, as to promise a considerable gain. In fact, it appeared by Mr. Brown's report that bills of *indisputable credit* might have been negotiated at Havana for an advance of twenty to thirty per cent, and the accounts will show that there was also an advance on the negotiations from Cadiz to Paris, and from thence to Amsterdam. If, therefore, the plan had succeeded in all its parts, $400,000 in Europe would have produced near $600,000 here, instead of $360,000, — the most which could otherwise be obtained. But, unfortunately, the credit of the United States was not so well established at the Havana as that merchants would hazard the purchase of American *public bills* to any considerable amount or at the usual price."

In the same Report the loss of this adventure in 1781 is stated at $2,509. In the quarter ending March 31, 1783, Brown exported from Havana specie obtained for flour to the amount of $72,247, the export duty on which was nine and a half per cent.

Probably in October Morris received a long despatch of July 26 from Franklin, about Laurens's visit and the money recalled from Holland. All of the six millions had been taken in specie to America, or had been spent in Europe, and the ten million loan had failed. "By these means you have really at present no funds here to draw upon." But, as we have seen, Congress had authorized Morris on June 4 to use the six millions, whether we are to

[1] Dip. Corr. Rev. xii. 44.

understand that Washington drew the bills or that Morris drew them. The arrival of the specie had been hailed as a great piece of good fortune; but it was now learned that it had come out of Franklin's six millions, and that the rest of that had been spent, while many bills had no doubt already been drawn against it. In this month the strain of the Yorktown campaign was at its greatest. Franklin ended his despatch by begging Morris to remit to him before December, when his acceptances would fall due, "otherwise I shall be ruined with the American credit in Europe." [1]

This last demand was painfully ludicrous, in view of the situation here. Instead of taking any steps to comply with it, Morris and Livingston wrote long despatches in November, urging that France must lend more money.[2] Morris's despatch covers thirty pages, and gives a description of the situation, a review of the year, and a statement of the needs of the next year. Bills for two and a half million livres, which had been given to Beaumarchais in 1779, drawn for three years, would have to be met in the next year. Livingston argued eagerly to Franklin that France must advance more money. "The total abolition of paper, the length of the war, the restricted commerce we have carried on for the first five years of it, the arrears of debt, and the slender thread by which public credit hangs, put it totally out of our power to make any great exertions without the immediate supply of money. Taxation will be carried as far as it can go, but this will fall very far short of our wants. The richest nations in Europe, unable to carry on a war by taxation only, are compelled to borrow. How then will it be expected that a nation which has had every difficulty to struggle with, — an enemy in the heart of its country, and all its considerable towns at one

1 Dip. Corr. Rev. xi. 407.

2 Ibid. xii. 27, 52.

time or another in their possession, a superior navy on its coast, and the consequent ruin of agriculture and commerce, — how, I say, can it be expected that such a nation should find resources within itself for so long and bloody a war? . . . Surely it is not possible that France, after having done so much for us, after having brought us within view of the desired haven, should oblige us to lose the advantage of all she has done. And yet, be assured that the most serious consequence may attend her stopping her hand at this critical time. Public credit, which is growing very fast, will drop to the ground. . . . You are perfectly acquainted, sir, with the natural resources of the country. You know the value of our exports and the security they afford for any debts that we may contract. . . . Congress are preparing for an active campaign. They have directed eight millions of dollars to be raised by a tax. There is not, however, the least idea that this, or even one half of it, will be collected in the time specified. You will not, therefore, suffer the court to deceive themselves by hopes of exertions founded on this measure, but urge again and again the absolute necessity of supplying money."[1]

In November Morris and Luzerne were engaged in a controversy as to whether Morris had drawn bills beyond the limit allowed him by the Minister. Morris was in the utmost financial necessity. The best answer he could make was: "I shall not dwell on the consequences of my efforts: enough of them are known to speak for themselves, and I leave to your knowledge and observation the comparison of our public affairs now with what they were exactly six months ago.[2]

In September Jay wrote to Franklin that he was sure that Morris would abandon "the singular policy of drawing bills without previous funds."[3] Morris did not aban-

[1] Dip. Corr. Rev. iii. 200. [2] Ibid. xii 23. [3] Ibid. viii. 23.

don it, however, because he had no other resource than his hopes of what might be obtained in Europe. The whole cause thus came to hang upon the European aid, and that meant upon Franklin's influence with the French court. There had been a promise that no more bills should be drawn without previous funds after April 1, 1781; but, in January, 1782, Franklin wrote that they continued to come, drawn on Jay, Adams, Laurens, and himself. He suspected that they were antedated to conceal a breach of the promise.[1] Were these drawn by Morris? Were they really old bills? How did the bills which were put in Morris's hands in June stand related to this promise? As late as May, 1783, Morris wrote: "The bills drawn by order of Congress at a long sight on their ministers, as well in Spain and Holland as in France, have involved the affairs of my department in a labyrinth of confusion, from which I cannot extricate them, and I very much fear that many of these bills will have been twice paid." [2]

November 5, 1781, the King of France borrowed for the United States, on his own credit, the ten millions which he had agreed in February that he would guarantee, but which, for political and other reasons, it had not been possible for the United States to borrow.

December 31, Vergennes wrote to Franklin: "I shall not enter into an examination of the successive variations and augmentations of your demands on me for funds to meet your payments." He promises to put a million at Franklin's disposal. "But I think it my duty, sir, to inform you that if Mr. Morris issues drafts on this same million, I shall not be able to provide for the payment of them, and shall leave them to be protested." He tells

[1] Franklin in France, ii. 30.

[2] Dip. Corr. Rev. xii. 359. Barclay wrote to Morris, October 23, 1783, that he found in John Adams's bill-book that one bill had apparently been paid twice (Dip. Corr. Rev. i. 494).

him also flatly that, if he has accepted drafts for more than that sum, he must look to himself how he meets them. Vergennes will only meet those of Morris, provided they do not exceed the remainder of the Dutch loan, after taking out this million.[1]

On the 1st of August previous, Luzerne had written to Vergennes [2] that Congress had neglected to provide financial resources, because there were rumours of another loan from France. Perhaps this letter caused the peremptory tone of the French minister at the end of the year. Morris and Hamilton thought that the States had been made negligent by relying on France.[3]

In October, 1781, Jay reported the Spanish Minister as saying that "the good disposition of Congress toward Spain had not as yet been evinced in a manner the king expected, and that no one advantage had hitherto been proposed by America to Spain to induce the latter to come into the measures we desire."[4]

In November, 1781, Jay wrote another begging letter, on account of $31,809 bills to be paid the next month. To this he never received any answer. He therefore turned to Franklin, writing: "It seems as if my chief business here was to fatigue you and our good allies with incessant solicitations on the subject of the ill-timed bills drawn upon me by Congress. It is happy for me that you are a philosopher, and for our country, that our allies are indeed our friends."[5] January 19, 1782, Franklin answered, telling the story of Gillon and the ships in Holland, but promising Jay part of the million livres which he had just obtained. "What I am to do afterwards, God knows."[6]

[1] Dip. Corr. Rev. viii. 54. [2] Durand, 251.
[3] Dip. Corr. Rev. xii. 52; Hamilton's Works, i. 245.
[4] Johnston's Jay, ii. 81. [5] Dip. Corr. Rev. viii. 42.
[6] Ibid. 57.

During the winter of 1781–82 the Spanish Minister expressed the king's displeasure at the silence of Congress about returns for this kindness, especially about the ships building in New England. Jay could only refer to the concession which he had made under the orders of Congress, about the navigation of the Mississippi; but Spain now treated this as a mere recognition of right, to which she allowed no value. March 2, 1782, Jay declared that he had nothing more to offer.[1] The French Minister at Madrid tried to persuade Florida Blanca to yield to the requests of the Americans. He wrote to Vergennes, March 30, 1782, that the American envoy was then in great distress on account of bills to the amount of $40,000 or $50,000, which had been protested. He thought that Florida Blanca was hostile to American independence.

Florida Blanca, in fact, entertained the deepest dread and suspicion of the United States. In 1787 he prepared a secret memorial for the Council of State, which was in fact a program of Spanish policy for the immediate future. It covered all points of internal and external policy, and was, in many respects, remarkably enlightened. As to the United States, however, he bitterly refers to the claim to navigate the Mississippi, based on a treaty with England; expresses apprehension at the possible growth of a powerful neighbour to the Spanish possessions, and speculates on the chances of internal discord in the United States, which he thinks very great. It should be the policy of Spain to watch and foster this discord and profit by it. He never had a disposition to help the United States.[2]

In April, 1782, Livingston wrote to Jay that the reasons of the Americans for sending a minister to Spain were "to solicit the favourable attention of his Catholic Majesty to

[1] Johnston's Jay, ii. 182.

[2] Obras de Florida Blanca, 228.

a people who were struggling with oppression, and whose success or miscarriage could not but be important to a sovereign who held extensive dominions in their vicinity."[1]

These reasons weighed very little at Madrid.

April 30, 1782, Congress resolved that they were surprised that their offer about the Mississippi had been fruitless, and directed Jay to urge a speedy concession of an equivalent by Spain.[2] August 7, they resolved to make no treaty with Spain, — that is, they withdrew this offer.[3]

In June Jay went to Paris, as one of the Commissioners to negotiate the peace. This chapter of the attempt to get aid in Europe was then closed. Unfortunately, the payment of the $150,000, which was obtained through this humiliating negotiation, was in default for several years, which was more humiliating still.

January 25, 1782, Luzerne informed Congress of the tenour of despatches to him dated September 7.[4] Therefore it was probably about the same date that Morris received Franklin's despatch of September 12, containing better news. Franklin had a promise of money with which to pay the bills for the purchases in Holland, so that he would not need the remittances for that purpose. "I shall finish the year with honour, but it is as much as I can do, with the aid of the sum I stopped in Holland, the drafts on Mr. Jay and on Mr. Adams much exceeding what I had been made to expect. I had been informed that the Congress had promised to draw no more bills on Europe after the month of March last till they should know they had funds here; but I learn from Mr. Adams that some bills have been lately presented to him, drawn June 22, on Mr. Laurens, who is in the Tower, which makes the proceeding seem extraordinary." He sees by the minutes of

[1] Dip. Corr. Rev. viii. 15.

[2] Secret Journ. iii. 98.

[3] Thomson Papers.

[4] Secret Journ. iii. 85.

Congress that they have stopped drawing on the other ministers, but not on him; which he says terrifies him, for he has promised Vergennes to accept no more unless he has funds, or that he does it at his peril. So he fears that the bills must go back protested. Gillon has sailed from Holland without taking under convoy the two vessels that were freighted to carry the goods purchased by Captain Jackson in Holland. "There has been terrible management there, and from the confusion in the ship before and when she sailed, it is a question if she ever arrives in America."[1]

The two ships under convoy returned. In November Franklin wrote further about this affair, which had wasted the help which he had begged with such pertinacity. His last aids have all been used up by the drafts on Jay and Adams, for Adams did not get any loan in Holland; and also by the enormous unexpected purchases in Holland by Jackson, which were to have gone in Captain Gillon's ship, but were left behind. He now hears from Amsterdam that the two ships which were to carry the goods have not yet sailed, because their contract was to sail under convoy of the "South Carolina" which left them. Now the owners demand higher freight, or that Congress should buy the ships. He expresses his distrust of Gillon. He had promised to pay for ten thousand pounds' sterling worth of goods, said to be shipped on Gillon's ship, and afterward allowed five thousand pounds more. Bills were sent in to him for fifty thousand pounds. He refused to pay; but Jackson finally persuaded him to do it, and he was obliged to go to the Minister to beg for more, and for goods bought in another country. At length he succeeded in getting it. Then the officers of the ship declared her overloaded, and the goods were put into two other ships.

[1] Dip. Corr. Rev. xi. 469.

Then these were left behind, and now he must buy them or pay increased freight, and he does not see how to make a new demand on France for this. "The very friendly disposition of this court toward us still continues, and will, I hope, continue forever. From my own inclination, as well as in obedience to the orders of Congress, everything in my power shall be done to cultivate that disposition; but I trust it will be remembered that the best friends may be overburdened, — that by too frequent, too large, and too importunate demands upon it, the most cordial friendship may be wearied; and as nothing is more teasing than repeated, unexpected large demands for money, I hope the Congress will absolutely put an end to the practice of drawing on their ministers, and thereby obliging them to worry their respective courts for the means of payment."[1]

In a letter to Jay in January, he complains of the waste in Holland and the abuse of French generosity to which he is driven. "I had worried this friendly and generous court with often-repeated after-clap demands, occasioned by these unadvised (as well as ill-advised), and therefore unexpected, drafts, and was ashamed to show my face to the Minister. . . . We have been assisted with nearly twenty millions since the beginning of last year, besides a fleet and army; and yet I am obliged to worry them with my solicitations for more, which make us appear insatiable."[2]

It was a common complaint against Franklin in America, that he was timid about asking aid of France.

December 4, 1781, Adams wrote from Amsterdam to the President of Congress that the goods left behind by Commodore Gillon were detained for freight and damages. He was trying to get them free and send them over. "This

[1] Dip. Corr. Rev. iii. 245.

[2] Ibid. viii. 57.

piece of business has been managed as ill as any that has ever been done for Congress in Europe, whether it is owing to misfortune, want of skill, or anything more disagreeable." [1]

In the accounts of the banker Grand, there is an entry for the purchase made in Holland by Jackson, "which was detained there," $227,635.

The painter Trumbull, Major Jackson, and several other Americans took passage in the "South Carolina." She met with a storm, and was obliged to go around Scotland. Trumbull says that the ship was saved by Captain Barney, who assumed command of her.

We next hear of Gillon, after he left Holland, in the public documents, at Corunna, in October. The Spanish Minister called on Jay to account for two men on board the ship, who were alleged to be Spanish deserters. After that a quarrel arose between Gillon and Colonel Searle, which Jay was called on to settle, but he could not quit his post.[2] At Corunna, Trumbull and some of the other passengers left the ship, "tired of the management of the "South Carolina."[3]

April 18, 1782, the Governor of South Carolina had news from Philadelphia that Gillon had arrived at Havana with five prizes, worth one hundred and fifty thousand hard dollars.[4] In May, Gillon, with his ship, helped the Spaniards to conquer the Bahamas, from which action there arose a claim against Spain.[5]

In June Franklin wrote to Morris a long recapitulation of this misconduct, and of the trouble and expense to which he had been subjected by it. The charges alone were nearly forty thousand florins. He asks where Gillon

[1] Dip. Corr. Rev. vi. 205.
[2] Ibid. viii. 26.
[3] Trumbull, 83.
[4] Gibbes, 168.
[5] Dip. Corr. U. S. iii. 132; vi. 330; Journ. Cong. ix. 134.

can now be found. "Perhaps, since his success in the West Indies, he may venture into an American port, in which case it would be well to secure him and make him account for the £10,000 sterling he received of me in consequence of his agreement with Colonel Laurens."[1] At about the same time Morris was writing to Franklin, in equal anxiety and dissatisfaction, about the same affair. If the cargo of the "Lafayette," he says, was like some that had been received, the capture of it was no great loss, for the clothing was too small. "The goods from Holland we still most anxiously expect. Would to God that they never had been purchased! Mr. Gillon, however, is at length arrived, and I hope we shall have those matters in which he was concerned brought to some kind of settlement."[2]

These goods now, which were left behind by Gillon, on which Franklin's and Morris's money had been spent, reached the United States in September, 1782, — nearly a year after Yorktown, and within a few weeks of the preliminary treaty of peace.[3] The only explanation ever suggested why Gillon escaped trial is by Chastellux's translator: "The universal esteem in which Mrs. Gillon, his wife, was held by every person in Carolina."[4] November 1, 1782, a committee appointed by Congress to inquire into the causes of the detention of the goods purchased in Holland, reported. On motion of the delegates from South Carolina, the report was referred to Morris. If he should find that the United States had cause of action for damages against Gillon as representing South Carolina, he was to submit to arbitration the dispute between the United States and South Carolina.[5]

1 Franklin in France, ii. 35.

2 Dip. Corr. Rev. xii. 203.

3 Ibid. viii. 119.

4 Chastellux, i. 192.

5 Gillon was in Congress in 1793–94, and died in 1794 (Lanman). The "South Carolina" was captured off the capes of Delaware at the end of 1782 (Almon, 1783, Part i. 227).

The total receipts of the year 1781 were $1,030,084. They consisted of the following items, fractions of a dollar being omitted:[1] —

Bills of exchange sold	$294,165
Specie from France	462,597
Paper money negotiations	62,001
Yorktown booty	71,439
Specific supplies of Pennsylvania	101,054
Prizes	34,717
Sundries	4,106

The expenditures were $723,459. The heaviest expenditures were: —

Salaries and expenses of civil officers	$15,302
Marine	87,608
Paymaster	140,965
Military and ordnance stores	39,573
Quartermaster-general	110,330
Army subsistence	114,997
Army clothing	60,560
Medical department	10,090
Payment of old accounts	115,196

Under the expenses we find: —

Household of the President of Congress	$4,197
Officers of Congress	3,291
Expenses of Congress	840
Officers of the Treasury department	2,053
Expenses of the Treasury department	1,038
Household of the Commander-in-chief	2,780[2]

Of the receipts, the bills of exchange consisted of $52,720 of bills used by Morris out of those put at his disposal by the Resolution of June 4, 1781,[3] and $19,425 in bills on France received for flour sold to the French army agents, — together, $72,145. The rest consisted of bills drawn on

[1] Reports of 1785 and 1790.

[2] Including $260 for silverware.

[3] See vol. i. p. 280.

the bankers, Le Couteulx and Grand, in the hope that they would have funds obtained from the French government. The total of bills drawn was $367,516, on which the loss below five livres and eight sous per dollar was $42,785, leaving a net product of $324,731. Of this, Morris spent $30,565 in buying paper money in his operation of "appreciation," so that the money for that was borrowed of France. Of the total of bills, $295,371 were drawn on the bankers. Of this, $221,296 fell on Le Couteulx. It exceeded the loans and subsidies from France put in his hands by $141,953; so that the United States had overdrawn their account with him by that amount. $74,075 were drawn on Grand in the shape of 400,000 livres in "conditional orders." The debt to Grand, however, at the end of 1781 was $1,158,895; whereas, at the beginning of that year, it had been $1,576,591,—a reduction of $417,696. This was because of the large amount of the French loans and subsidies deposited with him. The net reduction of the debt to the bankers for the year was $275,743; and the debt to both, January 1, 1782, was $1,300,848.

Of the old accounts paid, the largest amounts were to John Ross $79,399, and to William Bingham $18,518. Of pensions, the largest amount was $2,452 to the children of General Warren. Five hundred and twelve dollars were paid for educating three Indian youths at Princeton College by order of Congress. The delegates from the three southern invaded States were paid $7,813 from the federal treasury. The expenses of bringing the specie from Boston were $5,853. Sixteen dollars were paid to John Dolly for ringing bells on the surrender of York.

The following are the only criticisms on Morris which we have found belonging to the year 1781. The first is by Varnum of Rhode Island:[1] "Mr. Morris's personal credit here, as well as in Europe, is very extensive, and no other man could effect as much as Mr. Morris. We have already experienced the happy consequences of his appointment in a great retrenchment of expenses. He is now taking effectual measures to simplify the various departments, and calling to account those who have basely wasted the public funds. . . . The evils have been so multiplied, and the indemnities so certain, in the estimation of public servants, that sporting with public property has become familiar, and the multiplication of dependents in every department has been so enormous, the feeling as well as views of many individuals will be greatly affected by the necessary alterations." He goes on to speak of the difficulty of reform, and the vested interest in abuses which makes reformers unpopular. "From these reforms alone I can take on me to affirm that the public will annually gain several millions of specie dollars, — an important consideration, when we reflect what relief it will afford the people already groaning under the burden of enormous taxes. I must now take the liberty of subjoining that from the knowledge, integrity, and credit of the Financier, we may expect the most beneficial effects from his administration; but he must be supported by the States."

In November President Reed wrote to General Greene: Congress have lost authority by the failure of public credit. It was necessary to appoint a pecuniary dictator. "Mr. Morris, who had been long pursuing a gainful traffic from which others were excluded by embargo and restrictions, naturally presented himself as combining the necessary qualities; but his terms were high, and, at first blush, inadmissible. He claimed a right of continuing in private trade, of dismissing all continental officers, handling public

[1] To Governor Greene, July 2; Staples, 346.

money at pleasure, with many lesser privileges amounting to little less than an engrossment of all those powers of Congress which had been deemed incommunicable, and which we had sometimes thought they exercised with rather too much hauteur. However, Mr. Morris was inexorable, Congress at his mercy, and finally the appointment was made with little relaxation from the original conditions; since which the business of that august body has been extremely simplified, Mr. Morris having relieved them from all business of deliberation, and of executive difficulty with which money is in any respect connected, and they are now very much at leisure to read despatches, return thanks, pay and receive compliments, etc. For form's sake some things go thither to receive a sanction, but it is the general opinion that it is form only. But it would not be doing justice not to acknowledge that, humiliating as this power is, it has been exercised with much advantage for the immediate relief of our distresses, and that the public have received a real benefit from Mr. Morris's exertions. At the same time, those who know him will also acknowledge that he is too much a man of the world to overlook certain private interests which his command of the paper and occasional speculations in that currency will enable him to promote. It seems to have ever been a ruling principle with him to connect the public service with private interests, and he certainly has not departed from it at this time of day. His influence is also great, not to say irresistible, in the appointment of other officers not connected with his own department, of which we have had recent proof in the appointment of a minister for foreign affairs and that of the war department; Mr. R. Livingston having, after much opposition, been appointed to the former, and General Schuyler standing fairest for the latter." After speaking of the hostility to Schuyler, he adds: "This is Mr. Morris's doing, and it is wondrous in our eyes. . . . I say nothing of the whole appointment's wearing so much the appearance of cabal, when at the same time you consider that Mr. Gouverneur Morris is the Financier's assistant, and, censorious people say, his director." [1]

In December the Rhode Island delegates, in their report to the Governor,[2] wrote: "The established character of the Superintendent of Finance, his abilities, numerous correspondents in different parts of the world, and permanent property, give great advantages in the execution of the important trusts he is honoured with. The public debts that have accumulated previous to his coming into office were numerous, and the public creditors exceeding clamorous. They now think that the debts of the longest standing should be paid first. It appears to be justice, but policy forbids the measure, when our very existence as a people calls aloud that the wheels of the present movement be kept in motion."

[1] Reed's Reed, ii. 374. [2] Staples, 359.

CHAPTER XVII.

THE BANK OF PENNSYLVANIA AND THE BANK OF NORTH AMERICA.

IN a speech in the Pennsylvania Assembly, in 1786, on the Act to Charter the Bank of North America, Morris said that although the proprietary government "had no idea of a bank, the commercial men of the Province had, and I, as a merchant, laid the foundation of one, and established a credit in Europe for the purpose. From the execution of this design I was prevented only by the Revolution."[1] Silas Deane submitted to Congress a plan for a bank, with a capital of a million and a half sterling.[2] It was suggested in the scheme of reconciliation which the Carlisle commission brought to America that a bank might be formed to provide for the continental paper currency.[3] Hamilton had a bank scheme in mind, probably in 1779.[4] The first real step toward an institution of that kind was independent of all these plans.

On the 4th of June, 1780, Paine wrote to Joseph Reed, urging that a subscription should be raised to obtain recruits and supplies.[5] The idea took root. Paine was then Clerk of the Assembly of Pennsylvania. It was expected that Charleston would be taken, and many members of the Pennsylvania Assembly brought petitions from their constituents against taxation. A letter from the General set forth the sad state of the army. It produced great gloom. Paine says that he subscribed $500, and the next day

[1] Carey's Debates, 37. [2] Dip. Corr. Rev. i. 160. [3] Stevens, 440. [4] Hamilton, 107. [5] Reed's Reed, ii. 218.

M'Clenahan and Morris subscribed each £200 in hard money. On the 14th came the news of the loss of Charleston. On the 17th a meeting was held, at which it was resolved to open a security subscription to the amount of £300,000 of Pennsylvania currency, but in real money, the subscribers to execute bonds for their subscriptions and to form a bank thereon for supplying the army.[1] June 21, the Board of War informed Congress that a number of patriotic persons had formed a bank, whose object is the public service. They ask for a committee of Congress to confer with them. The committee was appointed, and next day reported the plan of the bank. The offer of the persons who formed it was to provide on their own credit, and by their own exertions, three million rations and three hundred hogsheads of rum, without profit to themselves, but asking security for their payment. The faith of the United States was pledged to them, and the Board of Treasury was directed to deliver to them bills of exchange drawn in their favour on the envoys in Europe, for a sum not exceeding a hundred and fifty thousand pounds sterling, as a guarantee of payment within six months.[2]

Morris described the bank, in a letter several years later, as "in fact nothing more than a patriotic subscription of continental money . . . for the purpose of purchasing provisions for a starving army."[3] A notice was issued by the bank: "All persons who have already lent money are desired to apply for bank-notes, and the directors request the favour of those who may hereafter lodge their cash in the bank, that they would tie it up in bundles of bills of one denomination, with labels, their names endorsed, as the business will thereby be done with less trouble and greater despatch."[4] Hamilton criticised this bank because its pur-

[1] Paine's Works, i. 372.
[2] Journ. Cong. vi. 65.
[3] Ford MSS.
[4] Lewis, 22.

chases were made with its "stock," that is, its capital, and not with its notes; so that it was only a particular subscription for a particular purpose, and not an institution.[1]

From these remarks about the bank we may infer what its plan of operation was. Continental or State paper was brought into it as a subscription, for which the subscriber obtained the (no doubt interest-bearing) notes of the bank, payable in six months. The supplies were bought with the currency which the subscribers had brought in. The bills drawn on the envoys were held as collateral security until Congress paid for the supplies. The bills might be negotiated; but it was the understanding that they would not be, for it was well understood that they were not drawn for value legitimately at the disposal of the drawer, but on the chances that the envoys could borrow or beg funds with which to pay them, if they should be negotiated and presented.

Reed belittled this bank enterprise, as he was bound to do from his party position. He said that he would support the bank, although there were secondary views and party spirit in it. The bank consisted of opponents of the Pennsylvania Constitution.[2] That the bank was a political engine is evident from the fact that when Washington tried to spur President Reed to greater energy, in July, 1780, he put the argument to him that the bank was in the hands of his political enemies and would be used against him.[3]

In May just previously, the ladies of Philadelphia had collected by subscription $300,000 in paper currency, of the value of $7,500. Reed compared this disparagingly with the bank subscription, which amounted to only $315,000 in paper. The subscription of the ladies included coloured women, the Marchioness de Lafayette, and the Countess de Luzerne.[4]

[1] Hamilton's Works, i. 223.

[2] Reed's Reed, ii. 216.

[3] Ibid. 220.

[4] Ibid. 261.

The bank was called the Bank of Pennsylvania, and began operations July 17, 1780, on Front Street, two doors above Walnut. The last instalment of the subscription was called up November 15, and the bank was wound up at the end of the year 1784.[1] November 29, the Pennsylvania Assembly appointed a committee to confer with the directors of the Bank of Pennsylvania on the practicability of an immediate supply of ten thousand bushels of corn and forage for the federal army on three or six months' credit, to be paid for in current money of that State, equal in value to gold and silver.[2] In May, 1781, Reed wrote to Washington that the notes of the bank would no longer circulate; that they soon lost credit, but that the bank ruined the paper money of the State.[3]

In May, 1781, before he had assumed the office of Financier, Morris submitted to Congress his plan of a bank.[4] "Anticipation of taxes and funds," he wrote, "is all that ought to be expected from any system of paper credit."[5] He proposed that Congress should apply to the States for power to incorporate the bank. In his use of language, "funds" meant separate forms or branches of revenue. By "anticipations" he meant paper evidences of debt issued for obligations of the government, with the intention that they should be cancelled by the revenue when it came in. His doctrine, therefore, was that paper ought not to be used except to anticipate taxes. His plan was to borrow of the bank. This loan he would obtain in bank-notes. He could pay out the notes for his obligations. The notes would be receivable (as he hoped) by the States and the

[1] Lewis, 22; see page 29.

[2] Penn. Journ. i. 542.

[3] Reed's Reed, ii. 300.

[4] Gouverneur Morris claimed that he planned the bank (Morris's Morris, i 15). Hamilton made suggestions for it. These three men very often acted together.

[5] Dip. Corr. Rev. xi. 364.

United States for taxes. Thus, either in taxes or requisitions, they would return to him, and he could return them to the bank in payment of the loan.

May 26, 1781, Congress approved of the plan of the bank as follows: There were to be four hundred shares of $400 each, with liberty to increase the capital. The state of the cash account and circulation was to be made known to the Superintendent of Finance every evening except Sunday; the States were to make the notes, if payable on demand, receivable in duties and taxes; the Superintendent of Finance was to have access to all books and papers; the States were to make laws to punish embezzlement in the bank as felony; no director was to be paid for his services. On the question to incorporate the bank, Massachusetts voted no; Pennsylvania was divided. Madison voted no. The States were asked not to charter any other bank during the war, and to pass the other votes called for by the plan.[1]

On the same day Morris wrote to Hamilton, in answer to Hamilton's suggestions of April 30, "I have thought much about interweaving a security[2] with the capital of this bank, but am apprehensive it would convey to the public mind an idea of paper being circulated on that credit; and that the bank in consequence must fail in its payments in case of any considerable run on it. And we must expect that its ruin will be attempted by external and internal foes."[3]

The next thing he had to do was to overcome prejudice and opposition and secure subscriptions. A writer over the signature of "Walsingham" had apparently already begun to break the way for him.[4] He started from the

[1] Journ. Cong. vii. 87.

[2] That is, some of the evidences of the public debt.

[3] Dip. Corr. Rev. xi. 366.

[4] Moore's Diary, ii. 422.

evils of depreciation and the causes of it. He attributed it chiefly to the quantity of the notes and to the measures which had been taken to prevent it. He denied that it was attributable to the tories, speculators, etc., and proposed a bank "where specie may be lodged in safety. Let bills be issued, signed by the Financier-general, subject to be exchanged at the pleasure of the holder for specie at this bank. One million of Spanish dollars, under the management of a gentleman of established credit and ample fortune, would serve as a fund for ten millions of paper dollars." As an alternative he proposes that the government should issue bills, and lay taxes to cancel them within twelve months. In the "Packet" of May 29, the plan of the bank was published, with the resolutions of Congress and an explanatory letter by Morris. In the last he said: "To ask the end which it is proposed to answer by this institution of a bank is merely to call the public attention to the situation of our affairs. A depreciating paper currency has unhappily been the source of infinite private mischief, numberless frauds, and the greatest distress. The national calamities have moved with an equal pace, and the public credit has received the deepest injury. This is a circumstance so unusual in a republican government that we may boldly affirm it cannot continue a moment after the several legislatures have determined to take those vigorous and effectual measures to which the public voice now loudly commands their attention. In the mean time the exigencies of the United States require an anticipation of our revenues, while at the same time there is not such confidence established as will call out for that purpose the funds of individual citizens. The use, then, of a bank is to aid the government by their moneys and credit, for which they will have every proper reward and security; to gain from individuals that credit which property, abilities, and integrity never fail to command; to supply the loss of that paper money which, becoming more and more useless, calls every day more loudly for its final redemption; and to give a new spring to commerce in a moment when, by the removal of all restrictions, the citizens of America shall enjoy and possess that freedom for which they contend."

On the 11th of June, 1781, he issued a circular explaining and recommending the bank.[1] In that and the following month he wrote long letters to Franklin, Jay, and Robert Smith, dilating upon his hopes and plans in regard to this, which was now his pet project. "This country by relying too much on paper is in a condition of peculiar disorder and debility. To rescue and restore her is an object equal to my warmest wishes, though probably beyond the strength of my abilities. Success will greatly depend on the pecuniary aid we may obtain from abroad, because money is necessary to introduce economy, while at the same time economy is necessary to obtain money." He then mentions the national bank. "I mean to render this a principal pillar of American credit, so as to obtain the money of individuals for the benefit of the Union, and thereby bind those individuals more strongly to the general cause by the ties of private interest."[2] "When once by punctual payment the notes of the bank have obtained full credit, the sum in specie which will be deposited will be such that the bank will have the interest of a stock two or three times larger than that which it really possesses."[3] A reason for establishing the bank is "that the small sums advanced by the holders of bank stock may be multiplied in the usual manner by means of their credit, so as to increase the resource which government can draw from it, and at the same time, by placing the collective mass of

[1] Dip. Corr. Rev. xi. 374. [2] Ibid. 378. [3] Ibid. 392.

private credit between the lenders and borrowers, supply at once the want of ability in the one and of credit in the other." He expects to supply the place of the other paper, which he intends to absorb as soon as possible, "and thereby to relieve the people from those doubts and anxieties which have weakened our efforts, relaxed our industry, and impaired our wealth." He hopes by the bank "to unite the several States more closely together in one general money connection, and indissolubly to attach many powerful individuals to the cause of our country by the strong principle of self-love and the immediate sense of private interest. . . . I am determined that the bank shall be well supported until it can support itself, and then it will support us. I mean that the stock, instead of $400,000, shall be £400,000, and perhaps more. How soon it will rise to that amount, it is impossible to foresee; but this we may venture to assert, that, if a considerable sum of specie can be speedily thrown into it, the period when its force and utility will be felt and known is not far off." [1]

He wrote to Franklin that the bank must control the exchanges by having control of all the bills, and he asked him to tell the bankers that he, Morris, intended to make the capital ten times what it was.

In 1786 he said that the subscriptions to the bank had not, up to September 1, exceeded $70,000.[2] In September the "Magicienne" arrived at Boston with the silver which John Laurens brought. The amount was $462,862. Morris put this in the bank; but half of it was drawn out and expended before the bank started.

In June, 1781, he reported to Congress that the nonpayment of the sums due to the Bank of Pennsylvania by Congress hindered the subscriptions to the new bank. Congress were not willing to sell the bills lodged as secu-

[1] Dip. Corr. Rev. vii. 439.

[2] Carey's Debates, 48.

rity, lest the minister at Madrid should be incommoded. Morris proposed that the bills be put at his disposal; he thinks he can pay the debt and cause the money to be subscribed to the national bank, and at the same time use the bills so that they will not be presented for a long time, or not at all. In the diary of July 4, he mentions that he met the directors of the Pennsylvania Bank, and proposed that they should transfer their subscriptions from the Pennsylvania to the national bank, and deliver up to him the bills of exchange which they held as security, while he would pay to the commissioners of the national bank what remained due to the old bank from Congress. They all agreed.[1]

Morris paid to the Pennsylvania Bank, in January, 1782, $20,572; in April, $7,081; in November, $5,929; in July, 1784, a fraction of a cent, which seems to be entered to mark that the account was closed.[2]

A meeting was held November 1 to organize the new bank. It consisted of the members of the Bank of Pennsylvania, and nine others.[3] December 31, the Act of incorporation was passed by Congress.[4] The bank commenced business January 7, 1782. Thomas Willing was President. The largest subscribers were: William Bingham, 95 shares; John Carter, 98; Robert Morris, 98; John Swanwick, 71; William Smith, 50; Jeremiah Wadsworth, 104.[5] Morris was never a director or other officer. The day that the bank went into operation he noted in his diary that he paid to it $200,000 for the subscription of the United States.[6]

There was much doubt about the power of Congress to pass an Act of incorporation.[7] The Virginia delegates

[1] Dip. Corr. Rev. xi. 376; Journ. Cong. vii. 107.
[2] Report of 1785.
[3] Lewis, 33.
[4] Journ. Cong. vii. 197.
[5] Lewis, 133.
[6] Dip. Corr. Rev. xii. 26.
[7] Madison Papers, i. 105.

reported to the Governor that they had consented to the Act on account of the utility of the bank, but that the States ought to ratify the Act of Congress.[1] The bank determined to seek a charter from Pennsylvania. Objections were made in the Assembly that the charter was perpetual, that the bank had power to hold real estate, and that Mr. Willing had encouraged negotiations with General Howe.[2] Nevertheless the Act was passed April 1, 1782.

March 9, Franklin congratulated Morris on the success of the bank. He had directed Bache to take a share for him.[3]

In May, 1782, a proposition was made to Morris to found a bank in New Hampshire, to which he replied: "From what you propose with respect to the establishment of a bank in New Hampshire, as well as from the ideas which you say are entertained of the increase of my private fortune, I am convinced that you and other gentlemen are alike mistaken as to the nature of the national bank and my official connections and transactions. . . . By accepting the office I now hold, I was obliged to neglect my own private affairs. I have made no speculations in consequence of my office, and instead of being enriched, I am poorer this day than I was a year ago. You will from what I have said see two sufficient reasons against adopting the plan you have proposed, — that I have not money, and that I have totally quitted commerce and commercial projects to attach myself wholly to a business which requires my whole attention."[4]

In the Report of 1785, Morris said, with regard to the Bank of North America, or, as he calls it, the national bank, that the event alone could determine whether the measure was rash or not. "To judge of an Act, the cir-

[1] Va. Papers, iii. 11.

[2] Lewis, 45; see vol. i. p. 211.

[3] Franklin in France, ii. 44.

[4] Dip. Corr. Rev. xii. 142.

cumstances of the time must be considered. Public credit was at an end. No means were afforded adequate to the public expense. Credit, therefore, was necessary. Various expedients had been used, and with considerable success, during the course of the year 1781. But it is of the nature of expedients to increase the evils which they postpone. The autumn of that year found America in the situation of that part of the federal army which then returned through Philadelphia from the capture of Yorktown,—crowned with laurels, but distressed by want. The plan of a bank had been long proposed; but out of a thousand shares two hundred had not been subscribed. And it was some time after the business of the bank was fairly set a going before the sum received upon all subscriptions put together amounted to $70,000.

"On the first day of the year 1782 there remained in the treasury, being part of those moneys shipped in the 'Magicienne,' about $300,000. A considerable sum was then due for past transactions, and Congress had not required the States to pay anything for the service of the coming year before the first day of April. One quarter's expense was therefore to be provided from other sources, even if the States should punctually comply with the requisitions made upon them. The treasury was $1,600,000 in arrears, as the state of anticipations will show,[1] and therefore bills of exchange could not be hazarded. Yet the expense which was unavoidable could not but exceed the sum in hand. These were the circumstances under which something more than $250,000 of the public money was invested in bank stock. It was principally upon this fund that the operations of that institution were commenced, and the accounts which end on the last day of March will show that the public obtained before that

[1] See the table, page 129.

day a loan of $300,000, being the total amount of their then capital.[1]

"This loan was shortly after increased to $400,000, as will appear from the accounts of the succeeding quarter, which accounts will also show the necessity of that increase, the sum total brought into the treasury from the several States not amounting to $30,000 upon the last day of June. But the direct loans of the bank were not the only aid which it afforded. Considerable facilities were obtained by discounting the notes of individuals, and thereby anticipating the receipt of public money. Besides which, the persons who had contracted for furnishing rations to the army were also aided with discounts upon the public credit. And in addition to all this, it must be acknowledged that the credit and confidence which were revived by means of this institution formed the basis of that system through which the anticipations made within the bounds of the United States had, upon the first day of July, 1783, exceeded $820,000. There was due also upon that day to the bank directly near $130,000. If, therefore, the sums due indirectly for notes for individuals discounted and the like be taken into consideration, the total will exceed one million. It may then be not only asserted, but demonstrated, that without the establishment of the national

[1] The account in the table on page 129 does not show the transactions of Morris with the bank during the quarter. They were as follows: —

Quarter ending.		*Borrowed.*		*Paid.*	*Bal. due.*
1782.	March 31 . . .	$300,000			$300,000
	June 30 . . .	112,000		$12,000	400,000
	September 30 .	300,000		300,000	400,000
	December 31 .	200,000	shares	200,000	
			cash	300,000	100,000
1783.	March 31 . .	200,000		200,000	100,000
	June 30 . . .	83,194	shares	53,394	129,800
	September 30 .	54,781		29,800	154,781
	December 31 .	balance paid.			

bank the business of the department of finance could not have been performed. The officer who was at the head of that department would be guilty both of ingratitude and injustice if he did not acknowledge his obligations to them, and he trusts that it will neither dishonour them nor him that their confidence was as extensive as prudence could possibly admit, and only confined by their duty and their means."

In 1784 he wrote in a private letter: "The bank has created a punctuality here in such [business] matters as to render it a pleasure to trust safe people in the course of dealings, and everybody feels the benefit of it."[1]

Morris borrowed of the bank during his administration $1,249,975. He repaid this in cash, except $253,394, which was paid by surrendering the stock owned by the United States. The bank paid in dividends to the United States, $22,867. The United States paid to the bank for interest on loans, $29,719.[2]

Livingston gave a somewhat highly coloured statement of the new arrangement in a despatch to Jay, February 2, 1782: "Order and economy have taken place in our finances. The troops are regularly clothed and fed at West Point and most of the other posts, at the moderate rate of ninepence a ration when issued; so that the innumerable band of purchasing and issuing commissaries is discharged. The hospitals are well supplied in the same way, and small advances of pay are made to the officers and men. Upon the whole, they were never in so comfortable a situation as they are at present. Our civil list, formed upon plans of the strictest economy, after having been many years in arrear, is now regularly paid off, and the departments in consequence of it filled with men of integrity and ability. Embargoes and other restrictions

[1] Ford MSS. [2] Report of 1790.

being removed, our commerce begins to revive, and with it the spirit of industry and enterprise. And what will astonish you still more is that public credit has again reared its head. Our bank paper is in equal estimation with specie. Nothing can be more agreeable than to see the satisfaction with which people bring their money to the bank and take out paper, or the joy, mixed with surprise, with which some who have hesitatingly taken bank-bills for the first time, see that they can turn them into specie at their option." [1]

To Dana he wrote, March 2: "The only money now in general circulation is specie, and notes from the American bank, which have the same credit as silver. Our taxes are collected in these; and by removing the restrictions on our commerce, together with the small loans we have made in Europe, we find not the least want of a circulating medium." [2]

From a full statement of the history of the bank, the derogatory and abusive statements about it cannot be omitted.

Gouge says that, when people went to the bank to get silver, "they found a display of silver on the counter, and men employed in raising boxes containing silver, or supposed to contain silver, from the cellar into the banking room, or lowering them from the banking room into the cellar. By contrivances like these, the bank obtained the reputation of possessing immense wealth; but its hollowness was several times nearly made apparent, especially on one occasion when one of the copartners withdrew a deposit of some five or six thousand dollars, when the whole specie stock of the bank did not exceed twenty thousand." [3]

Bancroft gives a tradition that the bank was accustomed to buy up its own notes, at a distance from Philadelphia, at

[1] Dip. Corr. Rev. viii. 5. [2] Ibid. 329. [3] Gouge, 13.

ten or fifteen per cent discount.[1] This, however, is not necessarily a fact injurious to its reputation. In view of the difficulty of transportation and communication in those days, the notes of a bank, at a distance from the place of issue, must have been at a discount equal to the important expense of sending them home for redemption; and if the bank bought them up, it would limit this depreciation and control it in a beneficial manner.

The following is only worth quoting because it is, once for all, a part of the record which we are not at liberty to omit, and because it shows how party animosity in those days could distort facts: —

"The Bank of North America was set up with the King of France's dollars, sent here to pay the revolutionary army when they were on the point of a mutiny; yet Mr. Robert Morris, with the assistance of his advisers, had the address to satisfy the soldiers with his own six months' notes, without ever allowing the honest fellows to palm a sixpence of the cash. The money was made into a bank, and the soldiers were paid with notes, with which they purchased shoes at ten dollars the pair, hats, etc., on the same reasonable terms, at various stores set up by this Robert Morris and his agents, in every quarter of the United States; so that in the end the soldiers never touched the money, although he made the profit." [2]

[1] Bancroft, x. 567.

[2] Callender, Letters to Hamilton, 78 (1802).

CHAPTER XVIII.

EXCHANGE, MINT, AND COINAGE.

ONE great cause of perplexity in studying the financial operations of the period of the Revolution arises from the changes which took place in the currency of different countries. This affected particularly the foreign exchanges; and as the relations between the United States and France were very important for the finances of the period, the rates and quotations of exchange often have great significance. The exchange between the United States and France was very complicated. The dollar was a Spanish coin. It was used by the Americans as the metallic unit, while they had a money of account in pounds, shillings, and pence. In France the dollar needed to be converted into livres and sous. The money of account in the different colonies did not rate the dollar at the same number of shillings and pence. Moreover, the old relations with England had established a habit, which was only partially suspended during the war, of regarding the relation between the dollar and sterling money as the one which was of the most interest and importance to the colonies.

In this period the English currency actually went over from silver to gold. The Spanish dollar underwent a deterioration by fraud or bad workmanship in the mint, and the American currencies underwent depreciation by excessive paper issues. All these elements entered into the quotation of the exchange. Even the merchants who were using the quotations do not seem to have understood them. They used them by habit and tradition, and by empirical rules. They were, however, perplexed and tormented by them when new elements entered in, which required variation in the customary rules.

We therefore find that the leading public men, and Morris perhaps first of all, early turned their attention to the project of a mint for the United States.

We can find a guiding thread through the perplexities of the coinage and exchange of the period only by establishing, as nearly as it is possible to do it, the par of the metals between the Spanish dollar, the French livre, and the English shilling.

The proclamation of Queen Anne of June 18, 1704, was based upon assays of the Spanish coins which had been made at the mint, under the direction of Sir Isaac Newton. The Seville piece of eight, or dollar, was rated at four shillings and sixpence sterling; the Mexico piece of eight, at the same; and the pillar piece of eight, at four shillings sixpence and three farthings. These pieces were said to weigh seventeen pennyweight and a half when of full weight, and it was forbidden to take them in the colonies at more than six shillings current money. Hence the currency in which a dollar was estimated at six shillings was called "proclamation money," or lawful money. The parity with sterling was, therefore, £1 equals $\$4.44\frac{4}{9}$. Wright says that four shillings eightpence for one dollar was the rate at which the British forces in America were paid in the Seven Years' War. At this rate, the New York currency, being eight shillings to the dollar, gave $171\frac{3}{7}$ as the par of exchange; and the Pennsylvania currency, being seven and a half shillings to the dollar, gave $160\frac{5}{7}$ as par of exchange. This produced an extremely complicated and mysterious method of quotation.[1]

In April, 1776, Morris bought bills for Congress at the rate of \$4.93⅓ for a pound sterling.[2]

If the piastre which Sir Isaac Newton had before him was worth exactly four shillings and sixpence, the pure contents of it must have been 386.709 grains troy. If its gross weight was 17½ pwts., then the fineness was .9207. De Veyrac, writing in 1719, stated the gross weight of the piastre at 549 Spanish grains, which would be equal to 419.3597 grains troy. He says that the fineness was eleven twelfths. This would give pure contents 384.4. The parity with sterling would then be: one piastre equals four shillings five and a half pence. It is probable that Sir Isaac adopted a round number, and that the pure contents of the Spanish dollar never exceeded 384.5 grains troy. In the course of the eighteenth century it deteriorated. The assays which were made under the direction of Robert Morris, in 1782, showed that the pure contents were 373 grains.[3] The parity for that dollar with English silver would have been four shillings and fourpence. Hamilton, in his mint Report of 1791, said that the average weight of the dollars then in circulation was 416 grains. The assays varied greatly. The one which he thought best gave 370.933 grains fine contents. The Spanish standard, he says, was, in 1761, .906¼, at which ratio of fineness, a coin of 416 grains should have had 377 grains fine contents. The actual price of dollars in London and Amsterdam was adjusted to pure contents 368 grains. The most important information, however, which he gives is, that the actual unit of account in America had been, as a means of escaping these changes, 24¾ grains of

[1] Wright, 324 (1765).

[2] Journ. Cong. ii. 130.

[3] Dip. Corr. Rev. xii. 93.

fine gold. In the mean time the English standard had become gold. The parity of this imaginary gold dollar with gold sterling was: one dollar equals four shillings four and a half pence.

Sir James Steuart, in 1760,[1] stated the pure contents of the French crown of six livres at 409.94 grains troy. Morris found the pure contents to be 414 or 415 grains. This would allow for a variation in the livre from 68 and a third to 69 and a sixth troy grains. Sixty-nine and a half grains, the weight of the modern silver full-weight franc, was nearest correct. The equality with the silver dollar assayed by Morris would be: one dollar equals five livres eight and a third sous.

The currency in which the transactions of the Revolution were chiefly carried on was the Pennsylvania currency, in which seven shillings and sixpence were rated at a dollar. In practice this currency offered especial facilities, because one ninetieth of a dollar was a penny. Hence the accounts were kept in dollars and ninetieths, which made it easy to pass from one denomination to the other. If now seven shillings and sixpence were equal to five livres eight sous, five livres were worth six shillings eleven and one third pence. A crown of six livres was worth one hundred pence, and a livre was sixteen and two third pence. This was the metallic par.

Morris once stated that sixteen millions of livres would sell in this country for $2,962,962, which would be at the rate of 5.4 livres to the dollar, or six shillings eleven and a fourth pence Pennsylvania currency for five francs. But the same sixteen million livres would be reckoned in France worth $3,047,619, which would be at the rate of 5.25 livres for a dollar, or seven shillings one and two thirds pence Pennsylvania currency for five francs.[2] This

[1] Political Economy, i. *ad fin.*

[2] Dip. Corr. Rev. xi. 497.

statement shows a margin of 2.75 per cent at that time for expenses of transmission. In other calculations he uses sixteen and two-thirds pence Pennsylvania currency for a French livre as par.[1]

In May, 1782, he urged Grand to ship coin to America. The new efforts of the English to blockade the coast had cut off commerce; therefore bills were not salable. He wanted six hundred thousand livres sent over in coin, preferably in gold. Four crowns are worth here only four hundred pence, but a louis is worth four hundred and fourteen pence, both being the same number of livres. English guineas are worth four hundred and twenty pence; a half johannes, seven hundred and twenty pence; a moidore, five hundred and forty pence; and a Spanish pistole, three hundred and thirty-six pence.[2]

The quotation for the crowns and the louis d'ors shows that gold was to silver in the United States at the time as fifteen and a quarter to one.

In an ordinance of Congress, of October 18, 1782, for the regulation of the post-office, it was stated that the current custom was to rate a pennyweight of silver at five ninetieths of a dollar Pennsylvania currency. This would give four hundred and thirty-two grains gross weight for a dollar. If it was eleven twelfths fine, three hundred and ninety-six grains of pure silver would be the dollar, which is a very high and exceptional rating.[3]

The committee on the debt, in 1783, converted the foreign debt into dollars at five livres and eight sous to the dollar.[4] At about the same time the salaries of the agents in Europe were ordered to be paid in bills on France or Holland, at five livres and five sous to the

[1] Dip. Corr. Rev. xi. 477; xii. 23. The statement, Ibid. xi. 422, is somewhat enigmatical.

[2] Ibid. xii. 159.

[3] Journ. Cong. vii. 386.

[4] Ibid. viii. 151.

dollar, or four shillings and sixpence to the dollar.[1] This was an old rating for the French money, which we find to have been used just before the war.[2] At this rating five livres would be worth seven shillings one and five sevenths pence Pennsylvania currency. Livingston declared that a buyer at six and a quarter shillings Pennsylvania currency gained nearly five and a half per cent.[3] This would make the par, five livres equals six shillings seven and a half pence Pennsylvania currency.

When we compare these historical statements of the usage of trade with a metallic computation, we see how various and perplexing the transactions were.

In Morris's administration of the treasury, we find that, in 1781, he sold bills of exchange at rates varying from five shillings and threepence to six shillings and sevenpence for five livres. Six shillings eleven and one-third pence being metallic par, he incurred a very heavy loss. We have seen that he tried to lessen this loss by undertaking to negotiate both his own bills and those of the French army agent; and he appears to have succeeded to some extent in his object, for he sold the bills which he bought of the French agent at six shillings and threepence. He made a profit on some bills which he bought of Holker, the French consul, of $327 by this rate. In 1782 he sold his bills at rates from six shillings and threepence to seven shillings. The loss for the year, as compared with the par, was $92,372. In 1783 he sold at about the same rate, and the loss was $54,491. In 1784 he sold at rates varying from five shillings and fivepence to seven shillings and sixpence, the result being a gain of $7,001.[4]

In his accounts he converted livres tournois, or of France, at five livres eight sous for a dollar; livres of

1 Journ. Cong. viii. 112.
2 Franklin, ii. 425.
3 Dip. Corr. Rev. ix. 128.
4 Report of 1790.

Martinique and Hispaniola, at eight livres five sous to the dollar; florins, at thirty-four and three-fourths ninetieths each; bank guilders, at thirty-six ninetieths each.

January 15, 1782, Morris submitted to the President of Congress a report on the coinage of the United States, as he proposed that it should be, with a discussion of the existing currency. It was actually prepared by Gouverneur Morris.[1]

Spanish dollars passed in Georgia at five shillings, in North Carolina and New York at eight shillings, Virginia and New England at six shillings, South Carolina at thirty-two shillings and sixpence, and in the other States at seven shillings and sixpence. In a paper written by Franklin, probably in 1764 or 1765, it is stated that the Spanish dollar had been rated at eight shillings in New York, and seven and a half shillings in Pennsylvania, for forty years.[2]

The common denominator for all the fractions of shillings and pence put equal to a Spanish dollar was fourteen hundred and forty. One of these parts would be equal to the sixteen hundredth part of a French crown. Twenty-four of them would be a penny in Georgia, fifteen in North Carolina or New York, twenty in Virginia and New England,[3] and sixteen in the other States, except in South Carolina, where forty-eight would be thirteen pence. The author of the report considered it a matter of the first importance to find a common unit into which all the vary-

[1] Sparks's Morris, i. 273, 281.

[2] Franklin, ii. 351.

[3] In the report of the proceedings of the Price Convention at Providence, in 1776, which is given in the New York Journals, ii. 329, it is stated that the prices are set at five shillings for a Spanish dollar. This specification is not found in the corresponding report in the Rhode Island Colonial Records. The New York report came from the Secretary of Congress, and not directly from the Convention. The prices set for Massachusetts and Connecticut are the same as for Rhode Island. In those States the quotation was certainly six shillings for a dollar.

ing currencies could be converted. He proposed two copper coins, to be called an "eight" and a "five," and to contain that number of the unit. Two of the "eighths" would be a penny of Pennsylvania currency, and three a penny of Georgia currency. Three of the "fives" would be a penny of New York currency, and four a penny of lawful, or Virginia and New England currency. The money unit would be equal to a quarter of a grain of fine silver in coined money. One hundred units would be the lowest silver coin, and might be called a cent. Since the unit would be equal to a quarter of a grain, the number of units in a troy pound would be 23,040. The mint price of a pound was to be 22,237 units. The difference, — 803 units, — being the charge for coinage, was assumed to be about equal to the cost of coinage. According to the best assays that Morris had been able to get, a dollar contained about 373 grains of fine silver, or, at the mint price, 1,440 units; and if crowns contained from 414 to 415 grains of fine silver, they would, at the mint price, be worth 1,600 units.[1]

When the dollar was divided into ninetieths, twenty ninetieths were equal to a shilling sterling, fifteen to a shilling New England, twelve to a shilling Pennsylvania, eleven and a quarter to a shilling New York, and sixteen and two thirds to a livre.

The accounts show payments to Benjamin Dudley, "employed in preparing a mint" during the year 1781. The total of them, however, for that year is only $177. Similar entries occur of payments to him during 1782. In October of that year, Samuel Wheeler provided sundries for the mint. Jacob Ekfield furnished dies for the "mint of North America," at an expense of five dollars and eighteen ninetieths. In March, 1783, Nathan Sellers delivered a

[1] Dip. Corr. Rev. xii. 91.

pair of moulds and a box to Mark Wilcox for the use of the United States, at a cost of a hundred and three dollars and thirty ninetieths. In April, John Swanwick provided dies, and in May there was a payment to A. Du Bois for sinking and case-hardening the same.

December 12, 1782, Morris informed Congress that dollars were rapidly going over to the enemy in exchange for light gold, which was causing a scarcity and loss of silver.

He proposed a rating for foreign coin, English silver to pass at one dollar and sixteen ninetieths per ounce, Dutch silver at one dollar and fifteen ninetieths, French silver at one dollar and fourteen ninetieths, and Portuguese silver at one dollar and thirteen ninetieths. English, Spanish, and Portuguese gold coin he rated at seventeen dollars per ounce, and French gold coin at sixteen dollars and sixty-eight ninetieths.[1] The English at New York were clipping the foreign gold coins, which is the fact referred to here by the "light gold."[2]

The clipping was attributed to Robertson, the English Barrack-Master. The Chamber of Commerce ordered that the coins should pass by weight.[3] The gold coins sent by the English found their way into the American part of the continent, "where they circulated in a variety of mutilated forms. The moidores and six-and-thirties had all of them holes punched in them, or were otherwise diminished at New York, before they were suffered to pass the lines, from whence they obtained the name of 'Robertsons' in the rebel country; but the profits, if any, of that commander on this new edition of the coin remain a secret. In the country almost all the specie of every denomination was cut by individuals, and appeared under the forms of half, quarter, and eighth parts, the latter of which received

[1] Dip. Corr. Rev. xii. 307. [2] State Dep. MSS. 137, ii. 191, 195.
[3] Jones's New York, i. 163.

the name of 'sharp shins.' By this arbitrary division of the money, which was never weighed, great frauds were inevitable." [1]

The exchange of silver for the light coin of gold which the English at New York had clipped produced trouble for the Quartermaster-general of the army. Morris charged him for all the full-weight gold coins which he sent to him a premium representing the excess of their value above the clipped ones which were in circulation. This compelled the Quartermaster-general to become a coin clipper, to which that officer answered: "'T is a shameful business and an unreasonable hardship on a public officer. I am not certain that I will receive any more bank gold on such odious conditions. Send a pair of good shears, a couple of punches, and a leaden anvil of two or three pounds weight. Will you inquire how the goldsmiths put in their plugs?" [2]

Morris believed that it was because there was no proper regulation of the coin at the peace, by a mint or otherwise, that a great part of the coin was exported.

January 7, 1783, Morris proposed that there should be a mint, to which Congress agreed. April 2, Dudley, the mechanic who was at work under his direction, brought him a silver coin, "being the first that has been struck as an American coin." April 22, Dudley sent in several pattern coins, to be submitted to Congress.[3] It appears that these coins were for a thousand units and five hundred units, according to Morris's scheme; and that specimens of them are still extant, for it is recorded that such specimens

[1] Chastellux's Trans. i. 328.

[2] Pickering's Pickering, i. 387, December 24, 1782.

[3] Hist. Mag., January, 1867. Extract from Morris's Diary. There are letters printed by Robert Morris about this man Dudley and his wife, which show Morris exerting himself for the comfort of humble people.

were shown to the Massachusetts Historical Society in 1869.[1]

Another report on the mint was submitted by the Board of Treasury, April 8, 1786. They proposed that there should be a mint charge sufficient to make a difference of two per cent between coin and bullion, and therefore that the mint price in the United States should be £3 3*s.* 3*d.* sterling, or £4 4*s.* 4*d.* lawful, for one troy pound of standard silver. The unit coin was to contain 375.64 grains of fine silver. There was to be a half dollar, a double dime, and a dime. Two pounds and a quarter avoirdupois of copper were to be a hundred cents. There was to be a gold eagle containing 246.268 grains of fine gold, and a half eagle in proportion. The mint price of a troy pound of standard silver was to be $9.92, and the mint price of a troy pound of standard gold $209.77. They found that the ratio of coined gold and coined silver in the United States was nearly 1 to 15.6. In England it was 1 to 15.21; in France, 1 to 14.458; in Spain, 1 to 14.85. The standard which they used throughout for both metals was eleven twelfths. They say that one hundred and twenty-six grains of the standard gold of Great Britain passes in the United States for two hundred and fifty-two pence sterling, and that gold is received at the banks in the United States at the rate of £48 sterling for a pound troy. They made a careful table of the value of coined and uncoined silver and gold in sterling and in New York currency.[2]

If the best specification of a dollar was twenty-four and three fourths grains of fine gold, then the true par with sterling was, £1 equals $4.5657; which would be 102.73, if the old assumed par, 4.44\frac{4}{9}$, was one hundred. The

[1] Mass. Hist. Soc. Proc., 1869–70, 295.

[2] State Dep. MSS.; Rep. Bd. Treas. No. 139, 131.

English mint value of a troy pound of standard gold was £46.725. This multiplied by 102.73 gives £48. The "pounds sterling" in America meant pounds in exchange.

This report of 1786 shows much closer study of the subject, and better mastery of it, than the report of Hamilton on the same subject. He thought, as above stated, that the actual unit during the revolutionary period had been 24.75 grains of pure gold for a dollar. His investigation of the ratio of gold to silver is so superficial and imperfect as to create a doubt whether he had before him the report of 1786, although the computations of the Board of Treasury were printed in a form for distribution. He thinks that the ratio in America is fifteen to one. Therefore the silver dollar should be something between three hundred and sixty-eight and three hundred and seventy-four grains of pure silver. He arrived at 371.75 grains of pure silver for the dollar by taking the average of the last two Spanish coinages. Evidently this average was nothing. The law of August 8, 1786, had determined that one half of one per cent should be taken on gold and two per cent on silver for coining. This entered into Hamilton's computation of the relative weight of the coins of the two metals. Jefferson's plan was to make a silver dollar with three hundred and sixty-five grains pure contents, and to derive from it the gold dollar at the ratio of fifteen to one.[1]

[1] Folio State Papers, Finance, i. 91.

CHAPTER XIX.

1782: PEREMPTORY REFUSAL OF AID BY FRANCE; MORRIS'S DISCONTENT; CHARGES AGAINST HIM; ARTHUR LEE'S ACCOUNTS; MORRIS EXPECTED TO DEFAULT; THE LOAN OF 1782 IN HOLLAND; STATE BORROWING; CONTRACTS.

WRITING to Nathan Appleton, January 22, 1782, Morris refused to make any more promises or to put out new scrip to pay the interest on old debts. He blamed Massachusetts for not passing the impost, although a great part of the debt was owned in that State. He refused to divert revenues to other purposes than those for which they were intended, and threw the responsibility on the States.[1] If he was wearied out, so was Franklin at that time. He had never had any orders to pay the bills drawn on other people. "Thus I stand charged with vast sums which I have disbursed for the public service without authority." February 12 he writes to Adams in regard to the bills: "This has, among other things, made me quite sick of my Gibeonite office, — that of drawing water for the whole congregation of Israel."[2]

Jay, however, sympathized with him, and recognized his services to the cause: "It seems as if trouble finds its way to you from every quarter. Our credit in Holland leans upon you on the one hand, and in Spain on the other. Thus you continue, like a keystone of an arch, — pressed

[1] Hist. Mag. vi. 169.

[2] Franklin in France, ii. 31, 33.

by both sides, and yet sustaining each. How grateful ought we to be to France for enabling you to do it!"[1]

January 25, 1782, the French minister transmitted to Congress despatches, addressed to himself, which he had just received, dated September 7. Vergennes assumed that Morris had stopped drawing, and he expressed his orders to the French Minister in the following plain language: "We have peremptorily declared to Dr. Franklin that we will not in future discharge any bills that have not been drawn with your consent. As to you, sir, we cannot but repeat our former instructions on this subject; and we direct you to authorize no drafts, even for a small sum." On the 28th of January the French Minister asked Congress to send power to Franklin to make a contract with the King of France for the repayment of the loans.

On the 8th of February, 1782, Congress resolved that they could not, "without injustice to themselves and their ally, withhold from him a knowledge of their present circumstances, or neglect to mention the ruinous consequences that may attend a refusal of those aids" which they still require; and they directed the Secretary of Foreign Affairs and Superintendent of Finance to explain to the American Minister in France the "extensive advantages which have resulted from money supplied by his Most Christian Majesty to these United States," and their need of at least twelve million livres for 1782. They directed Franklin to borrow that amount at an interest not exceeding that allowed on national security in Europe.[2]

Morris had expected this sum of twelve millions when he issued notes to the officers of the army with which to buy clothing. In the spring he learned that France would advance but six millions. He also learned that the ten-million loan in Holland, which he had expected to have

[1] Dip. Corr. Rev. viii. 55. [2] Secret Journ. iii. 85 fg.

almost entirely at his disposal, had been largely cut into.[1]

We may suppose that the instructions just quoted reached Franklin in May; but in April he had written to Adams, urging him to push the loan in Holland, because there was rising enthusiasm for America there, and it was reported that bankers were willing to undertake it. Morris had sent to Franklin advice of large drafts, not knowing that nearly all of the last loan had been consumed in purchasing goods. May 2, Adams replied that there was great eagerness to become the American banker, but he could not find that any one of the persons who came forward could really command the money. Loanable capital is not plentiful, and there are many loans in the market.[2] On the 25th Franklin wrote to Laurens, expressing the hope that he would obtain a loan in Holland. He says: "We have pressed rather too hard on this court, and we still want more than they can conveniently spare us."[3]

In April, 1782, the Prussian Chargé d'Affaires at Paris informed Frederick II. of an interesting incident. The Controleur-general, at the council table, made the statement that the expense of supporting the army in America was sixty million livres per annum. The King, who had not seemed to be paying attention, woke up at this and said: "It is a big price to pay for succouring people from whom we cannot expect to gain either fidelity or reimbursement."[4]

May 16, 1782, Morris made another strenuous appeal to the States:[5] "I write sir, to apprise you of the public danger, and to tell you I shall endeavour to fulfil engagements which I have entered into already, that I may quit

[1] Franklin in France, ii. 34.
[2] Dip. Corr. Rev. iii. 398.
[3] Ibid. 431.
[4] Circourt, iii. 159.
[5] Dip. Corr. Rev. xii. 152.

my station like an honest man; but I will make no new engagements, so that the public service must necessarily stand still. What the consequences may be I know not; but the fault is in the States. They have not complied with the requisitions of Congress; they have not enabled me to go on; they have not given me one shilling for the service of the year 1782, excepting only the State of New Jersey, from which I received $5,500 a few days ago, and this is all that has come to my hands out of two millions which were asked for. Now, should the army disband, and should scenes of distress and horror be reiterated and accumulated, I again repeat, that I am guiltless; the fault is in the States. They have been deaf to the calls of Congress, to the clamours of the public creditor, to the just demands of a suffering army, and even to the reproaches of the enemy, who scoffingly declare that the American army is fed, paid, and clothed by France. That assertion, so dishonourable to America, was true; but the kindness of France has its bounds, and our army — unfed, unpaid, and unclothed — will have to subsist itself or disband itself. This language may appear extraordinary, but at a future day, when my transactions shall be laid bare to public view, it will be justified. This language may not consist with the ideas of dignity which some men entertain; but, sir, dignity is in duty and in virtue, not in the sound of swelling expressions. . . . I have borne with delays and disappointments as long as I could, and nothing but hard necessity would have wrung from me the sentiments which I have now expressed."

This circular was submitted to a committee of Congress. They were disinclined to send it. Morris proposed sending members of Congress to visit the States.[1] May 22, Congress voted to send two members to the South and two to

[1] Dip. Corr. Rev. xii. 161.

the East, to urge the States to comply with the requisitions.[1] However, the circular was sent off; but it seems to have produced nothing but irritation. June 16, Morris wrote to Lovell: "I find the publications of 'No Receipts' are by no means very pleasing. Men are less ashamed to do wrong than vexed to be told of it."[2]

On the 24th of May, 1782, the Financier made a report on the state of the finances. In connection with this, a motion was made in Congress hostile to Morris, for a committee to inquire into the authority under which the appropriation of the loans and subsidies in Europe had been made; but it was lost, and the Financier was only called upon to report the general purposes to which those resources had been applied.[3] The charges which were current in Virginia against Morris had, at this time, reached such definiteness that they could be enumerated under six heads: first, that he had robbed the Eastern States of their specie; second, that he was partial to Pennsylvania, being commercially connected with half the merchants of Philadelphia; third, that he was partial to the disaffected; fourth, that he had established a bank for sinister purposes; fifth, that his plan and the plan of Pennsylvania was to keep Virginia poor; sixth, that he and the Secretary of Congress, with others, were engaged in speculation in tobacco under the Yorktown license. He wrote a long letter at the end of May to Daniel Clark, refuting each of these charges in detail.[4]

In June Madison wrote to Edmund Randolph that he saw malice was entertained against Morris, for which he knew of no reason. "I am persuaded that he accepted his office from motives which are honourable and patriotic. I have seen no proofs of misfeasance; I have heard of many

[1] Journ. Cong. vii. 295.

[2] Dip. Corr. Rev. xii. 195.

[3] Secret Journ. i. 237.

[4] Dip. Corr. Rev. xii. 169.

charges which were palpably erroneous; I have known others somewhat suspicious vanish on examination; every member in Congress must be sensible of the benefit which has accrued to the public from his administration. No intelligent man out of Congress can be altogether insensible of it. The court of France has testified its satisfaction at his appointment, which, I really believe, lessened its repugnance to lend us money."[1] The prime mover in these attacks in Congress was Arthur Lee. We have notes of a debate which took place July 25.[2] Lee said that more money was reserved in France for certain purposes than was necessary. He moved for a committee on the report of the Financier. It was then proposed to stop drawing bills; but this alarmed those who expected bills for their interest.

In the midst of this Arthur Lee interposed a request that he might be paid by bills of exchange the balance which had been found due him, instead of by the loan-office certificate which he had received. By a vote of May 29, 1781, he had been allowed to present invoices and receipts as vouchers, also bankers' accounts showing cash deposited; and if he could not give these, it was ordered that the accounts should be kept open for later completion. The accounts were to be stated as ordinary and extraordinary, and no other voucher was to be required for either than the word of Mr. Lee.[3] If poor Deane had found such treatment as this, he would no doubt have come to stand as one of the heroes of the Revolution. Lee had not rendered an account of 68,853 livres expended for Virginia, but turned over to the United States. Morris demanded this account.[4] Lee, however, was allowed to include that sum in his settlement. Morris

[1] Madison Papers, i. 137.
[2] Thomson Papers, 65.
[3] Journ. Cong. vii. 91.
[4] Dip. Corr. Rev. xii. 139.

said that there were no funds on which the bills could be drawn; but in spite of the state of the finances and all other considerations, it was voted that Lee should have bills of exchange for £2,238; and Morris was forced to incur either the odium of the public creditors, by drawing the bills for Lee which he could not give to others, or the enmity of Lee, by refusing to pay him. In October, Morris alleged that all loan-office certificates must be treated alike; therefore that he could not convert those held by Lee without a special order of Congress.[1] The original order for the payment to Lee, among the papers in the State Department, is a scrawl without date. There are many interlineations and changes in the amount ordered to be paid. The words: "And that the certificates given to Mr. Lee for that balance be cancelled," are in a different ink, and perhaps in a different handwriting.[2] Lee charged for three months that he served the country at London before his appointment. According to the Thomson Papers he put in that item in 1782; but a vote of Congress appears, March 4, 1785, allowing him $1,977 for services and expenses at London, in addition to £200 sterling which the Committee of Secret Correspondence allowed him at the time.[3]

The entry in Morris's accounts shows the payment to Lee, who is called "Agent at Vienna," of $10,746, December 10, 1782. The payment came out of money begged in France.[4]

It was asserted that Lee's enmity to Morris caused him to persuade Virginia to repeal her consent to the impost.[5] That enmity certainly pursued Morris and cost him much harm. Its personal and political consequences force the causes of it upon our attention.

[1] State Dep. MSS. 137, ii. 19. [2] Ibid. 5.
[3] Journ. Cong. x. 50. [4] Elliot, v. 29. [5] See page 65.

August 22, 1782, Clark, Osgood, and Duane came as a committee to pester Morris with questions as to why he had done certain things. The attitude of that entire party was, not to do anything to help or to support the efforts which were made; but if the officer was forced to do what no one wanted to do, but what could not be helped, to take the highest grounds of strict correctness for the purpose of criticising him.[1]

In a communication to Congress, August 1, 1783, Morris stated that the States had paid on the requisition of 1782 as follows: South Carolina, the whole, by means of supplies to the troops serving there; Rhode Island, nearly a quarter; Pennsylvania, above a fifth; Connecticut and New Jersey, each about a seventh; Massachusetts, about an eighth; Virginia, about a twelfth; New York and Maryland, each about a twentieth; New Hampshire, about one one hundred and twenty-first; North Carolina, Delaware, and Georgia, nothing at all.[2]

On the 1st of August Morris notes in his diary that people expected him to default that day on the notes given to the officers in the previous February. When he gave them out he expected that four millions of dollars would be paid in on requisitions in April and July. Instead of that, he had not received fifty thousand. He was compelled to raise the money by selling bills on France. The amount was $140,266. Thirty-nine thousand dollars he redeemed, paying part and getting an extension on the rest. The remainder he was ready to pay. "So that the hopes and expectations of the malicious and disaffected will in this instance be disappointed."[3] His bills on France, however, had simply adjourned the difficulty and thrown the burden over on the agents in Europe, as we shall soon see.

[1] Dip. Corr. Rev. xii. 253. [2] Ibid. 395. [3] Ibid. 241.

We may suppose that the despatch was received in September, which Franklin wrote June 25, on receipt of the orders of Congress to borrow twelve millions. "I had already received the promise of six millions, together with the clearest and most positive assurances that it was all the King could spare to us, that we must not expect more; that if drafts and demands came upon me beyond that sum, it behooved me to take care how I accepted them, or where I should find funds for the payment, since I could certainly not be further assisted out of the royal treasury. Under this declaration, with what face could I ask for another six millions? It would be saying, You are not to be believed; you can spare more; you are able to lend me twice the sum, if you were but willing. If you read my letter to Mr. Morris of this date, I think you will be convinced how improper language capable of such a construction would be to such a friend."[1]

About June, 1782, a despatch was received from Franklin, dated March 4, in which he said: "The accounts we have of the economy introduced by Mr. Morris begin to be of service to us here, and will by degrees obviate the inconvenience that an opinion of our disorders and mismanagement had occasioned."[2] In a despatch of August 12, to Morris, he says: "Your conduct, activity, and address as a Financier and provider for the exigencies of the State are much admired and praised here; their good consequences being so evident, particularly with regard to the rising credit of our country and the value of bills. No one but yourself can enjoy your growing reputation more than I do."[3] In this despatch he transmits the treaty which he had made on the 16th of July for a settlement of the debt to France. It was probably received in October, and was ratified by Congress January 2, 1783.

[1] Dip. Corr. Rev. iii. 368. [2] Ibid. 311. [3] Ibid. 498.

In this treaty were summed up the monetary obligations of the United States to France up to that time, leaving out of account three million livres given before the treaty of alliance, and the six million livres which were a gift in 1781. The total was eighteen million livres. It was promised that this sum should be repaid in twelve equal annual payments, beginning the third year after the peace, with five per cent interest from the date of this treaty. Arrears of interest to this time were forgiven. In another article, however, it was said that the five per cent interest should commence upon the signing of the treaty of peace. The ten million livres borrowed in Holland were to be paid in ten equal annual payments, beginning on the 5th of November, 1781, with interest at four per cent, to begin from the date that the loan was contracted; but the King assumed the expense of all the commissions and bank charges of contracting the loan.[1]

At home, however, during this summer, there was little improvement. The people were utterly weary of the war, anticipated peace, and could not be stimulated to any interest or activity. The requisitions of 1782 were for $8,000,000, of which only $125,000 had been paid up to September 1.[2] On the 27th of June Morris submitted to Congress a draft of a resolution that loan-office interest should be paid out of the five per cent impost, and not by bills on Europe; because such bills, "without producing a full value to the parties, are very injurious to the finances."[3] As there was no impost, this could not be adopted.

In September Livingston wrote to Franklin: "The melancholy tale of our necessities is sufficiently known to you. It has been too often repeated to need repetition. Mr. Morris, who writes from an empty treasury, amidst per-

[1] Treaties and Conventions, 254. [2] Dip. Corr. Rev. xii. 267.
[3] State Dep. MSS. 137, i. 639.

petual duns, will speak more feelingly. In short, money must be obtained for us at any rate, whether we have peace or war. France having already done much for us, and it not being probable that we shall extend our demands beyond the present, she may think it wise not to let us open account with a new banker, since the debtor is always more or less under obligations to the creditor." [1]

On the 27th of that month Morris wrote to Franklin, urging him to get another loan from France. "The people are undoubtedly able to pay; but they have easily persuaded themselves into a conviction of their own inability, and in a government like ours the belief creates the thing."

In October he also addressed the governors again: "Our enemies hold up to contempt and derision the contrast between resolutions to carry on the war at every expense and the receipts of nothing in some States, and very little in all of them put together." [2]

In June, 1782, the second American loan was started in Holland, this time without an indorsement by France.[3] August 18, Adams wrote that he had obtained 1,300,000 or 1,400,000 guilders.[4] This may be regarded as the turning-point in the finances of the Revolution, for the United States now began to borrow as an independent nation; and although its credit fluctuated greatly in the next few years, yet it was this power to borrow in Holland which, as we shall see, enabled Morris to finish his administration with a certain measure of dignity and success. We may suppose that he knew of the success of the Dutch loan in November.

In the autumn, however, new demands were directed to France. Lafayette told Fleury, the French Finance Min-

[1] Dip. Corr. Rev. iv. 18.

[2] Ibid. 289.

[3] Franklin in France, ii. 26.

[4] Dip. Corr. Rev. vi. 372.

ister, that he must let America have twenty million livres that year. He said that he would not.[1] Franklin also wrote to Vergennes, under the instructions of Congress, asking for another loan, because another campaign would probably be necessary.[2] In October, however, Vergennes wrote to Luzerne, approving of his firmness against Morris's demands: The more exacting the Americans are, the less they will get. If peace comes the King will cease to pay the American army, "which will then be as useless as it has habitually been inactive. But it will be dangerous, I think, to announce this to Congress in the present state of things. If they ask you for aid for the next year, say only that you are ignorant of the King's intentions; but do not conceal from Mr. Morris that we are astonished at the demands which they continue to make on us, while the Americans obstinately refuse to pay taxes, and that it seems to us much more natural to levy on them than on the subjects of the King the taxes necessary for the defence of their cause. As to the payment of interest [on the American loans], you may declare peremptorily that the King will not undertake it, and that any dissatisfaction which may result from this determination will serve only to measure at their just value the gratitude and attachment of the Americans for France."[3] Franklin also wrote on the 5th of December: "It is in vain for me to repeat again, what I have so often written and find taken so little notice of, that there are bounds to everything; and that the faculties of this nation are limited, like those of all other nations. Some of you seem to have established as maxims the supposition that France has money enough for all her occasions and all ours besides, and that if she does not supply us, it is owing to her want of will or to my negligence."[4]

[1] Dip. Corr. Rev. vi. 480.

[2] Franklin in France, ii. 39.

[3] Circourt, iii. 288.

[4] Dip. Corr. Rev. iv. 48.

Another source of trouble and vexation was the continued attempts of several of the States to obtain supplies, or contract loans, or obtain subsidies in Europe. April 27, 1782, Morris wrote to the Governor of Virginia in regard to a loan which Virginia had obtained from the King of France. Franklin asked Morris that the United States should assume this as a part of its own debt to France. Morris refused, and complained of these applications by the separate States abroad.[1] In June the delegates of Virginia reported to the Governor that the French Minister said that the means of transportation at the disposal of France were so occupied that it was doubtful if they could be used to bring out the supplies purchased for Virginia.[2] They also reported that, out of the loan made by France to the United States for this year, a deduction of seven hundred thousand livres had been made on account of stores purchased for Virginia by the French Minister; so that Virginia had become indebted to the federal government to that amount.[3] In September David Ross informed the Governor that he had received from Europe clothing for fifteen hundred or two thousand troops.[4] The Governor wrote to Morris, asking him to buy these goods.[5] October 23, Morris informed the Governor that Barclay, the agent of the United States in France, had been instructed to ship the military supplies in France which belonged to Virginia, and that the United States would take them, Congress having authorized this.[6] November 29, he wrote again to the Governor, and expressed a hope that any opinion which he had uttered on this matter would not be misconstrued.[7] From this it appears that more of the fault-finding had been developed in this connection. In November Vergennes declared to Barclay that there

[1] Dip. Corr. Rev. xii. 138. [2] Va. Papers, iii. 185. [3] Ibid. 202. [4] Ibid. 312. [5] Ibid. 328. [6] Ibid. 353. [7] Ibid. 384.

was great inconvenience in furnishing articles for the States, to be paid for by the United States. The States ought to negotiate with Mr. Morris.[1] Franklin informed Morris, in December, that Penet, the agent of Virginia for borrowing money, was bankrupt and had absconded. His creditors were worrying Franklin, who had nothing to do with his affairs. The States, by attempting to borrow money in Europe, have hurt our credit and produced nothing. "We have put our faith in every adventurer who pretended to have influence here, and who, when he arrived, had none but what our appointment gave him." [2]

The general failure of all resources in the autumn of 1782 affected Morris's contracts for the support of the army. He had a contract with Comfort Sands, made in February, 1782, to supply the clothing which was lacking on account of the loss of the "Lafayette." [3] Writing to Oliver Phelps in March, Morris said that other nations had adopted contracts as the best method of supplying armies. "The experience of other countries could not satisfy America. We must have it of our own acquiring. We have at length bought it; but the purchase has nearly been our ruin." [4] Contracts were used in 1776 at New York, both in the State and continental service. There was some clashing.[5] May 6, the Superintendent of Finance was directed to appoint inspectors for the two chief armies to oversee the contracts of supplies, and report fraud, negligence, or waste of public property, in order that those who were guilty might be subjected to court-martial.[6]

This system of contracts was employed, therefore, during the summer for the Northern army. We shall see that jealousy was occasioned in the Southern army. Septem-

[1] Va. Papers, iii. 383. [2] N. J. Corr. 330.
[3] 5th Series Mass. Hist. Soc. Coll. iv. 243.
[4] Dip. Corr. Rev. xii. 127. [5] N. Y. Journ. i. 352, 387.
[6] Journ. Cong. vii. 284

ber 11, the contractors wrote to Morris that the sub-contractors would hold them liable for the difference between specie and Morris's notes. The taxes do not come in fast enough to provide the receivers with funds to meet Morris's drafts. These drafts being given out to all the agents of the government, quartermasters, clothiers, etc., as well as contractors, are paid out below specie par. When they made their contract, they placed more dependence on Morris's personal than on his official character. They cannot be responsible for the supply of the army on their contract. They must have monthly payments in specie, or a guarantee against loss on the drafts. He refused to give the guarantee, for the reason that the contracts would then be useless.[1]

On the 23d of September he wrote to Ezek Cornell, who was the inspector of the Northern army, as follows: "This day's post has brought me a state [statement] of receipts for the week [that is, what the receivers of taxes had received on account of the Confederation]. The whole amount is short of seven thousand dollars; and of that which is received, I do not touch one thousand in specie. The rest is paid in paper, which was an anticipation. My engagements are very numerous and weighty; and although I have determined to incur no new expense, not even the slightest, yet those already incurred are sufficient to ruin the credit I had taken so much pains to establish, unless I can procure a respite." He declares that he will have to cancel the contracts and leave the army to impress supplies.[2] On the 5th of October Cornell replied that Colonel Wadsworth had taken up the contract. The writer has also adjusted the accounts of Sands, and he advises Morris to accept the settlement agreed upon, lest the sub-contractors should sue Sands, and make trouble on account of

[1] State Dep. MSS. 137, i. 833 and fg.

[2] Ibid. 847.

Sands's due bills not being paid. If the settlement is accepted, Sands will pay his due bills and close everything up. Cornell also urges Morris to give the soldiers two months' pay, and to direct a quarter of a dollar per week to be paid to privates, and a half dollar to non-commissioned officers, that they may have something to amuse themselves with. Being well clothed and fed, they will then be very comfortable.[1] Morris sent a circular to the governors, informing them of this trouble with the contractors. He thought the contractors had a right to demand indemnification; but he did not dare give it, because they would no longer be under any restraint. His new contracts were made at an advance of one third.[2]

It appears that there was an arbitration between the treasury and the contractors, for the expense of it — sixty-three dollars — appears in the accounts.

October 18, 1782, Congress adopted an ordinance regulating the post-office. The postage was set in pennyweights and grains of silver, each pennyweight to be five ninetieths of a dollar "as at present." For a distance not exceeding sixty miles the postage was to be one pennyweight eight grains; between sixty and a hundred miles, two pennyweights; between one hundred and two hundred miles, two pennyweights sixteen grains; and so on, increasing sixteen grains for every hundred miles. An ounce was four letters.[3]

In December, 1782, Joseph Reed wrote in reference to Morris that he was a Colossus, who bestrode not only all the other officers in Congress, but even Congress itself.[4]

[1] State Dep. MSS. 137, i 854.

[2] Dip. Corr. Rev. xii 287; Madison Papers, i. 186.

[3] Journ. Cong. vii. 386.

[4] Reed's Reed, ii. 390.

CHAPTER XX.

THE IMPOST; TAXATION UNTIL 1789.

THE one point to which the financial difficulties must constantly return was taxation. Without that there was no finance, but only paper-mongering and bill-kiting. An import duty was also the tax called for by the situation. No one, in fact, disputed these assertions as abstract propositions.

The first proposition for an impost — that is to say, for an uniform import duty — came from the Price Convention at Hartford, Connecticut.[1] February 3, 1781, Congress recommended the States to vest the power in Congress to levy five per cent on all imports, after May 1, 1781, except arms, ammunition, and clothing, or other articles imported for the United States or any State; also excepting wool cards and cotton cards and wire for making them, and salt during the war.[2] This was as far as they dared go, although there was a proposition to ask for a general power to regulate commerce and lay duties on imports.

The Articles of Confederation had not yet been adopted. This was a proposition to amend them. There was a sanguine expectation on the part of Morris and those who sympathized with his views that the States would soon, in spite of some reluctance, accept and consent to this proposition. The result put them in the position of having quite misjudged the situation. It will be noticed that the

[1] Hamilton's Republic, i. 553. [2] Journ. Cong. vii. 72.

plan was proposed just before Morris was appointed. That it would be adopted was one of the most important and essential assumptions on which he founded his projects for the administration of the finances. His disappointment in respect to it frustrated his plans, and gave to his career as Financier a direction and character totally different from what he had expected.

Virginia immediately assented to the impost. Massachusetts remonstrated against it.[1] Rhode Island also objected.

January 3, 1782, Morris sent to the governors a copy of a letter addressed especially to Massachusetts, Rhode Island, and Maryland, which had not consented to the five per cent impost. He throws on them the responsibility for the failure of the public credit and all the disasters to be expected. "The hope of our enemy is in the derangement of our finances."[2] Virginia, however, withdrew her assent to the impost. Madison, writing to Edmund Randolph, said that many held the opinion that Arthur Lee's enmity to Morris caused him to induce Virginia to take this action.[3] Arguing on the necessity of the impost, Morris wrote to the President of Congress, February 11, 1782: "Let us apply to borrow wherever we may, our mouths will always be stopped by the one word 'security.' The States will not give revenue for the purpose, and the United States have nothing to give but a general national promise, of which their enemies loudly charge them with the violation."[4] The subject now went over until the next December. In August, 1782, Morris replied to the Rhode Island objections, which were immediately afterward repeated in more elaborate and emphatic form to Congress.[5]

[1] Secret Journ. i. 215.
[2] Va. Papers, iii. 5.
[3] Madison Papers, i. 111.
[4] Dip. Corr. Rev xii. 100.
[5] Staples, 387.

Hamilton came into Congress in November, 1782, and during that winter an earnest attempt was made to carry the impost. December 6, the Superintendent of Finance was ordered to represent to the States the necessity of their paying in $1,200,000 to meet the interest on the debt, and $2,000,000 for current expenses. It was also voted to send a deputation to Rhode Island to ask that State to consent to the five per cent impost. A letter was adopted to be sent to Rhode Island. On the 12th of December a letter from the Speaker of the lower House of Assembly of Rhode Island was read, stating the reasons of that State for refusing, namely, First, that the tax would bear hardest on the most commercial States; second, that it would introduce officers into the State unknown to, and unaccountable to, the State; third, that it would give Congress power to collect money from the commerce of the State indefinitely as to time and quantity, and for the expenditure of which Congress would not be accountable to the State.[1]

It is noteworthy that these objections were the complete echo of those made against the English taxes before the war.

Reports were published in the Rhode Island newspapers that letters had been received from Adams to the effect that his loan was being rapidly taken, that the credit of the United States was very high, and that the only danger was of borrowing too much. A committee of Congress having been appointed to consider this statement, they reported that it was untrue; as it was, in so far as it stated that the Dutch loan was providing enough money to meet the necessities. The committee declared that they suspected some member of Congress of being responsible for the publication. They were instructed to go to Providence

[1] Journ. Cong. viii. 25

and find out who it was. On the 17th Mr. Howell of Rhode Island declared that he was the man, and proposed the revocation of the vote of investigation. This motion was lost, no one but the Rhode Island men voting for it.[1] It appears that the committee went to Rhode Island, for an entry of their expenses appears in the accounts, — $1,000.

The answer of Congress to the Rhode Island objections is understood to have been written by Hamilton. In it, it is asserted very positively that, under the Articles of Confederation, Congress has "an absolute discretion in determining the *quantum* of revenue requisite for the national expenditure. When this is done, nothing remains for the States separately but the mode of raising it. No State can dispute the obligation to pay the sum demanded, without a breach of the Confederation; and when the money comes into the treasury, the appropriation is the exclusive province of the federal government." Congress has a right to appoint officers in the States for the collection of taxes.[2] These doctrines were rather high for the States-rights party, even the moderate members of it, especially in Virginia.[3]

In this connection, however, Hamilton made a proposition which showed that he had clearly perceived one of the mistakes which Congress had made. He proposed to revise the requisitions and lower them to the point where the States could meet them. He said that they produced despair and apathy when they were too large.[4] It is certain that they were unnecessarily large; and in the retrospect, a few years later, people might have argued with very great reason that the expenditures had been restricted by the neglect or refusal to provide Congress with money.

[1] Journ. Cong. viii. 29; Staples, 412.

[2] Elliot's Debates, i. 135.

[3] Jones's Letters, 116.

[4] Madison Papers, i. 233.

The perversity of the Rhode Island delegates, in opposition to all the rest, and their method of pursuing their purpose, gave great offence, and exposed them to formal censure. The anarchical, anti-federal, States-rights doctrines cropped out in distinct form, as a premonition of the form under which, in an independent union, the old colonial fallacies would present themselves.[1] Hamilton was in the thick of the fight with these elements from the very first. February 19, 1783, he made a speech in which he said that it was useless to answer the points put forward by Rhode Island, because they were not the real motive of her opposition. Under existing arrangements she was taxing Connecticut, and she did not want to be disturbed.[2]

January 30, 1783, a committee of Congress presented a report on the finances, which was probably prepared by Hamilton. The five per cent impost recommended February 3, 1781, had been rejected by one State, another had withdrawn its assent, and a third had made no answer. Of the eight millions demanded for the service of 1782, only four hundred and twenty thousand dollars had been received. The loans obtained in Europe had produced, as available for that year, only $833,000, so that the total available resources were only a little over a million and a half. The estimated expenditure was $5,713,000, without counting interest on former debts, which would alone exceed all the money at their disposal.

In the spring of 1783 the Legislature of South Carolina reconsidered the vote on the impost. While it was pending, on the 8th of March, General Greene wrote a letter to the Legislature, as he had often done before during the war. In it he maintained nationalist doctrines, which were then unpopular in the State, and he urged that something should be done for public credit and the support of

[1] Staples, 393; Madison Papers, i. 220, 232. [2] Mad. Papers, i. 342.

the army. This made the Legislature very angry. They construed it as congressional and military dictation. They repealed the five per cent tax.[1]

On the 18th of April the project of revenue was adopted in Congress by nine States, Rhode Island alone voting no, and New York being divided, because Hamilton voted no.[2] This project provided definitely for only a part of the revenue which would be necessary to pay the interest on the debt. The States were left to provide the remaining part that would be necessary in any way they saw fit. Hamilton and Morris were both greatly discontented with it. It required still the ratification of the States; and Hamilton wrote to Governor Clinton that he voted against the plan because it had little more chance of success than a better one, and, if adopted, would fail in execution.[3] In March, when that plan was pending before Congress, Morris submitted a plan, in which there was not a uniform five per cent rate, but a classified tariff, and some export taxes, a land tax, a house tax, and an excise. The collectors were to be appointed by Congress. The plan sounds as if it must have been at least inspired by Hamilton.

In response to the project of taxation of April 18, Massachusetts addressed Congress, September 25, 1783. The half-pay for the officers and the large salaries caused dissatisfaction to the people of that State. They think it necessary to expressly inform Congress that the things complained of "are extremely opposite and irritating to the principles and feelings which the people of some Eastern States, and of this in particular, inherit from their ancestry." This is why Massachusetts has not been able to grant the impost, although she saw the necessity of sustaining the public credit. A committee of Congress reported on this, that, at

[1] Johnson's Greene, ii. 386. [2] Journ. Cong. viii. 139.
[3] Hamilton's Works, viii. 117.

the time the half-pay was adopted, Congress was extremely anxious to retain officers, and did not know how else to do it; that the position taken by Massachusetts would lead to a dissolution of the Union; and that the commutation was fixed and now irrevocable on principles of justice.[1]

If each State was to rejoin to the requisitions of Congress by this sort of remonstrance and argument, according to local views and prejudices, it was evidently all over with the Union.

We have seen that when Morris came into office he had a rational plan of action, which of course rested on taxation. Therefore, from the very beginning, he had insisted on that policy, not only with respect to the impost, but by the use of other taxes.

In August, 1781, he sent a communication to Congress, in which he urged a plan of taxation. He wanted not only import duties, but a poll-tax, a land tax, and an excise on spirits.[2] He wrote to Jay that people resist taxes while the expenditure is wasteful. He counted on his reforms in the expenditure to make taxation more productive.[3]

In February, 1782, he made to Congress another proposition for taxation. He proposed a dollar on each hundred acres of land, a poll-tax of a dollar on each freeman and male slave between sixteen and fifty, except "such as are in the federal army, and such as are by wounds or otherwise unfit for service." His language leaves it ambiguous whether this exception applies to slaves. He also proposed an eighth of a dollar per gallon tax on spirits.[4] In April he wrote to General Greene: the States at present "content themselves with the assertion that each has done most, and that the people are not able to pay taxes."

June 11, 1782, he wrote to Jenifer of Maryland: "The

[1] Journ. Cong. viii. 275.

[2] State Dep. MSS. 137, i. 121.

[3] Dip. Corr. Rev. vii. 423.

[4] State Dep. MSS. 137, i. 347.

taxes required are very moderate when compared either with the real wealth of the people or the former expenses which they have borne." Every State thinks its own quota the largest, "and would be very happy to apologize to the world for doing nothing, with the thin and flimsy pretext that it has been asked to do too much. . . . It is a vain thing to suppose that wars can be carried on by quibbles and puns; and yet laying taxes payable in specific articles amounts to no more, for with a great sound they put little or nothing in the treasury." [1] Addressing the President of Congress, July 29, he made the assertion that in America three days' labour would produce sustenance for a week. It would not be unreasonable to ask two days in a year as a contribution for the payment of the public debt, especially with an exemption for inability. He proposed to get this contribution by a poll-tax. "Labour is in such demand among us that the tax will fall on the consumer. An able-bodied man who demands a hundred dollars to go into military service for three years cannot be oppressed by the annual payment of one dollar while not in that service." [2] July 30, he addressed the governors, calling their attention to the fact that Congress had ordered the continental and State taxes to be collected separately. If they were collected together, the same person would be collector of both, and the executions to enforce both would issue from the Treasurer of the State. Therefore a preference would be given to State taxes; and if there was no occasion for an execution for the State taxes, none would issue for the continental; also, if the collector was in arrears on different taxes, he would apply all his collections to that one which was demanded most sharply of him, and let the other wait the longest time. He quotes a letter which he has received from one of his agents [probably Hamilton],

[1] Dip. Corr. Rev. xii 192.

[2] Ibid. 230.

that the collectors are in arrears for every State tax since 1776 in the State where the writer is, and are using the money collected on continental taxes to pay the arrears of the old State tax.[1] In January, 1783, Morris wrote to President Dickinson of Pennsylvania, that the quota of Pennsylvania for 1782 was $1,120,794, of which there had been paid only $107,925. "Laws not executed only substitute deception for denial."[2]

The first appearance of receipts from taxes in Morris's accounts is in June, 1782. In the quarter ending at that time, Rhode Island paid in $9,645; New Jersey, $15,912; Pennsylvania, $4,657.

November 3, Morris wrote to Luzerne: "Whatever may be the wealth of the inhabitants of America, and however capable they may be of bearing heavy taxes, this at least is certain, that they have neither been accustomed to them, nor have the Legislatures hitherto adopted the proper modes of laying and levying them with convenience to the people. Taxation requires time in all governments, and is to be perfected only by long experience in any country. America, divided as it is into a variety of free States, possessing sovereign power for all domestic purposes, cannot therefore be suddenly brought to pay all which might be spared from the wealth of her citizens. The amount even of that wealth is very disputable. Our extensive forests, though they are valuable as property, are by no means productive to the revenue; and many of our people have endured such losses that they require alleviation, instead of being able to bear burdens. Besides this, the use of many articles not strictly necessary are become so even by that use, and therefore the mode of living, being habitually more expensive than in other countries, requires greater wealth. A good prince would not suddenly render the lot

[1] N. J. Corr. 321. [2] Penn. Archives, ix. 740.

of his subjects worse; how then are we to expect that the people themselves will do so?" When we remember that this argumentation was addressed to the nation which was paying the bills, we can hardly suppose that it would be found very conclusive. Since the paper has been put out, he says, a large part of the revenue must consist in paper, and there is no other way but to take the paper in taxes and destroy it. He goes on to argue that the war will be fatal to Great Britain, but that it will give commerce to France, and the King's honour is pledged. The subjects of France will for ages obtain advantages in commerce for the money now spent.[1]

In 1782 Hamilton made a report on the tax system of New York to Morris, and gave at the same time an intelligent criticism of it. He took the office of Receiver of continental taxes in New York, in order to help Morris in his plans. He is the only subordinate Morris ever had at his disposal who was capable of responding, or did respond, to the demands which the Financier found it necessary to make on State officers for information or intelligent co-operation.

On account of the predominance of the rural interest, the city of New York was made to bear about one third of the State taxes. It ought not to have been over a quarter. The general aim of the tax system was, by means of Commissioners, to apportion taxes "according to circumstances and abilities, collectively considered." That is to say, they made an experiment of those notions about taxation which always present themselves easily to inexperienced persons, whatever may be their professional or political position. They wanted to reach "equality of sacrifice," taking into account all a man's circumstances and abilities. The consequence was, as Hamilton says, that a man's mode of life

[1] Dip. Corr. Rev. xii. 4.

and the impression which he made on his neighbours by his bearing and mode of business told more than anything else. In the Legislature there were constant cabals of the members from the different counties to try to evade the burden, for the tax in the first place was apportioned in quotas on the counties. There were on an average sixteen supervisors in a county. They apportioned the county quota on the smaller districts, under a similar system of special combination. The assessors were officers in the townships, who apportioned the taxes on individuals according to their judgment, as above stated. At this point, therefore, special advantages and exemptions were won by those who were in friendship with the assessors, so that the system was one of favouritism, as any system of apportionment of social burdens by a commission endowed with discretion must always be. In all this there was no haste. The collectors were another set of officers whose functions began when those of the assessors were completed. They did their work nominally under the oversight of the supervisors, but really under no oversight. It depended on the zeal of the collector, and the good-will of the people in his district, what amount of taxes was collected. The collectors paid to the county treasurers, and they to the State treasurers. There was no responsibility and no coercion in the system.[1]

We may here add what seems necessary with regard to the history of taxation during the latter part of the period which we are studying.

June 10, 1782, Luzerne made a report from Philadelphia: "No influence can persuade the people to tax themselves. We had great hopes before the recent disasters to commerce; but almost all the legislatures without exception allege their inability, which they say results from this cause.

[1] Hamilton's Works, viii. 63.

. . . Mr. Morris is obliged to have recourse to dangerous expedients for the execution of the engagements which he has contracted. He had reduced the pay of the officers of the army, and they had consented, in the hope of being paid regularly; but he is forced to suspend certain payments, and the result is trouble in the army." He refers to the revolt of the Connecticut line. The anticipation of peace prevents new levies. An ex-Governor of Virginia has proposed that no taxes be laid till the middle of next year. It met much support, but has been rejected. The army of the South is even worse off than that of Washington.[1]

Livingston wrote to Adams, December 19, 1782: "It is extremely difficult in a country so little used to taxes as ours is to lay them directly, and almost impossible to impose them so equally as not to render them too oppressive on some members of the community, while others contribute little or nothing. This difficulty is increased by the continual change of property in this country, and by the small proportion the income bears to the value of land." [2]

He wrote again to the same, February 13, 1783: "Our distress for money has rather increased than diminished. This object will demand your attention full as much if the war should be terminated as if it should continue. The army and the other public creditors begin to grow very uneasy, and our present exhausted situation will not admit of internal loans or such taxes as will suffice to give them relief." [3]

Morris wrote to the governors, July 11, 1783, that he had anticipations out for more than a million. It is another exhortation to raise taxes. He combats the notion that we have funds in Europe, or that there is no hurry about taxes, because the notes which he has issued

[1] Circourt, iii. 286. [2] Dip. Corr. Rev. vii. 5. [3] Ibid. 24.

are at six months, and refers to his reports to answer the question what becomes of the money paid in taxes.[1]

To Gerry he wrote, August 26, 1783: "The ability of the States . . . has never been put to the proof by prudent and vigorous taxation, because other countries not so wealthy bear much heavier taxes without inconvenience, and because these very States have borne it, though under another name; for the depreciation of the paper money, which wiped away not less than twelve millions annually, was in effect a tax to that amount."[2]

To Franklin he wrote, September 30, 1783: "Our people still continue as remiss as ever in the payment of taxes. Much of this, as you justly observe, arises from the difficulties of collection; but those difficulties are much owing to an ignorance of proper modes and an unwillingness to adopt them." They all admit that there must be taxes, but each wants to shift them on his neighbour.[3]

Hamilton wrote that in Massachusetts, in 1780, taxes were so heavy that there were real signs of distress. The Legislature stated them at £600,000, and they reduced them, although they were contracting a loan.[4]

In 1785 Massachusetts had a debt of over £1,400,000 currency, and a tax of £100,000. The population was 363,000. The debt amounted to £4 3*s.* 2*d.* per capita, — that is, $13.97; and the tax amounted to five shillings and sevenpence, or ninety-three cents per capita.[5]

In 1796 Gallatin wrote: "During the war Pennsylvania raised some enormous taxes, far beyond her abilities, the arrearages of which are not yet finally paid."[6] From

[1] Dip. Corr. Rev. xii. 376. [2] Ibid 403. [3] Ibid. 417.

[4] Hamilton's Works, iii. 92.

[5] Hist. Mag., March, 1871; from Chickering's Statistics of Mass.

[6] Gallatin's Writings, iii. 166.

March 20, 1778, to March 21, 1783, Pennsylvania undertook to raise by taxation £20.9 millions in continental, £367,281 in State currency, and £745,297 in specie. These amounts were distributed in quotas on the counties. The amounts due August 1, 1784, were £3.1 millions continental, £136,681 State, and £476,239 specie. It was stated that the counties had contributed very unequally.[1] The specie value of what they had paid could not be put higher than two million dollars. This amount had been paid in five years by a State in which there were sixty thousand adult males. We have a later statement that between 1782 and 1787 the amount of taxes paid into the State was £74,739, and that the amount due and unpaid for the same period was £251,379.[2]

May 6, 1784, the Legislature of New York laid a tax of £10,000 on Suffolk County, £13,000 on King's, and £14,000 on Queen's, which was called the "back tax," as compensation to the rest of the State, because those counties had not shared the burdens of the war from 1776 to 1783.[3] June 10, 1784, Benjamin Hawkins of North Carolina wrote to Washington that a tax laid by that State amounted to only sixpence on every hundred acres of land, and a poll-tax of one shilling and sixpence on all white males over twenty-one years of age and on all slaves from twelve years old to fifty.[4]

In Virginia in 1784 begins a series of judgments awarded against the sheriffs of the different counties for balances of taxes due on previous years, with interest.[5] By a report of the Solicitor-general in February, 1785, it appears that the delinquencies of taxes for 1783 were nearly $200,000. Many of the largest and wealthiest counties were most

[1] 9th Assembly, 49.
[2] Lloyd's Debates, i. 69.
[3] Onderdonk's Suffolk & Kings, 110.
[4] Letters to Washington, iv. 69.
[5] Va. Papers, iii. 591.

delinquent, and those which had been occupied by the enemy during the war were less delinquent.[1] In December, 1785, the sheriffs of twenty-eight counties pray for relief and remission of taxes. They have not been able to collect the taxes, on account of the poverty of the people and the scarcity of money.[2] If they distrain the property and try to sell it, there are no bidders for it.[3] In October, 1786, the Solicitor of the State reported to the Governor that, on account of the errors in the returns of taxable property, he could not get judgment against the sheriffs for the taxes of 1785.[4] In that year the delegates of that State in Congress made a plan for new taxes to supply a deficiency of $434,582. They make an enumeration of the subjects of taxation. They propose to tax carriages, and also to take a fraction of the fees of various court officers; also to tax physicians, surgeons, and apothecaries, improved lots of land, retail merchants in large cities and small towns at different rates, and to lay a two per cent duty on imports, and six shillings per hogshead of tobacco. With all this they do not, by their own calculation, provide one half the deficiency.[5]

All through 1786 the sheriffs in Virginia were complaining of the impossibility of collecting taxes, and petitioning to be relieved from their responsibilities. In 1787 a report of David Ross to the Governor showed that many counties were in arrears of taxes since 1782, and that in some cases the collectors had speculated in paper money, buying it up at a discount and paying the arrears therewith.[6] At the end of 1787 the sheriffs of nine counties were still petitioning for relief from back taxes.[7] In April, 1789, the Solicitor of the State reported to the Governor a list of

[1] Va. Papers, iv. 10.

[2] Chastellux first found a class of poor persons in Virginia. He attributed the existence of this class to the system of great estates (Chastellux, ii. 190).

[3] Va. Papers, iv. 77.

[4] Ibid. 178.

[5] Ibid. iv. 215.

[6] Ibid. 230.

[7] Ibid. 377.

the sheriffs, with their deficiencies in the collection of taxes, for the years since 1782.[1] In March, 1790, a State agent reported that he found in several counties considerable sums of money in the sheriffs' hands, collected from delinquents on the specific tax of 1782, which they had not paid over.[2]

If any one has doubts of the intimate connection between finance and politics, and about the constant influence of the former on the latter, he should study the Virginia Papers. They throw a very important and most unedifying light on the political position of the Virginia anti-federalists. We have seen in the preceding pages ample proof that the distress and havoc of the war was perhaps greater in Virginia than anywhere else, while the inefficiency of the war efforts was perhaps more striking in that State than anywhere else; and we have seen that the reason of this great cost on the one side, and small result on the other, was the faults of the administration. After the war was over this same inefficiency of administration produced the result that little or nothing was done to bring the finances into order, or to discharge the obligations of the war, while some other States were rapidly and easily regulating their finances and paying their debts.

On account of the maladministration through this period, the persons who had suffered hardship by impressments and damages had in some cases received no vouchers for the loss, while in other cases they had received extravagant and undue compensation. Confusion, loss, and injustice prevailed on all sides. Then, when it was proposed to adjust the accounts between the States and the Union, Colonel Davies, the agent of Virginia, set to work to collect vouchers; and, as that was possible only in very few cases, to collect secondary and incidental evidence of the expenditures in the State; that is, he had to try to remedy

[1] Va. Papers, iv. 595.

[2] Ibid. v. 121.

the negligence and waste of the past. This he was called upon to do, not on behalf of the individual sufferers, but on behalf of the State; and his task resolved itself into an attempt, not to simply set in order and present the true facts of the case, but to inflate to the greatest possible degree the claims and charges which the State might make against the Union. Those States which had managed their affairs with comparative order and regularity were, therefore, to suffer doubly by the misbehaviour of those which had allowed everything financial to fall into chaos; for they all vied with one another in making their claims against the Union as big as possible, when it came to the settlement, just as they had all vied with one another, during the war, in their efforts to make their contributions to the common cause as small as possible. Those which had the fewest books and vouchers were the freest in swelling the figures of accounts made up by construction out of secondary and incidental evidence. In view of all these facts, we see that the Virginia anti-federalists were trying either to obliterate all the accounts, in order that nobody might be paid, or else, if all were to be paid, to create questionable accounts on behalf of their own State. We have here, therefore, very strong evidence indeed in favour of the fact which Hamilton alleged as his controlling motive in assumption, and a strong reinforcement of his argument that the different States had behaved very differently in keeping accounts and in their methods of charging expenditure; and that it was hopeless to do justice between them, if each was left to act for itself. We have also a strong justification of his plan of allotting an assumed sum between the States, in order to cut off the operation by which, while each vied with the others in swelling its demands, the aggregate of their demands against the Union was being increased beyond all limit.[1]

[1] Hamilton, 154.

CHAPTER XXI.

MORRIS'S UNPOPULARITY IN THE SOUTHERN STATES; MORE HETEROGENEOUS TASKS; THE MEMORIAL OF THE ARMY OFFICERS; THE OVERDRAFT OF JANUARY, 1783; MORE APPEALS TO FRANCE.

THE States from Virginia southward became greatly irritated against Morris during 1781 and 1782. The causes and consequences of this fact were important.

General Greene wrote to Reed, May 4, 1781, that the power of the Southern States to support war was not nearly so great as had been supposed. The whigs and tories were butchering each other, and the whigs would do nothing unless the tories were forced to do as much. He complained of the lack of energy. The people would do nothing when the enemy had passed away from the immediate neighbourhood.[1]

After the downfall of the continental paper in May, 1781, at Philadelphia, specie came into general circulation there. Inasmuch as the paper remained in use south of the Potomac, specie did not come in there. The Southerners took into their heads an ineradicable notion that Morris had obtained large amounts of specie from France, which belonged to all, ought to have been shared among all, but had been kept at Philadelphia unfairly. This opinion and the ill-humour produced by it are fully expressed by Johnson, who indeed seems to be not free from the same state of mind.[2] The Southern States also thought

[1] Reed's Reed, ii. 351. [2] Johnson's Greene, ii. 253, 360, 373.

themselves abandoned by the rest when it came their turn to be overrun. In this they were not peculiar, for each State, when it was the seat of war, thought the same.

When Morris took office Congress recalled and turned over to him all the bills which they had drawn and placed in the hands of various agents. This step was essential to the new system, and to correct the abuses of the old. Among the rest were some bills on Franklin, which had been appropriated to the use of the Southern army, and put in the hands of Burnet, the purchasing agent there.[1] Johnson says that Burnet spent $20,000 of them in defiance of Morris. The latter treated these bills as generally available, and disregarded the previous appropriation of them.

Johnson finds a grievance in the fact that Morris demanded that the Southern army should wait for the goods which John Laurens had brought to Boston. It was no doubt long to wait, especially for men who were in the direst necessity; but if the bills had been sold in order to buy clothing here, and the clothing which had been bought in Europe with the money borrowed there had been left unused, there would have been a double expenditure of the slender resources which Morris was striving so hard to economize. When every dollar was needed five or six times for separate and great necessities, he could not allow two of them to be spent in supplying one necessity.

Perhaps Morris meant sympathy and condolence when he wrote to Greene: "The Superintendent of Finance in particular, circumstanced as the American Superintendent is, must give the fullest applause to an officer who finds in his own genius an ample resource for the want of men, money, clothes, arms, and supplies." He did not leave Greene entirely neglected, for he sent an agent to be with

[1] See vol. i. p. 282.

the army, with a small sum, to intervene in the direst extremity,[1] — which was reached and passed.

Speaking of this agent, Hall, Johnson relates the matter as follows: "If the money at this time deposited in his hands was intended for the occasional use of the army, he certainly did great injustice to the views of Mr. Morris; for his having money of the United States or of Mr. Morris in his hands for the use of the army, appears to have come accidentally to the knowledge of General Greene, and when the latter, on the 6th of November, required of him an advance of 1,200 guineas, he intimates in his answer of the 8th 'that the money had been confided to him by Mr. Morris to take up his notes or those of his bank;' we presume at their depreciated value, for he says: 'Should I part with it, I shall be exceedingly censurable, particularly after Mr. Morris's instructions to me, wherein he says that every shilling of it to him is worth pounds.' He admits, however, 'that he was authorized to let General Greene have small sums upon the most pressing occasions.' General Greene conceived that this most pressing occasion had arrived, and notwithstanding Mr. Hall declared that he should be bankrupted by the demand, insisted upon and obtained the 1,200 guineas."

When Morris began to supply the army by contract, at the beginning of 1782, he did not extend the system to the Southern States. This led to new dissatisfaction. Governor Harrison of Virginia, in a letter to the Council, in January, 1782, after complaining of the State laws which had robbed the executive of all necessary power, went on to say: "It has long been matter of wonder and indignant surprise to me that Congress and its ministers have not taken the measures for supplying your army that they have taken in every State to the north of us; that is, by

[1] Marshall's Washington, iv. 557 n.

contract. With us, they depend on this State for everything, though they know it can only be obtained by force; and when their wants are supplied, they even refuse to give us credit for what they have obtained, but insist on our full quota of money being paid into their treasury. It is this kind of partial conduct that is the true cause of our distress, and that will in the end, if not amended, be attended with ruin both to you and us."[1] In the Virginia Papers there are several instances to be found in which this gentleman was over-hasty in assuming that he had a grievance against somebody. It is not true that credit was refused to Virginia; but her own State documents show that through the faults of her own administrative system she had no vouchers upon which to make claim in proper form. Morris replied to this complaint of Governor Harrison, repelling the strictures on Congress and himself, and urging the Governor to perform the duty of Virginia in supplying the Southern army.[2] In February the Virginia delegates, having conferred with Morris, reported to the Governor that he would provide for the Southern States by contracts as soon as taxes were laid there. This was his ground from which he would not swerve.[3] June 21, Congress asked him to report why he had not supplied the Southern army by contract.[4] The answer is not at hand, but it no doubt was to this effect, for contracts were not introduced there.

In February, 1782, Greene said of Virginia and North Carolina: "They both appear like two great overgrown babies who have got out of temper, and who have been accustomed to great indulgence."[5]

In the same month the Deputy Quartermaster, Claiborne, having written to Pickering what complaints were

[1] Johnson's Greene, ii. 311. [2] Va. Papers, iii. 77. [3] Ibid. 76.
[4] Journn. Cong. vii 302. [5] Reed's Reed, ii. 378.

current in Virginia, the latter was provoked to this indignant outburst: "That your government, too, should complain, as you suggest, is to me a matter of astonishment. Good God! from what sources are public moneys to be derived? Is it imagined that the Financier has the power of creation, that the appointment of that officer was to rid the State of all further trouble and expense; that it was to receive moneys from, instead of supplying the public treasury?" The Quartermaster goes on to say that the state of things everywhere else is the same as in Virginia; that he has carried on his department almost wholly by persuasion and impresses. The States have furnished the Financier no funds.[1]

In April Colonel Carrington declared: "Nothing but the most criminal negligence in the different States can frustrate Mr. Morris's views of giving our finances the firmest basis. Of this I am a little fearful. The jealousies and the intolerable indolence which prevail are really alarming."[2]

Another matter which produced new cause of dissatisfaction and suspicion was the exportation of tobacco from Virginia under the capitulation of Yorktown. Morris was authorized to buy for the United States the goods of the storekeepers in Yorktown, paying for them with tobacco, and giving a special license to the storekeepers to carry the tobacco to New York. The federal government thus made gain out of its own restrictions, as sovereigns have done for centuries. The citizens who were debarred from the same enterprise, and whose exclusion created the profit of the special licenses, although they thought the restriction a proper and necessary war-measure, watched the transaction with suspicion. The possibility of course suggested itself that those who were charged with the execu-

[1] Va. Papers, iii. 63.

[2] Ibid. 144.

tion of the transaction might easily enlarge it somewhat for their own benefit. This possibility soon grew into a suspicion, and then into an allegation. It seems that Morris, in his great necessity for money, having found the profit which he could win by this transaction, may have carried it further for the account of the Union. In July, 1782, the Virginia Assembly voted that the Governor should forward the views of Congress and the Financier in regard to the exportation of a specified amount of tobacco, the Assembly being satisfied with the explanations given.[1] Further complaint seems to have been made, however, for an investigation was made by Congress in February, 1783. It resulted in a report that the amount of tobacco shipped had never surpassed the limit set in the original resolution allowing it.[2]

Greene, in his eagerness to provide clothing for his soldiers, who were almost naked, made a contract for a supply. He had the same fate as others who were led by zeal to take personal risks. He fell under suspicion of illegal trading and collusion with contractors, and never cleared himself while he lived. His transaction was partly carried out by bills on Morris. This matter became mixed up with Virginia affairs,[3] and contributed to the Virginia hatred of Morris. The report spread far and wide that "the American general, employing the funds of the public, had, through the agency of Banks, opened a lucrative commerce with Charleston; and in a short time it was superadded that Mr. Robert Morris, particeps in the iniquity, had given him an unlimited right of drawing, in order to furnish a capital for speculation."[4] We have seen above that complaint was made of Morris, at the time of

[1] Va. Papers, iii. 193.

[2] Journ. Cong. viii. 92.

[3] Va. Papers, iii. 363, 396, 402, 428, 435.

[4] Johnson, ii. 365.

the Yorktown expedition, that he did not provide for the officers taken prisoners at Charleston. In 1783 Greene wrote to Washington: "The people of this State [South Carolina] are much prejudiced against Congress and the Financier. Those who came from the northward think they have been amazingly neglected by both in their distresses. . . . This State has contributed more than any other State, it is true, towards the continental expenses; but necessity obliged them." [1]

In May, 1782, Morris was ordered by Congress to prepare a report on the state of commerce of the United States, together with a plan for the protection thereof; and it was ordered that he, as Agent of Marine, should apply to the commanders of the fleets of France and Spain for protection to commerce; also that he should prepare a draft of an application to France for the protection of the trade of the United States.[2] May 14, he made these reports, which were ordered to be transmitted to Franklin. In his statement of commerce, after stating what it might be, he says that none of it exists except the export of provisions to the West Indies and tobacco to Europe. The trade cannot be carried on without convoys. With convoys, tobacco would be cheaper in Europe, and European goods in America. The enemy, by depressing American commerce, gain two things: they obtain resources, and they carry on contraband trade. "The history of human affairs demonstrates the inefficacy of penal laws to prevent such a commerce when the temptation is great; and therefore, although the dispositions of the several Legislatures cannot be questioned, yet as long as the enemy can send their goods from New York, Charleston, and Halifax cheaper than the fair trader can import them, that contraband will subsist." He puts the insurance at forty per

[1] Letters to Washington, iv. 5. [2] Secret Journ. iii. 102.

cent, which makes a loss on the exportation of tobacco. The profits must all be sought on the importation from France. With convoy, he showed a profit of ten per cent on the exportation. The reason for this subject being taken up at this time was that the trade had suffered greatly from the English cruisers in the spring of 1782.[1]

In August he informed Congress that the fourth class of the lottery had been drawn. He asks how the prizes are to be paid. He refused when he took office to have anything to do with the lottery, and he now leaves it to Congress to give directions in the matter. He is too busy to attend to it, to say nothing of other reasons. The letter implies disapproval of the lottery.[2]

In September the "Magnifique," a seventy-four gun ship of the French navy, having been lost in Boston Harbour, Morris proposed that Congress should make a present to the King of France of the seventy-four gun ship "America." His chief reason was that there was no money in the treasury with which to fit out that ship for the United States.[3]

In September the goods at last arrived which had been purchased in Holland in the previous year, at the time of John Laurens's embassy. Morris wrote to Franklin, complaining of the wasteful purchases in Europe: "The purchase of unnecessary things because they are cheap appears to be very great extravagance. We want the money as much as anything else; and the world must form a strange idea of our management if, while we are trying to borrow, we leave vast magazines of clothing to rot at Brest, and purchase others to be shipped from Holland. . . . The detention of our goods has obliged me to purchase clothing and other articles at a great expense, while those

[1] Dip. Corr. Rev. iii. 355. [2] State Dep. MSS. 137, i. 725.
[3] Dip. Corr. Rev. xii. 254.

very things were lying about at different places in Europe."[1]

Morris wrote to Washington about this clothing, that it was unfit for soldiers' use. He was selling it to pay debts incurred for clothing, including $12,000 for needlework due to people in extreme indigence.[2] In January, 1783, he wrote to Franklin that he had been obliged to sell part of the goods which arrived from Holland to save his credit. Thus the purchase of these goods had in the first place subjected Franklin to extreme distress, and then Morris was obliged to sell them, to save himself from bankruptcy.

On the 6th of January, 1783, a committee of officers arrived from the army, at Philadelphia, with a memorial to Congress. Anticipating peace, they feared that the disposition would be to get rid of the army as soon as possible, and having once got rid of them, to pay no attention to any of their subsequent remonstrances or complaints. The committee of Congress to whom their memorial was referred held a conference with Morris. Instead of being in a position to undertake any new burden, he was obliged to tell them that his department had reached such a crisis that he had been on the point of asking for a confidential committee to whom he might intrust the facts.[3]

On the 8th of January, 1783, Morris had a conference with such a confidential Committee of Congress. He told them that he had overdrawn on France three and a half million livres, and must draw more, relying on Adams's loan. This was the result of his operations of the last two years, and especially of the loan issued in the previous February, to provide the officers with clothing. By drawing and redrawing he had secured extensions, which had

[1] Dip. Corr. Rev. xii. 271. [2] Ibid. 279.
[3] Elliot's Debates, v. 21.

now produced this result. He wanted the support of a Committee of Congress for the new drafts which must now be made. The Committee agreed to obtain this authorization under the seal of secrecy. Only one member doubted if it was right to do this; but the others told him that it was unavoidable, for credit abroad and the public service at home. They felt the evil of it when negotiating for peace.[1] On the 11th Morris wrote to Franklin: "Imagine the situation of a man who is to direct the finances of a country almost without revenue (for such you will perceive this to be), surrounded by creditors whose distresses, while they increase their clamour, render it more difficult to appease them; an army ready to disband or mutiny; a government whose sole authority consists in the power of framing recommendations. Surely it is not necessary to add any colouring to such a piece, and yet truth would justify more than fancy could paint."[2]

Morris therefore knew early in January, 1783, that his account with Grand was overdrawn. Luzerne asked him to explain the reasons. He said that it was due to two millions and a half of bills on behalf of Beaumarchais, which were due in June, 1782. He had hoped that the French government would make some provision for these bills. As they had been running three years, and had been sold over and over again, it was necessary to provide for them. The Dutch loan also produced a million less than he expected, and he had been forced to buy things in America in the place of those which had been left in Europe.[3] On the 13th he wrote to Franklin: "If one bill should be protested, I could no longer serve the United States."[4] In Livingston's despatches of January to Frank-

[1] Madison Papers, i. 251.
[2] Dip. Corr. Rev. xii. 310.
[3] Ibid. 316.
[4] Ibid. 313.

lin, he urges the necessities of the United States. He uses the revolt in the army as an argument that more help must be obtained from France, and he expresses fears of disorder in the United States. "I do not pretend to justify the negligence of the States in not providing greater supplies: some of them might do more than they have done; none of them all that is required. It is my duty to confide to you that if the war is continued in this country it must be in a great measure at the expense of France. If peace is made, a loan will be absolutely necessary to enable us to discharge the army, that will not easily separate without pay."[1] He also wrote to Lafayette: "If the war continues, we shall lean heavier upon France than we have done. If peace is made, she must add one obligation more to those she has already imposed, — she must enable us to pay off our army, or we may find the reward of her exertions and ours suspended longer than we could wish." [2]

Before these letters could have been received in Europe, on the 25th of February, 1783, Vergennes and Franklin entered into a supplementary treaty by which France lent the United States six million livres more, at the rate of a half a million per month during the year 1783, with interest at five per cent. In the treaty the substance of the treaty of July 16, 1782, was repeated. The present loan was to be repaid in six equal annual instalments, beginning at 1797, and the interest was to run from the 1st of January, 1784.[3]

In 1788 a statement was drawn up at the French treasury to show when and at what rates the payments would fall due. It is as follows, in millions of livres: [4] —

[1] Dip. Corr. Rev. iv. 462.
[2] Ibid. x. 21.
[3] Treaties and Conventions, 258.
[4] Dip. Corr. U. S. iii. 390.

	Instalments of the principal.	Interest.	Total.
1787 . . .	2.5	1.6	4.1
1788 . . .	2.5	1.485	3.985
1789 . . .	2.5	1.370	3.870
1790 . . .	2.5	1.255	3.755
1791 . . .	2.5	1.140	3.640
1792 . . .	2.5	1.025	3.525
1793 . . .	2.5	.910	3.410
1794 . . .	2.5	.795	3.295
1795 . . .	2.5	.680	3.180
1796 . . .	2.5	.565	3.065
1797 . . .	2.5	.450	2.950
1798 . . .	2.5	.325	2.825
1799 . . .	1.	.200	1.200
1800 . . .	1.	.150	1.150
1801 . . .	1.	.100	1.100
1802 . . .	1.	.05	1.050
	34.	12.1	46.100

This loan of February, 1783, passes as an unnoticed incident in the midst of the new appeal which was being made.

On the 10th of March Vergennes wrote to Luzerne: Franklin informs him that he is ordered to borrow four million dollars, and to ask the continued favours of the King; it is the last request of the kind he would have to make; he said that without this assistance the continental army could neither be kept together, nor disbanded without danger. "I informed His Majesty of the embarrassments of Congress, and of their inability to provide for their necessities by means of taxes, which the imperfections or the weakness of a rising administration did not permit them to levy. . . . Since the nation has reached the period of maturity consecrated by its emancipation and political independence, it seems that it ought to be sufficient for itself, and not to require new efforts of the generosity of its allies. . . . Notwithstanding the difficulties which His Majesty experienced in his own finances, he determined

. . . to grant to Congress a new loan of six millions of livres."[1]

This letter could not have been received here until May, but in March Luzerne informed Morris that he had reported during the last year the reforms introduced by Morris into his department; also that he thought a public revenue was about to be established, and had encouraged the extension of a loan for the next year. These assurances had brought about a new loan. He now finds himself deceived in the opinions he had expressed, and must report now that he was mistaken. "The King has not been able to make this last effort without great difficulties. . . . With regard to the resources which you may seek in other places besides France, the letters which I have had the honour to read to you do not allow any success to be looked for until the United States shall have established a permanent public revenue; and the delay and repugnance with which they proceed in doing this being known in Europe, the inclination for lending money to Congress which may have existed has disappeared. . . . Without the speedy establishment of a substantial public revenue, and without the vigorous execution of the engagements entered into by Congress, the hope of obtaining loans in Europe must be given up."[1]

[1] Dip. Corr. Rev. xi. 171. [2] Ibid. 125.

CHAPTER XXII.

MORRIS RESIGNS; CONSENTS TO CONTINUE IN ORDER TO PAY OFF THE ARMY; ISSUES NOTES FOR THAT PURPOSE; FAULT-FINDING WITH HIM; LAST VAIN APPEALS TO FRANCE; THE LOAN IN HOLLAND; THE OVERDRAFT OF 1784; MORRIS QUITS OFFICE; THE SUBSEQUENT ORGANIZATION OF THE TREASURY.

WE are now in a position to see what had been the course of things during Morris's administration. The year 1781 constitutes the grand crisis of the Revolution. At the beginning of that year the Americans were on the verge of failure. France was obliged to put her assistance, both pecuniary and military, on a new plane. Morris took charge of the finances. France provided loans and gifts on a far greater scale than before. The ship "Lafayette" was fitted out with a large cargo of the most essential supplies. She was unfortunately captured, and these goods had to be replaced from the subsidy. Then came the enormous waste by the bad proceedings in Holland and the abandonment of the goods which had been obtained at great expense. In America the expenses of the Yorktown campaign had to be met, and the bills drawn upon Europe fell upon Franklin when his subsidy was exhausted. Morris was also struggling to extricate himself from the mischiefs entailed upon him by the paper system, and engaged in a dangerous system of drawing and redrawing. He had also ventured on large expenses for the payments to the officers. This all depended upon a hope that at last definite and trustworthy resources would be obtained from taxation. At the beginning of the year 1783 the effect of all these measures had accumulated, while the hope of the impost was destroyed by the opposition of Rhode Island. Every plan which he had had when he undertook the office had therefore failed. Every belief and expectation which had justified him in the measures which he had adopted had come to naught. He could not see that Congress or the States were willing to view the situation as it was, or to take the steps which were imperatively necessary. Nor did anybody else have any proposition which was adequate for meeting the situation.

On the 24th of January, 1783, he sent his resignation to the President of Congress. "To increase our debts while the prospect of paying them diminishes, does not consist with my ideas of integrity. I must therefore quit a situation which becomes utterly unsupportable." An injunction of secrecy was put on his letter and on the fact of his resignation.[1] Madison says: "This letter made a deep and solemn impression on Congress. It was considered as the effect of despondence in Mr. Morris of seeing justice done to the public creditors or the public finances placed on an honourable establishment; as a source of fresh hopes to the enemy when known; as ruinous both to domestic and foreign credit; and as producing a vacancy which none knew how to fill, and which no fit man would venture to accept."[2] February 26, Morris asked that the injunction of secrecy should be raised from his resignation, because he must inform certain persons whose interests would be affected by it. Congress complied. The next day he wrote to Washington that Congress wished to do justice, but "they will not adopt the necessary measures, because they are afraid of offending their States." March 5, Congress

[1] Dip. Corr. Rev. xii. 326. [2] Madison Papers, i. 274.

appointed a committee to devise the steps to be taken in view of Morris's resignation.

His resignation brought out very diverse criticisms. Madison shows that he thought Morris's letter abrupt, and calculated to give an opportunity to his enemies.[1] Arthur Lee and Bland, in commenting upon it, disparaged his administration, and threw "oblique censure" on his character. Lee blamed him for his revelations of the state of the finances. Wilson and Hamilton defended him. In general, his letters were considered reprehensible in Congress,[2] "as in general, also, a conviction prevailed of the personal merit and public importance of Mr. Morris."[3]

On the 12th of March Morris noted in his diary that a ship had arrived with six hundred thousand livres in specie, ordered in October, 1782: "And this day also appeared a virulent attack on my public and private character, signed 'Lucius,' in the 'Freeman's Journal,' replete with falsehoods."[4] These articles in the "Freeman's Journal" ran through March and April. Morris was abused especially for his resignation, which was said to reflect on the honesty of the States and of Congress. It was said that he had stabbed credit. "So much has a sudden and enormous acquisition of wealth by speculating on the distresses of the war pampered your pride and inebriated your understanding. Remember, sir, what you were, and think what you may be." He is charged with ruining the citizens of Boston, and with buying certificates from distressed owners. The letters of "Junius" had stimulated a large number of

[1] Madison Papers, i. 513.

[2] Charles Biddle (128) tells a story that the Board of War once wanted to remove Morris from the office of Financier. Colonel Grayson asked Richard Peters to help. Peters said that he would, if they would change one word in their memorial. It was said in it that the Board complained. "Strike out the word 'Board,'" said he, "and put in the word 'shingle,' and I will sign it directly."

[3] Ibid. 371.

[4] Dip. Corr. Rev. xii. 337.

imitators in England and America. These letters are one of the best examples of the style of the provincial imitator of "Junius." Arthur Lee, when younger, had affected this style. If he did not write these letters he must have inspired them.

March 17, Morris wrote to the President of Congress: "I must observe on the misconstruction which men totally ignorant of our affairs have put on that conduct which severe necessity compels me to pursue. Such men, affecting an intimate knowledge of things, have charged the destruction of public credit to me, and interpreted the terms of my resignation into reflections upon Congress. . . . On the day on which I was publicly charged with ruining your credit, those despatches arrived from Europe which tell you it was already at an end. The circumstances which I alluded to in my letter of resignation were not yet known in Europe. It was not yet known that Rhode Island had unanimously refused to pass the impost law, and that Virginia had repealed it." [1]

When this letter from Morris was read, in which he said that the credit of the United States was at an end, Bland said that, if Morris thought that, then it was absurd for him to be Superintendent of Finance.

On the 29th of March Lee made a motion in Congress for an investigation of Morris's department; but it was rejected, on the ground that such an investigation would be unsuited to the modes of business in Congress, that the subject-matter was already partly before Congress, and that the measure was unsuitable in other respects.[2] In the same month Joseph Reed wrote to a correspondent in England: "Mr. Morris has been for a long time the *dominus factotum* whose dictates none dare oppose, and from whose decisions lay no appeal; he has, in fact, exercised the power

[1] Dip. Corr. Rev. xii. 343.

[2] Madison Papers, i. 425.

really of the three great departments, and Congress has only had to give their fiat to his mandates. I believe things have gone better, they certainly could not go worse, than before; but we are like to be at sea again shortly. The newspapers, which I presume Burnett will carry, contain his [Morris's] letters to Congress, which will probably be the subject of as much speculation with you as with us." [1]

Hamilton, although he was very friendly to Morris and sympathized deeply with him, did not approve of his letter of resignation. He wrote to Washington, April 11: "As to Mr. Morris, I will give your Excellency a true explanation of his conduct. He has been for some time pressing Congress to endeavour to obtain funds, and has found a great backwardness in the business. He found the taxes unproductive in the different States; he found the loans in Europe making a very slow progress; he found himself pressed on all hands for supplies; he found himself, in short, reduced to this alternative, either of making engagements which he could not fulfil, or declaring his resignation in case funds were not established by a given time. Had he followed the first course, the bubble must soon have burst; he must have sacrificed his credit and his character, and public credit, already in a ruined condition, must have lost its last support. He wisely judged it better to resign. This might increase the embarrassments of the moment, but the necessity of the case, it was to be hoped, would produce the proper measures, and he might then resume the direction of the machine with advantage and success. He also had some hope that his resignation would prove a stimulus to Congress. He was, however, ill advised in the publication of a letter of resignation. This was an imprudent step, and has given a handle to his personal enemies, who, by playing upon the passions of

[1] Reed's Reed, ii. 393.

others, have drawn some well-meaning men into the cry against him. But Mr. Morris certainly deserves a great deal from his country. I believe no man in this country but himself could have kept the money machine a-going during the period he has been in office. From everything that appears, his administration has been upright, as well as able. The truth is, the old leaven of Deane and Lee is at this day working against Mr. Morris. He happened in that dispute to have been on the side of Deane, and certain men can never forgive him. A man whom I once esteemed, and whom I will rather suppose duped than wicked, is the second actor in this business."[1]

The two Morrises and Hamilton had a project in March to unite the army interest with that of the public creditors, in order to bring pressure to bear on Congress which should force them to do justice to both. This project easily bore the appearance from the outside of a conspiracy to overawe Congress by the army. Washington also wrote to Hamilton that it might be construed by the army as a conspiracy to defeat the claims of the army until those of the certificate holders were satisfied.[2] Hamilton refuted these misconstructions of the enterprise. He said that there were two parties in Congress, — a national and a State-rights party. "The advocates for continental funds have blended the interests of the army with other creditors, from a conviction that no funds [taxes] for partial purposes will go through those States to whose citizens the United States are largely indebted."[3]

In April Congress appointed a committee, of which Hamilton, Madison, and Peters were members, to confer with Morris about his continuance in office. They reported as his statement: "That his continuance in office was

[1] Letters to Washington, iv. 20. [2] Washington, viii. 418.
[3] Letters to Washington, iv. 17.

highly injurious to his private affairs, and contrary to his private inclinations, but that he felt the importance of the exertions necessary to be made at the present juncture toward the reduction of the army in a manner satisfactory to them and convenient to the public; that therefore, if Congress should think his services toward effecting that object of importance, and should desire them, he would be ready to continue them till arrangements for that purpose could be made, and the engagements taken by him in consequence, as well as those already entered into, could be finally completed; that in this case he should hope for the support of Congress. Whereupon, resolved that the Superintendent of Finance be informed that Congress are of opinion the public service requires his continuance in office till arrangements for the reduction of the army can be made, and the engagements that shall be taken by him in consequence, as well as those already entered into, shall be finally completed."[1] He told them that the amount of three months' pay which was stated by the General to be indispensable was $750,000. No important part of this can be provided. The most which can be done is to risk a large paper anticipation. He would have to become personally liable on leaving the office for about half a million, and depend on his successor to save him from ruin, and risk his integrity, by which he seems to mean here, as elsewhere, his commercial credit.[2]

In the manuscript of this report in the Department of State a paragraph is struck out, in which the committee quote Morris as saying that he thought it essential, if he remained in office, that Congress should stimulate the States to supply money, and should get a further loan from France.[3] The conference of the committee with Morris

[1] Journ. Cong. viii. 184.

[2] Dip. Corr. Rev. xii. 346.

[3] State Dep. MSS. Reports, iv. 387.

does not seem to have resulted in a clear understanding. In a letter of the 1st of May, he restated the conditions of his continuance in office. They were that Congress should explicitly ask him to go on, and should pledge themselves to support him; also that the purpose of his continuance should be distinctly expressed, namely, to issue the paper notes for disbanding the army and to redeem the same. He expressly withheld his approbation from their plan of providing for the debt by the Act of April 18, by which they laid an impost for $900,000 and left the States to provide a million and a half more by unspecified supplementary taxes.[1]

Congress passed a resolution, May 2, that the Superintendent of Finance be directed to take the necessary arrangements for carrying the views of Congress into execution, and that he be assured of their firm support toward fulfilling the engagements he has already taken, or may take, on the public account, during his continuance in office.[2] On the same day they put on the Secret Journal a resolution proposed by Hamilton, that the payment of the army and other obligations made it necessary to raise taxes. They urged the States to lay taxes. They proposed a further application to France for three million livres in addition to the six million already obtained for this year.[3]

This is the point at which Robert Morris performed his greatest public service. It was known that the army would rebel if an attempt was made to disband it without pay. No one knew how to make any pretence of paying it, unless Robert Morris would do it. This also was what enraged his enemies and brought them to silence for a time, until they had used him for public services which no one

[1] Dip. Corr. Rev. xii. 353.
[2] Journ. Cong. viii. 189.
[3] Secret Journ. iii. 341.

else could render. Then, as will be seen, they began to yelp and snarl again. Magnanimity never was a colonial virtue. For the moment he was indispensable. We cannot tell in what way or form Morris put his name upon the notes which he issued to pay the army.[1] If those notes had been simple certificates of indebtedness of the United States, it appears that nothing could have been done with them. In effect he indorsed them, and it was his name and credit which made them available.

In January Morris had argued to Luzerne that it was very important, in order to bring the peace negotiations to a favourable conclusion, to keep the army up to a good state of efficiency.[2] In the conference between him and the Committee of Congress, in the middle of May, the committee maintained that it was desirable, for economic reasons, to disband the army, but that for political reasons it ought to be kept up. The Secretary of War said that the men would not continue in the field, under their present enlistment, if the war should break out again.[3] Morris then urged that they be disbanded at once, so as to reduce expenses. "We are keeping up an army at great expense, and very much against their inclination, for a mere punctilio." He thought it foolish to doubt of the sincerity of Great Britain, as it was the fashion to do.[4]

On the 3d of May he consented to go on for the particular purpose of paying off the army. On the 12th he issued a circular to the governors of the States, explaining the new state of things, and calling on them for the necessary support. "Nothing would have induced me to continue in office but a view of the public distresses. These distresses are much greater than can easily be conceived. I am not ignorant that attempts are made to infuse the

[1] See chapter xxv.
[2] Dip. Corr. Rev. xii. 321.
[3] Ibid. 367; Morris's Diary.
[4] Ibid. 364.

pernicious idea that foreign aid is easily attainable, and that of the moneys already obtained, a considerable part remains unappropriated." The only reliance is on the States.[1]

Although he had consented to go on, he was under no delusion as to the probable course which things would take. He had not been at the centre of political activity for eight years without acquiring a just estimate of congressional promises. May 29, he wrote to Washington that some designing men had construed his resignation as a factious desire to raise civil commotion. Unless he is greatly mistaken, the interests of the army and of the public creditors will be given up. The expenses have been kept on in spite of his remonstrance, and the revenue lessened, the States growing more remiss. If he now issues notes for the amount, it must be at six months. He would have been quit of his office long ago but for his desire to procure relief for the army.[2]

At the end of May he wrote to Franklin about his continuance in office. "In what country of the world," he asks, "shall we find a nation willing to tax themselves?"[3] "The distresses we experience arise from our own misconduct. If the resources of this country were drawn forth, they would be amply sufficient; but this is not the case. Congress has not authority equal to the object, and their influence is greatly lessened by their evident incapacity to do justice. . . . Nothing should induce me in my private character to make such applications for money as I am obliged to in my public character. . . . If these notes are not satisfied when they become due, the little credit which remains to this country must fall, and the little authority dependent on it must fall too." He urges Franklin to get another loan from France and to ship 1,800,000 livres.

At the time of the mutiny in Philadelphia, in June,

[1] Dip. Corr. Rev. xii. 357. [2] Ibid. 373. [3] Ibid. 370.

Morris received orders from the President of Congress to go to Princeton, from which place he wrote on the 30th: "In obedience to the orders of Congress, signified by your Excellency, I left Philadelphia on Tuesday evening, and proceeded to this place, having previously, according to your advice and opinion, put a stop to the business of my department until further orders. I am now waiting such orders as Congress may think proper to give, and must pray leave to suggest that the public service may be materially injured unless I should speedily return to Philadelphia and resume the business committed to my care."[1] It seems that there must have been some misunderstanding; for Boudinot, the President of Congress, wrote to Morris on the same day, giving him permission to return to Philadelphia, and saying there is "no entry on our Journals relating to your leaving the city."[2]

June 5, Morris wrote to Governor Livingston that he had issued notes to pay the army. They must be paid when due. His only dependence is on the requisitions of last year and this year.[3] On the 6th Washington wrote to General Heath, and quoted Morris that he could not make the notes for the army at two, four, and six months, but must make them for six months, on account of the remissness of the States, and that he added: "I must entreat, sir, that every influence be used with the States to absorb them, together with my other engagements, by taxation."[4] On the 11th Morris wrote to Governor Livingston a circular letter, in which he says: "On the States I am to rely for payment of the anticipation, amounting, as you will see, to more than a million; and you will observe that this great

[1] State Dep. MSS. 137, ii. 593.

[2] State Dep. MSS., Letters of President of Congress, xvi. 221. The accounts show an entry of $61 for the expenses of the two Morrises on this journey.

[3] N. J. Corr. 332.

[4] Ibid. 339.

anticipation has been made for that service which all affect to have so much at heart, — a payment to the American army." But for this payment to the army the revenues of 1783, even as they are collected, might have absorbed the notes which he must issue. He argues eagerly against those who say that since the notes have six[1] months to run, there is no hurry about providing for them. Provision should be made to pay them at their maturity.[2] On the 28th of July he wrote to the governors again. On the 30th of June last his payments exceeded his receipts by more than a million of dollars. All the taxes since 1781 did not amount to $750,000. The paper will lose its value unless punctually redeemed. The receivers of taxes have been instructed to exchange it, but must be provided with specie for that purpose by taxes. "I might also appeal to the clamours against me for opposing claims I could not properly comply with. Long have I been the object of enmities derived from that origin. I have therefore the right to consider such clamours and such enmities as the confession and the evidence of my care and attention."[3] There is a slanderous report that he has speculated in the paper. Those who discount it are covered with infamy, but he shows that they make a market for the paper which would not otherwise exist.

On the 11th of July the Superintendent of Finance was ordered to direct all the receivers of continental taxes to receive the notes issued in payment of the army, and also to report the reasons why the troops lately furloughed did not receive part of their pay previous thereto, according to the intentions of Congress. They also asked him to state the means by which he expected to redeem the notes issued by him in payment of the army.[4] July 15, he re-

[1] In the N. J. Corr. it is printed twelve.

[2] N. J. Corr. 341.

[3] Ibid. 343.

[4] Journ. Cong. viii. 214.

ported that the non-commissioned officers and privates had been paid one month's pay in specie and three months' pay in notes, and that the officers had been paid four months' pay in notes.[1] He construed the inquiries of the 11th as censure on him. He replied with a history of the last few months, and, in answer to their last inquiry, said that he relied on their promise, when they induced him to continue in office, for the means to redeem the notes.[2] On the 30th he informed them, in answer to other resolutions, that the receivers of taxes had been long since notified to accept all notes signed by him. They now ordered him to publish that fact.[3] They then asked him why the settlement certificates were not made payable to bearer. He answered that they would become paper money and depreciate, if payable to bearer; but being transferable on the books, they were bought and sold as debt.[4]

From these proceedings we perceive that Congress, the immediate exigency being passed and Morris having shouldered the burden, returned to their *rôle* of strict supervisors and exacting masters. It will speedily appear that they did not take up the task of providing for the postponed difficulty any more than they had provided for the difficulty before.

June 17, a committee to examine the department of finance made a report to Congress. "It appears to them the business of that office has been conducted with great ability and assiduity, in a manner highly advantageous to the United States, and in conformity with the system laid down by Congress." Accounts have been punctually kept. Accountability has been enforced. States have been called upon for accounts of specific supplies furnished; but answers have not been obtained, and persons intrusted with

[1] Dip. Corr. Rev. xii. 379.
[2] Ibid. 380.
[3] Journ. Cong. viii. 230.
[4] Dip. Corr. Rev. xii. 393.

public money neglect or refuse to settle their accounts, and there is no means of compelling them. Order and economy have been introduced into the office. No less than two hundred and fifty persons whose pay amounted to $126,300 per annum have been discharged from the department of commissary of issues. The whole amount brought into the public treasury from the 14th of May, 1781, to the 1st of January, 1783, amounts to $2,726,334, and the total expenditure to $3,131,046. In 1782 the expenditures exceeded the receipts by $404,713, which was supplied by the notes of Morris.[1]

In a letter to the Governor of Virginia in July, 1783, Morris had occasion to describe the system of administration of the treasury under him. He informed the Governor that the expense of feeding the troops in Carolina would be borne by the United States; but a regular account, with vouchers, must be transmitted to him. He will send it to the Comptroller of the Treasury, who will certify the amount due by the United States to the party. For this amount Morris will issue a warrant, and the payment will be made in paper, which being delivered to the Receiver for Virginia, will be acknowledged by him, and remitted on account of the State quota. It will then be paid to the Treasurer on Morris's warrant in his favour; and as all the warrants are recorded by the Register, as well as the receipts on them, the treasury books contain the evidence of all the receipts and payments in the simplest form, "and, being accessible to every citizen of the United States, must furnish incontestable proof of the verity of my accounts as exhibited."[2]

In the same month he wrote to the President of Congress that the States show no disposition to respond to the call of Congress; therefore he urges that expenses be

[1] Journ. Cong. viii. 202.

[2] Va. Papers, iii. 510.

greatly reduced.[1] From this we learn that in midsummer, 1783, he already foresaw that none of the assurances under which he had continued in office would be made good.

August 19, in a letter to the Governor of Virginia, he refers to some resolutions of the Virginia Assembly which were intended to refer to himself and his contractors, endeavouring to investigate frauds, which he says are extremely difficult to trace out under the old system. "This is one of the many evils which arise from a defective and unmethodical system; and the evils of such system are (I am sorry to say it) the reasons why many are desirous of seeing it re-established. So long as I continue in office, your Excellency may rely upon my most zealous aid in the investigation which the Assembly of Virginia have instituted. If I had met with that support which, though unmerited by my abilities, was due to my zeal for the public service, I believe that I should have continued in office until, all accounts being settled and all debts provided for, I could have left to my successor the pleasing prospect of future wealth, unclouded by any dismal retrospect of past poverty. But all other things out of the question, there is such a disposition among men to traduce and vilify, that no prudent man will risk a fair reputation by holding an office so important as mine."[2]

In August he wrote to the Paymaster, refusing to make more anticipations. He will have great difficulty to honour those already made, which have already exposed him to groundless clamours. "It becomes impossible to serve a people who convert everything into a ground for calumny. . . . My desire to relieve the army has been greatly cooled from the information that many of them have joined in the reproaches I have incurred for their benefit."[3]

[1] Dip. Corr. Rev. xii. 387.

[2] Va. Papers, iii. 524.

[3] Dip. Corr. Rev. xii. 399.

In September he sent a communication to Congress, in which he stated that the account sent to him by the banker Grand, on the 20th of July, 1782, afforded the only knowledge he had of the bills paid by Grand, and that this account shows why the foreign obligations of the United States cannot be stated. He was surprised to find that "the bills drawn before my administration had not been so advised of as that even the amounts could be known." He cannot tell the expenses for clothing, as he did not order it, and does not know the expenses for loading, unloading, etc. "It is very painful to me, sir, that I am obliged also to inform Congress of my utter inability to render account of the goods I have received." Invoices of clothing had not been received, partly on account of reshipment, changes, etc. "No clothing fit for soldiers (or at least very little, if any), except linen, arrived here before the preliminary of peace. The linen was immediately issued. The greater part of the clothing having arrived after the peace, and it being then evident that the greater part if not the whole of the troops would be disbanded, no measures were taken for making up and issuing clothes for the army." The purpose was to avoid expense. The cloth was sold, and soldiers were allowed for the clothing due them. The money was used to pay the anticipations. Thus he defends himself from blame in not giving clothing to the Massachusetts troops. He did it as soon as he knew of their distress.[1]

September 10, Arthur Lee made a motion, which was carried, that Morris should be called upon to state an account of all notes issued on the credit of the United States and the amount outstanding.[2] He answered this on the 10th of November, giving the daily issues and redemptions. This account shows the method in which the paper

[1] State Dep. MSS. 137, iii. 61. [2] Journ. Cong. viii. 250.

money book-keeping was carried on. First stands an account of the United States with the Treasurer. On the credit side are receipts of notes delivered to the Treasurer from December 26, 1782, to January 11, 1783. They are called subsistence notes, and the amount is $163,720; on the debtor side stand the notes paid out, and the balance is made by the notes on hand, $33,560. Then there is another account, on the creditor side of which is put that which was the debtor side of the former one, namely, the notes issued for subsistence; and on the debtor side the notes redeemed by the Treasurer appear. The issues are brought down to October 1, 1783, and the redemptions to September 1. Out of the net issue of $130,160, there remained $34,028 outstanding and to be redeemed.[1] September 20, Madison wrote to Jefferson: "The department of finance is an object of almost daily attack, and will be reduced to its crisis on the final resignation of Mr. Morris, which will take place in a few months."[2]

In November Morris wrote to Jay that the members of Congress, instead of supporting him, as they promised to do, were trying to frustrate his plans so as to ruin him personally.[3] He was then preparing a report to Congress on an extract from the Journal of the Assembly of Pennsylvania, November 5, which implied inattention on his part to the orders of Congress and an assumption of powers.[4] In this report he said: "Congress have before them full evidence that many persons, late officers in the civil department, refuse to account at all."[5]

In May, 1783, Grand made a complaint to the Commissioners for Peace. The last account which he sent to Morris had shown a balance due to himself of 413,892 livres, which would have put him in great perplexity but

[1] State Dep. MSS. 137, iii. 291. [2] Madison Papers, i. 573.
[3] Jay's Jay, ii. 135. [4] Dip. Corr. Rev. xii. 424. [5] Ibid. 430.

for aid obtained from the royal treasury. He was liable to pay a million livres more than he had to receive. The bearers of Morris's bills were becoming very urgent upon him. The Commissioners answered: "We see the difficulties you are in, and are sorry to say that it is not in our power to afford you any relief."[1] On the 28th of June Franklin and Jay sent Grand's statement to Vergennes. "Before the peace was known in America, and while Mr. Morris had hopes of obtaining the five per cent duty and a larger loan from his Majesty, the immediate, urgent necessities of the army obliged him to draw bills and sell them to the merchants to raise money for the purchase of provisions to prevent their starving or disbanding." They say that the loan in Holland is going on well; but it would be a great calamity that Morris's bills should be protested. They asked the counsel of the Minister, and begged for this one more loan.[2]

The applications to France for another loan failed. France was in earnest financial distress. In April, 1783, Franklin had written to Livingston: "The finances here are embarrassed, and a new loan is proposed by way of lottery, in which it is said by some calculators the King will pay at the rate of seven per cent. I mention this to furnish you with a fresh, convincing proof against cavillers of the King's generosity toward us in lending us six millions this year at five per cent, and of his concern for our credit in saving by that sum the honour of Mr. Morris's bills, while those drawn by his own officers abroad have their payment suspended for a year after they became due. You have been told that France might help us more liberally if she would; this last transaction is a demonstration to the contrary."[3]

In November he wrote again on the same subject. He

[1] Dip. Corr. Rev. x. 139, 148. [2] Ibid. 177. [3] Ibid. iv. 103.

spoke of the late failure of the *Caisse d'escompte*, occasioned partly by its having gone too far in assisting the government with money, and by the inability of the government to support the credit of the institution, though extremely desirous of doing it, — a fresh proof that their refusal to lend more to America was due to a real want of means.[1]

Jay wrote to Morris, July 20, that the French Minister said: "It was easy to be a Financier, and draw bills, when others provided the funds to pay them. . . . He intimated that his court was not treated with a proper degree of delicacy, and said that 'you treated them as your cashiers.'"[2] Luzerne and Marbois were not pleased with Morris's applications for money. Morris was not surprised that France would not lend any more, much as he desired it; "for we certainly ought to do more for ourselves before we ask the aid of others."[3] It is easy to imagine how cutting the sarcasm of the French Minister must have been to him, for it stated just the light in which his career as Financier might be construed by enemies or irritated friends.

In November the Peace Commissioners wrote that they were depending for their support on the bounty of a subject of France, the banker Grand, — "a bounty to which he tells us in his letter that he will be forced to set limits."[4]

The United States had then been independent for two months.

In August, 1784, we find another complaint by Grand, that, although the account of the United States is overdrawn fifty thousand livres, and he has letters from Morris, yet no notice is taken of the fact, and no provision made for it.[5]

In July, 1783, Adams wrote to Livingston that there was a great scarcity of money at Amsterdam. The *agio* of the

1 Dip. Corr. Rev. iv. 174. 2 Jay's Jay, ii. 125.
3 Dip. Corr. Rev. xii. 417. 4 Dip. Corr. U. S. ii. 246. 5 Ibid. 35.

bank had fallen to one and a half per cent, and the bank had been closed. No other loan was in as good credit or sold as well as the American. "In short, there is not one power in Europe whose credit is so good here as ours." On the same day he wrote to Morris that the arrival of a few cargoes of American produce for the payment of interest would have the best effect on American credit.[1] Before this letter could have been received, Morris wrote to Willink, August 6, that, the exchange on Amsterdam being high, and the need of money great, on account of the disbanding of the army, he proposed to draw on Willink at ninety days, intending to ship tobacco, and expecting that the loan would bring in money.[2] October 23, he wrote again that he had drawn for 750,000 guilders, at one hundred and fifty days' sight, to take advantage of the high exchange, and trusting to the success of the loan.[3] The notes which he had given out to the army when it was disbanded were now pressing upon him; and as nothing had been done at home to provide for them, he was driven to rely upon the loan in Holland.

The fluctuations of American credit in Holland are well shown by the amount of bonds sold in different months of 1783: in July, 195,000 florins; in August, 70,000; in September, 25,000 (news of the mutiny); in October, 10,000; in December, 18,000.[4]

December 31, he wrote to Willink again, apparently having received disquieting news with regard to the Dutch loan. His advices from there were down to September, when it appeared that the news of the mutiny at Philadelphia, in June, had acted unfavourably on the loan. Morris made light of the mutiny, and urged the bankers to support the bills.[5] In December there was great complaint of

1 Dip. Corr. Rev. vii. 113. 2 Ibid. xii. 396. 3 Ibid. 421.
4 Report of 1785. 5 Dip. Corr. Rev. xii. 437.

Morris's bills on the part of the Dutch bankers.[1] The bills continued to come, however, and as late as February 13, 1784, Adams wrote to Jay, begging him to make Morris stop, as he, Adams, was borrowing at usurious rates.[2] Adams, who had gone over to England, was growling because he had to return to Holland to borrow money to meet Morris's bills.[3] In a letter to the President of Congress, March 9, 1784, he says that he has raised money to prevent Morris's bills from being sent back. March 27, he wrote that this money was raised at a very dear rate.[4]

A certain number of bonds of a thousand guilders each, and bearing four per cent interest, were to be divided by lottery among the subscribers to the loan. The lottery bonds were to be drawn every other year from 1785 to 1797.[5]

In the mean time Morris had become extremely alarmed, and well assured that the bills would go to protest. On the 13th of January, 1784, he wrote to Le Couteulx, urging him to take up one of the bills which had been drawn on Holland, in case the loan there should leave a deficiency.[6] On the 12th of February he wrote to Franklin, urging him to make a series of drawing and redrawings, in order to protract payment beyond June or July, and promising to ship tobacco at once. He thanks God that the taxes now exceed the expenditures, which last are reduced almost to nothing. The next day he wrote to Franklin again, stating the whole financial situation. It included a debt to the bank of $340,000. He sold his bills of exchange for notes of individuals, which he discounted at the bank. He now proposes an elaborate scheme of drawing and redrawing between Amsterdam, London, and Paris, in order to win

[1] Adams, viii. 163, 166. [2] Ibid. 180. [3] Ibid. i. 408.
[4] Dip. Corr. U. S. ii. 104. [5] Journ. Cong. x. 163.
[6] Dip. Corr. Rev. xii. 443.

an extension of time.[1] At the same time he wrote again to Le Couteulx, urging him to help Franklin sustain the bills drawn on Holland, and stating that he was forwarding tobacco to sustain the bills.[2]

On the same day he wrote to Grand, calling on him likewise to help sustain the Dutch bills with any funds he had; and also to Willink, who had evidently reproached him for drawing these bills. The deficiency was 600,000 guilders; or, deducting the tobacco, 500,000. He makes excuses for this overdraft. He says that by a circuitous negotiation the payment might have been prolonged, and he reproaches the Dutch bankers for not having made it. He had himself bought 400,000 guilders out of the million. As it was stated in the letter of October 23 that he had drawn 750,000, we now see that there had been further drafts, bringing it up to a million. The reason why he bought the bills himself was because the London exchange was higher than that on Amsterdam, so he bought Amsterdam and sold London. He had also drawn another bill at six months' sight for 1,400,319 guilders, to replace bills drawn more than two years before at six months' sight on Jay and protested, involving twenty per cent damages. On this same 12th of February he wrote another letter to Willink, dilating on the magnitude of American resources, and quoting Lord Sheffield's pamphlet as the highest testimony to those resources.[3]

From these letters we see that on that date he was well aware that his account in Europe was heavily overdrawn, and we also have here a clear revelation of the disastrous system of running bills against time, in which he had been engaged. It is impossible to resist the conviction that his subsequent errors and misfortunes must be attributed in a large degree to the bad habits and desperate methods to

[1] Dip. Corr. Rev. xii. 461. [2] Ibid. 452. [3] Ibid. 454.

which he was habituated in the administration of a bankrupt treasury. In a private letter to Tench Tilghman, in March, he refers to this operation between the English and Dutch exchanges, on his own account, and gives as a reason for it that his own name and his private credit were threatened.[1]

John Adams always gave himself credit for having saved Morris and the credit of the United States in January, 1784. In a letter to the President of Congress, a year later, he refers back to the hard journey which he made to raise money to pay Morris's bills.[2] In a letter to Arthur Lee, January 31, 1785, he wrote: "I am not well enough acquainted with the history of the late Financier to know whether I agree with you in opinion of him or not. Has he produced his accounts of his administration as Financier? I cannot guess the reason why he should be so attached to the French and Franklinian interests as you think he is. He certainly has received little or no aid from either. The bills he drew upon Mr. Grand would have gone back protested if I had not procured the money to pay them. More than £600,000 sterling have I furnished him in the most profitable manner possible, not in soldiers' clothes, or arms, but in dollars from the Havana, and in cash received in Philadelphia for bills of exchange sold at a handsome profit, and another £100,000 is ready for him, if he has not already drawn for it, as it is probable he has. In short, his whole operations for two years past have been supported by me, and nothing at all has been done toward it by French or Franklin." [3]

As soon as the overdraft was known in America, Congress resumed its usual function of finding fault with the Financier and asking him why he had done so. March 17,

[1] Ford Collection. [2] Dip. Corr. U. S. ii. 154.
[3] Lee's A. Lee, ii. 252.

1784, he reported that he was compelled to draw on Holland in order to meet the notes which he had issued to pay off the army; but the Dutch loan failed, and bills to the amount of $530,000 were protested for non-acceptance. "Should they come back protested for non-payment, the consequences will be easily imagined. Besides this, there are $400,000 and the salaries of all the foreign ministers to be paid in Europe during the current year."[1]

On the 30th Congress issued a circular to the States. When the army was furloughed, the soldiers were promised three months' pay. The Financier issued his notes to discharge this promise. These notes were partly redeemed by money supplied by the States. For the rest, he drew on Holland. Some of these bills have now gone to protest, amounting, with the damages, to $636,000. The States are called upon to provide this amount at once, in the usual proportion of the requisitions.[2]

Things were, however, about to turn for the better. The failure of Morris's bills did not hurt the credit of the United States, because it was justly perceived that the country, having now won its independence, was in a position to establish its finances, and that this default was really the climax of the preceding trouble. In April, 1784, Franklin received news from the Dutch bankers that they were in a situation to honour every draft of Morris of which they had advice.[3] All through this year the Dutch loan was advancing. January 10, 1785, Adams reported to the President of Congress that his two loans were almost full, and he drew the contrast between the situation then and a year earlier.[4] It was the success of this loan which enabled Morris to pay off his notes in the course of 1784, and close up his administration.

[1] Dip. Corr. Rev. xii. 478.

[2] Secret Journ. i. 263.

[3] Franklin in France, ii. 43.

[4] Dip. Corr. U. S. ii. 154.

April 9, 1784, Luzerne addressed a communication to the President of Congress, asking what measures had been taken to pay France and the guaranteed loan in Holland.[1] In August Marbois wrote to Vergennes: "I do not consider Mr. Morris capable of aversion or affection for any foreign power; but I have sufficient reason to believe that his eagerness for resources may render him capable of very reprehensible irregularities, and that if he is not bound by the instructions of Congress, he will trouble himself very little about his obligations to His Majesty."[2]

The following incidents in the last months of Morris's administration may be noticed.

In the spring of 1784 Schweighauser, who had been agent of the United States at Nantes, caused an attachment to be levied on guns and arms, in order to recover a debt due him by the United States. Morris protested against this to Marbois and also to Franklin, saying that it was astonishing to find a subject countenanced in arresting the property of a sovereign power in this enlightened age.[3] In 1786 Jefferson, then Minister to France, examined these arms. There were thirty thousand bayonets, fifty thousand gunlocks, thirty cases of arms, and twenty-two cases of sabres. They had been under water on account of an overflow of the river, and were said to be a solid mass of rust; but on examination he found them better than the report. There were also eighteen hogsheads of gun-flints and ten anchors. They are too good to be abandoned, if they could be withdrawn by consent of the parties, without any notice of their having been in the hands of justice. These were a part of the goods bought with money when it was so hard to beg or borrow it, and

[1] Dip. Corr. U. S. i. 99.

[2] Lomenie, ii. 187.

[3] Dip. Corr. Rev. xii. 495.

when the financial administration of the United States was reduced to the most humiliating straits for want of it.[1]

In a letter to Reed, March 30, 1784, Morris condemns the loan offices, and wants to get rid of them.[2] Writing to the President of Congress, April 29, he enlarges on this point. The officers have not conformed to the rules prescribed for them. "It is an expensive and a pernicious establishment, without being attended with a single good effect to compensate the mischief." May 6, at Morris's request, three Commissioners were appointed to superintend the treasury, and were permitted to inspect it.[3]

Subsequent developments only too fully justified his opinion about the loan offices. The Committee of Congress on Finances reported, in 1788, with respect to the loan offices of the Revolution, that those of New Hampshire and Massachusetts had closed their accounts. From Rhode Island no account had been received nor return of any settlement. Connecticut had settled by commissioners, but the settlement had not yet been inspected. New York was substantially in the same position. The offices in New Jersey had been examined by the Commissioners, but the settlement was not finished. Those in Pennsylvania had not been examined at all. Delaware and Maryland were in the same position as New York. The papers of the first loan officer in Virginia were said to be lost. No settlement had been reached. The second had settled his accounts with the State Commissioner. In North Carolina, South Carolina, and Georgia, no settlement had been reached. In the last two the State was said to have appropriated the amount. The Commissioners had returns of books and papers only from New York, New Jersey, Maryland, Georgia, and Pennsylvania. The liquidated

[1] Dip. Corr. U. S. iii. 117, 250. [2] Dip. Corr. Rev. xii. 483.
[3] Waln, 352.

certificates were not cancelled in New York. It was said that a lot of them had been stolen and negotiated by one of the clerks. Whether others had been taken in a similar manner was unknown.[1]

June 1, the statue of General Montgomery, supposed to be in the care of Mr. Hughes of North Carolina or his executors, was ordered to be delivered to the Superintendent of Finance, to be transported to New York, and set up wherever the Legislature of New York should order, at the expense of the United States. Congress had ordered it early in the war. The ship that brought it over was forced to run into North Carolina, and it had lain there since. It was set up on the wall of St. Paul's Church, New York City.[2]

June 3, the Superintendent of Finance was ordered to provide goods for presents to the Indians, in connection with Indian treaties.[3]

October 11, 1784, Morris published an advertisement, giving notice that all his notes would be duly paid at maturity.[4] On the 1st of November he returned his commission to Congress. "It gives me great pleasure to reflect that the situation of public affairs is more prosperous than when that commission issued. The sovereignty and independence of America are acknowledged. May they be firmly established and effectually secured! This can only be done by a just and vigorous government. That these States, therefore, may be soon and long united under such a government is my ardent wish and constant prayer."[5]

We may now turn our attention to the personal aspects of the last year of Morris's administration. The most reasonable explanation of the animosities which he had aroused lies in the fact, to which incidental reference has

[1] Journ. Cong. xiii. 114. [2] Ibid. ix. 199. [3] Ibid. 225.
[4] Dip. Corr. Rev. xii. 502. [5] State Dep. MSS. 137, iii. 753.

been made many times in the above extracts, that he held a predominant position at Philadelphia; but we also meet at every step with evidences of the narrow and stupid prejudices entertained by many public men of the period. Mr. Howell of Rhode Island wrote to Governor Greene, December 24, 1783, that he looks to the land as the resource with which to pay the debt. He is alarmed that Massachusetts should have consented to the impost, and thinks that Morris will stick to office until funds, that is, revenue, are provided to pay the evidences of the debt which are in his hands and those of his friends.[1] February 2, 1784, Samuel Osgood wrote a long letter to Samuel Higginson, comparing opinions with him about the seat of the federal government and the administration of the treasury. He favoured an alternate residence of Congress, because otherwise the single residence would be placed at Philadelphia. Opinions differed, however, as to the force of the argument which was deduced from this as affecting Morris. Some argued that it would force his resignation, or reduce his influence, if the residence was not at Philadelphia; but Osgood seems to argue that Morris would have more influence if he was at a distance from Congress. Higginson had said that people objected to the impost "from want of confidence in the person who is at the head of the treasury, and from a belief that his plans are artfully laid to subvert the liberties of the people." To this Osgood rejoined that the treasury is "a department that ought to have the most vigilant eye exercised over it. It is at best a very dangerous affair to the liberties of the people." Osgood goes on to say: "I will tell you very freely that I am clearly in opinion that in mere money transactions he has saved the United States a very large sum." The annual expense is only half as much under

[1] Staples, 461.

him as before. He has also introduced regularity of accounts. This should be fairly admitted, because it is impolitic, "when a person is to be attacked," to depreciate his real merit. "His notions of government, of finance, and of commerce, are incompatible with liberty. . . . I hope it will be generally agreed that if it was necessary to create an omnipotent Financier in 1781, that necessity does not exist now." He has a plan that the Confederation shall assume the State debts, but then reapportion them among the States, and let each of them pay its share as it sees fit. "What a field will be open if the ravages occasioned by the enemy are to be liquidated! Yet this is set on foot by the Superintendent of Finance, probably to balance the claims of some States; and will it not have its effect?"[1]

William Lee recorded on the cover of his letter-book, apparently about 1783, the following opinion: "Mr. Robert Morris seems to be the most dangerous man in America, from the particular attention that is paid to every creature, dependent, and connection of his that appears in Europe, by Franklin and John Adams, — two men that are rivals in all the low cunning and tricks of politics. This conduct puts one in mind of the theology of the native Indians of North America on the first discovery of that continent. They never worshipped an all-powerful, good, and gracious divinity, but they paid their adoration and erected temples to a wicked, malignant, artful, and malicious being, such as the devil is painted to be by the European; because they said that a good being would not, nor could he from his nature, do them any harm, but it was necessary by adoration, sacrifices, etc., to appease the malignant spirit of the wicked demon."[2]

[1] Mass. Hist. Soc. Proc. March, 1862, p. 467.

[2] See page 272.

On the 5th of April, 1784, a report was made to Congress on the state of the debts, and a budget was presented for the current year, which was the first effort of that kind. It was stated also in decimals of a dollar, and not in ninetieths. The budget called for six millions of dollars, — one half to be paid in cash, and one half in indents or certificates of interest due. On the 12th of April Congress changed the amount demanded from six millions to four.[1] Very naturally the tax-payers inferred that if they did not pay any taxes, probably it could be reduced to two. It was such proceedings as this which gave point to the complaints out of doors, that a party wanted to organize a federal government on a grand scale, with many officers, large salaries, a great establishment, etc.

In fact, the later developments literally justified such a view of the case. In the budget of 1787 the expenses were estimated at only a half million dollars. Congress had cut down the whole establishment to dimensions more conformable to the popular taste, and, in fact, much more fitted to the circumstances of the country.[2] In a treasury report of 1788 it was said that the requisition in 1784 exceeded what was needed, and that in 1786, by mistake, $333,000 were called for more than was needed.[3]

A committee had reported a new organization of the treasury department March 30, but nothing was done about it until late in May.[4] May 28, a committee reported a new plan for that department. In their report they say: "The committee are of opinion that the United States have derived very great advantages from the arrangement and management of their finances under the administration of the Hon. Robert Morris as Superintendent thereof; but as he has signified his resolution to retire from

[1] Journ. Cong. ix. 71.
[2] Ibid. xii. 129.
[3] Ibid. xiii. 79.
[4] Ibid. ix. 68.

the said office, your committee are of opinion that it will be expedient to make seasonable provision for such event, and they propose a Board of Commissioners." They fixed the salary of these at $2,500 each. There were to be three, and they were to take up the business on the 10th of November, or sooner if Morris was ready to surrender it. No Commissioner might engage, directly or indirectly, in commerce. The term of the Commissioners was to be three years.[1] Congress found great difficulty in electing a Board which would serve. Samuel Osgood and Walter Livingston were elected on the 25th of January, 1785,[2] and Arthur Lee was elected as the third member, July 27, 1785.[3] Thus there was no Board of Treasury or other head of that department at all from November 1, 1784, to January 25, 1785; and it does not appear that Osgood and Livingston proceeded to act as a Board, for Jay wrote to the President of Congress, April 1, 1785, urging that the Commissioners of the Treasury ought to convene and proceed to business.[4] In 1788 the Committee on the Finances fixed the date upon which the new Board of Treasury took office after Morris's resignation as the 21st of April, 1785.[5]

[1] Journ. Cong. ix. 179.
[2] Ibid. x. 7.
[3] Ibid. 175.
[4] Dip. Corr. U. S. ii. 156.
[5] Journ. Cong. xiii. 107.

CHAPTER XXIII.

REVIEW AND SUMMARY OF MORRIS'S ADMINISTRATION ; THE COST OF THE WAR.

THE authorities for the business of the treasury under the administration of Robert Morris are the two Reports constantly referred to in the present volume as the Reports of 1785 and 1790. The latter is an abbreviated and compendious statement, prepared by Joseph Nourse, under an order of the federal House of Representatives. It adds some information and puts some things in a clearer light.

November 2, 1781, Congress passed an Act for appointing receivers, in the several States, of the continental revenue. February 12, 1782, Morris issued instructions to these receivers. They were to report at the end of each month the sums received by them, and to publish this report in the newspapers of the State, "to the end that every citizen may know how much of the moneys collected from him in taxes is transmitted to the treasury of the United States for the support of the war, and also that it may be known what moneys have been at the order of the Superintendent of Finance." It was intended that the federal department of finance should publish a report of receipts and expenditures quarterly. In explaining why this was not done, Morris said: "It will be sufficient to observe that in the end of July, 1783, the anticipations upon the public funds by a paper circulation, and other auxiliary achievements, exceeded $800,000. This anticipation was founded on credit, that is, on opinion. It is a misfortune that secrecy should be necessary for the support of public credit. The officer who withholds a true state of affairs subjects himself to blame; but there are moments when he ought to withhold that state, and in such cases he must bear the blame and leave his justification in the hands of time."

In 1785 he published the Report of that year, which presents the quarterly reports which should have been regularly published under the plan described in the above paragraph.[1]

The sums which came into the treasury during Morris's administration — February 20, 1781, to November 1, 1784 — were as follows:[2] From taxes, gross, $2,050,590; net, $2,025,099, which was paid by the States as follows: —

New Hampshire	$3,000	
Massachusetts	332,677	
Rhode Island	74,555	
Connecticut	132,403	
New York	52,657	
New Jersey	124,348	
Pennsylvania	431,773	
Delaware	2,140	
Maryland	129,413	
Virginia	352,113	
North Carolina	0	
South Carolina, supplies	373,598	
cash	41,916	
Georgia	0	
	$2,050,590 Net	$2,025,099
Cash paid by Pennsylvania to Morris with which to buy specific supplies, and which was spent for the United States		153,830
Supplies and vessels sold		346,224
Bills of exchange sold, including Havana bills and bills for flour		3,265,540
Specie imported, French loans		574,521
Borrowed of the Bank of North America		1,249,975
Loans and advances from individuals		94,394
Booty of Yorktown		45,948
Prizes		76,749
Commercial transactions, gross sales		230,015
Contingencies		31,906
Sundry sums due the treasury on balance of account		83,224
		$8,177,431[3]

[1] On that Report see further, page 208.

[2] Report of 1790.

[3] See note, vol. i. p. 281.

The expenditures were: —

For the civil establishment	$484,552
For the military establishment	5,233,311
For the marine establishment	746,514
For loans and advances repaid, including Bank of North America	1,336,009
Cost of merchandise, ships, etc.	236,305
Sundries	118,752
Cash balance	21,986
	$8,177,431

The sum received for bills sold, to draw funds from Europe, was: —

In 1781 . .	$294,165		
In 1781 . .	30,565	specie value of Penn. paper to the am't of	$111,828
In 1782 . .	1,077,490		
In 1782 . .	213	" " " " "	534
In 1783 . .	1,692,021		
In 1784 . .	129,739		
	$3,224,196		

By the Report of 1790 the total amount of expenditures and advances *at the treasury* of the United States, during the war, in specie value, was estimated as follows: —

1775 and 1776 . . .	$20,064,666	
1777 . . .	24,986,646	
1778 . . .	24,289,438	
1779 . . .	10,794,620	
1780 . . .	3,000,000	
1781 . . .	1,942,465	
1782 . . .	3,632,745	
1783 . . .	3,226,583	
1784 . . .	548,525	to November 1.
	$92,485,693	

This table shows how the country lapsed into dependence on France after the alliance was formed. The round number opposite 1780 is very eloquent. It means anarchy and guesswork.

Of the goods purchased in France with money loaned to the United States, Morris sold $334,420 worth to realize. What these goods cost is not known.

Morris's commercial transactions for the account of the United States produced a profit, on a part, of $21,881; and a loss, on a part, of $10,915. Net gain, $10,966 on transactions to the amount of $99,027. The tobacco transactions, chiefly in connection with the capitulation of Yorktown, were kept separate from the other commercial transactions. They produced a gain of $13,109.[1]

Morris's transactions in the attempt to appreciate the Pennsylvania paper covered $233,117 in paper, on which the profit which he won for the United States was $32,998.[2]

From a letter of Morris to Washington, August 29, 1782, we learn that it cost $3⅓ per month to feed a soldier.[3]

We have compiled the adjoining table from the Reports of 1785 and 1790, in order to show the movement of the treasury during Morris's administration. He uses the word "Anticipation" in a peculiar way. In column 1 is given the floating debt, to which he gives that name. In column 2 is given the surplus or deficiency of the account of receipts and expenditures. The deficiencies in this were met by printing and issuing his notes. They were, therefore, "Anticipations."

The floating debt included the current deficiencies in column 2, the overdrafts on the two bankers (3 and 4), the excess of the borrowings from the Bank of North America over the stock in that bank owned by the United States (5), the bills drawn on envoys without funds (6 and 7), the old debts assumed and paid (8), the bills payable, so far as they exceeded the bills receivable, if at all (9), and the overdrafts on Willink & Co. (10). When any of these accounts presents a surplus, it diminishes the antici-

[1] Report of 1790. [2] Ibid.

[3] Dip. Corr. Rev. xii. 253.

	1	2	3	4	5		6	7	8	9	10	11	12	13	14
	"Anticipations."				B'k of N. Amer.										
DATE.	Floating Debt.	Current Deficit, M's Notes.	Grand.	Le Couteulx.	Debt to.	Stock in.	Bills on Holland.	Bills on Jay.	Old Debts paid.	Receivable in excess, +; payable, —.	Willink & Co.	Taxes.	French loans and subsidies.	Bonds sold in Holland.	Total expenditures.
Feb. 20, 1781	*$2,536	—	Overd. 1,576	—	—	—	218	376	378	—	—	—	—	—	—
Jan. 1, 1782	1,606	Surplus 306	" 1,158	Overd. 141	—	—	218	60	263	— 74	—	—	1,356	—	747
Apr. 1, 1782	1,728	" 11	" 1,012	" 41	300	252	218	51	232	—136	—	—	285	—	643
July 1, 1782	1,264	M's Notes 20	" 1,096	—	400	253	218	—	205	— 80	Dep. 484	30	215	484	467
Oct. 1, 1782	159	" 218	" 205	—	400	253	—	—	197	+ 2	" 606	154	774	123	965
Jan. 1, 1783	692	" 380	" 947	Dep. 395	100	53	—	—	74	+230	" 130	†543	555	56	1,555
Apr. 1, 1783	793	" 577	" 686	" 395	100	53	—	—	74	+ 72	" 122	205	555	74	1,290
July 1, 1783	552	" 824	" 289	" 188	129	—	—	—	30	+138	" 392	218	555	346	1,021
Oct. 1, 1783	643	" 602	Deposit. 81	" 81	154	—	—	—	23	+ 61	Overd. 88	172	—	106	505
Jan. 1, 1784	677	" 230	" 10	" 16	—	—	—	—	23	+128	" 579	201	—	10	409
Apr. 1, 1784	213	" 183	" 10	" 16	—	—	—	—	23	+123	" 157	162	—	402	118
July 1, 1784	Surplus, 174	" 118	" 10	Overd. 1	—	—	—	—	9	+233	Dep. 59	306	—	276	224
Nov. 1, 1784	Antic. 40	Surplus 21	" 28	" 18	{ Antic. on taxes " on funds in Europe			153 88 }		+178	Overd. 7	56	—	35	205

* In all cases the three figures for thousands of dollars are omitted.

† This figure is very misleading; $343,000 of it were supplies credited to South Carolina on her taxes.

pations. It will therefore be found that column 1 is the balance of all the columns down to 10.

Columns 11, 12, and 13 are entirely different.

One chief purpose of the table is to ascertain and show how Morris extricated the department from the position in which he found it. To this end the quarterly payments of taxes, the French loans, and the bond sales are given. The figure for the taxes here given is the total amount paid by the States in the period. In Morris's accounts only the amounts received at the treasury were put into the receipts where they acted on column 2. All the taxes paid were a resource. This column, as here given, therefore has no book-keeping connection with columns 1 to 10. In column 12 it is shown at what rate the French court paid over to the American bankers, during the period, the loans and subsidies granted. We take account only of the sums paid to the bankers. Other sums were spent for supplies, and are not in the books at all. Others were sent in specie, and are already included in columns 5 or 9. Column 12 therefore especially shows how the French loans paid the overdrafts on the French bankers of the United States. In column 13 the sales of bonds are given by quarters to show at what rate and at what points of time they became available to carry the load.

Finally, column 14 is added, giving the total expenditures; because it was by diminishing them, while winning the resources in columns 11, 12, and 13, that he performed his task.

It is plain that the operations in columns 12 and 13 consisted in funding the floating debt. No account was kept in the books of the loans thus contracted, or of the interest on them, or on any other part of the debt. The "anticipations on funds in Europe," left by Morris when he went out, were a provision by him to pay the first interest on the loan obtained for the United States by France in Holland in 1781.

He also gave out "anticipations on the taxes" in settlement of the Quartermaster-general's accounts. The arrears of taxes in the hands of the receivers were then only $16,636. The large plus balances in column 9 consist almost entirely of ships and cargoes bought and not yet sold. Therefore it was only for a moment, and by special manipulation, that Morris got in his notes, and made a favourable situation which enabled him to escape. A careful study of this table, however, will excite wonder at what he succeeded in doing. Modern men are satisfied to see a man do well, even with reasonable means. The men of his time expected a man to do much with nothing. Hence they made light of what he had done.

Morris's detractors argued that he deserved no great credit for his management of the finances as compared with his predecessors, because in his time everything turned in his favour. It is true that if things had remained as before, he could not have restored the finances; for the miracle of carrying on a war without means has never yet been performed by anybody. The events which gave him an opportunity to restore the finances, by intelligent and energetic action, were as follows.

The first was the collapse of the paper currency and its absolute removal from circulation, in May, 1781, just before he took office. As soon as it was out of the way, specie came in. He was able to throw aside all the trammels in which the treasury operations had been entangled by the paper system. It is true that he did not succeed in his attempt to relieve himself entirely from these anticipations, which, inasmuch as they were anticipations, would have used up the revenues of his time; but it was a great gain for him to be able to conduct his current operations at least in terms of specie. The second thing in his favour was the great help granted by France in 1781, and especially the importation of a part of this in specie. This enabled him to found the bank, from which he borrowed six times what he put into it. The chief use of the bank to him, however, was to discount the notes which he took for bills of exchange. Then also it was possible for him to reduce the expenses in a way which his predecessors had not had the courage or the opportunity to accomplish, because in their time the abuses of the old method had not gone far enough to force acquiescence in the reforms. In Morris's time, and chiefly, as it appears, by his exertions and merit, the expenditures were greatly reduced for an army of a given size. When the war came to an end, it was possible for him to reduce the entire establishment to a very low scale. Next we notice that the efforts to introduce taxation bore fruit which, although it was trivial in one point of view, was large enough to be very important to him in his desperate circumstances. Finally, when his need was the greatest, and these advantages and opportunities proved inadequate, the rise of American credit made the loan in Holland possible, and this carried him through to the result. This also explains what colour of truth there was in John Adams's claim that he enabled Robert Morris to extricate himself from his office with credit. It belonged to Adams's idiosyncrasies always to think of that point in a public transaction in which he had stood, as the centre of it, and of that activity in it which he had executed, as the leading one.

According to the best records we possess, the cost of the war to the United States, reduced to specie value year by year at the official scale of depreciation, which, being always below the truth, makes these figures too high, was, as above stated, $92,485,693, *at the treasury.*

There were also certificates of indebtedness out for $16,708,009. There had been expended in Europe, which never went through the treasury, $5,000,000. The States were estimated to have expended $21,000,000. Total, $135,000,000. Jefferson calculated it at $140,000,000, by adding the debts incurred and the continental currency.[1] The debt contracted by England during the war was £115,000,000, for which £91,000,000 were realized.[2] The Comptroller of the Treasury of France said that it cost 60,000,000 livres a year to support the army in America.[3] Vergennes told Lafayette, in November, 1782, that France had expended 250,000,000 livres in the war.[4] There is an often-repeated statement that the war cost France 1,200,000,000 livres,[5] or 1,280,000,000,[6] or 1,500,000,000.[7] Arthur Young put it at £50,000,000 sterling.[8] Probably if 60,000,000 a year for five years, or $60,000,000, was taken as the amount directly expended for and in America by France, it would be as fair a computation as could be made of her contribution to American independence. She had large expenditures elsewhere in the' prosecution of her war against Great Britain, and her incidental losses of ships, etc., were great.

When England abandoned the effort to subdue the colonies, she was in a faı better position for continuing it than either of her adversaries. George III. was by no means stupid in his comments and suggestions about the war. No Englishman of the period said things which now seem wiser in the retrospect. As early as September, 1780, he said: "America is distressed to the greatest degree. The finances of France, as well as Spain, are in

[1] Jefferson, i. 401.
[2] Elliott's Funding, 1236.
[3] Circourt, iii. 159.
[4] Dip. Corr. Rev. vi. 470.
[5] Circourt, iii. 260, Editor's note.
[6] Durand, Preface.
[7] Steuben, 93.
[8] Pinkerton's Voyages, iv. 350.

no good situation. This war, like the last, will prove one of credit."[1] This opinion was fully justified in 1782. French finances were then hastening toward bankruptcy, so that France could not continue the war expenses or the loans and subsidies to America. English credit was high. October 2, 1782, Vergennes wrote to Montmorin,[2] that the English fleet was stronger than at the beginning of the war, while the fleets of France and Spain were weaker; that French finances were greatly weakened, while English credit was high; that England had recovered influence in Russia, and through Russia on Prussia and Austria. He wanted peace and reconciliation with England in order to act with her in eastern Europe. If England had chosen to persevere in the war, the matter of credit would have been the most important element in her chances of success, aside from the natural difficulties of the enterprise.

[1] George III. ii. 336.

[2] Circourt, iii. 331.

CHAPTER XXIV.

THE BURDEN OF THE WAR UPON THE PEOPLE.

IN view of the pitiful story of weakness and failure during this period, the question naturally arises whether it was due to the exhaustion of the country by the distress of the war and the calamities of the times. We have ample material with which to answer this question.

From the very beginning of the contest it was difficult to enlist soldiers, because of the attractions of other enterprises. Rush wrote to R. H. Lee, December 21, 1776, that the Eastern States had great difficulty in filling their quotas, on account of the rage for privateering. The continental soldiers were eager to serve their time out in order to go to sea. Ten thousand men of New England were then so engaged.[1] We have heard Morris complaining at the same time of the same thing,[2] and we have seen instances of embargoes on ships and men.[3]

An interesting specimen of the life of one of these soldiers and sailors is given in the "Adventures of Ebenezer Fox." He served a tour of militia duty for a few months. Charles Biddle's memoirs show how a man of superior position spent the time of the war. He did a few weeks of military duty on an excursion to New Jersey. The rest of the time he was pursuing gainful voyages between the West Indies and North Carolina.

In the summer of 1777 the last-named gentleman rode through New Jersey. "Nothing in the country at this

[1] Lee's R. H. Lee, ii. 161. [2] See vol. i. p. 204. [3] Ibid. 133.

time had the appearance of distress. The people everywhere as we passed appeared cheerful and contented."[1]

Graydon says that, fortunately, at the beginning of the war, few were aware of the price at which independence was to be acquired. If they had been, it would not have been achieved. If there had been as much disaffection to independence in 1776 as there was in 1777, it would never have been begun. "Still, it may be observed that as whigism declined among the higher classes, it increased in the inferior, because they who composed them thereby obtained power and consequence." They got military rank and public occupation, instead of agricultural and mechanical work.[2]

In 1779 Franklin wrote to his daughter that when she told him how dear everything was, he thought she was going to say that everybody was economizing; but she said, "There never was so much pleasure and dressing going on." She had written to ask him for black pins and feathers from France. After preaching frugality, he declined to furnish her with any such stuff. "If you wear your cambric ruffles as I do, and take care not to mend the holes, they will come in time to be lace; and feathers, my dear girl, may be had in America from every cock's tail."[3] He also wrote to the President of Congress, in October, 1779: "The extravagant luxury of our country, in the midst of all its distresses, is to me amazing. When the difficulties are so great to find remittances to pay for the arms and ammunition necessary for our defence, I am astonished and vexed to find upon inquiry that much the greatest part of the Congress interest bills come to pay for tea, and a great part of the remainder is ordered to be laid out in gewgaws and superfluities."[4]

[1] Biddle, 100.
[2] Graydon, 285.
[3] Franklin, viii. 375.
[4] Dip. Corr. Rev. iii. 116.

In June, 1779, Pickering was having the regulations printed which Steuben had prepared for the army. He writes to excuse delay: "We expected to send you more copies of the regulations, of which the bookbinder gave us encouragement; but his workmen failed him. It is not so easy to get work executed in America as in Europe. Here, under the present scarcity of hands, you can place no dependence on your workmen, — to-day they are with you, and to-morrow on board of a privateer, with hopes of making their fortunes." [1]

A French officer wrote, in 1779, that New Hampshire had not suffered from the war. Her people were enriched by privateering. "Patriotism is null at Philadelphia. It has become almost farcical. Fortune is the idol in every State. All who are well off are corrupt at heart, and so athirst for peace that this would be welcome at any price." [2] The thirst for gain was noted by many observers, both foreign and domestic. They often spend their rhetoric in denunciation of it. The chief value of their observations is in the proof they furnish that there were new chances of gain offered, not only in privateering, but also in more legitimate enterprises. The chances of gain, especially when presented to people who had not previously enjoyed them, awakened the appetite for gain.

In June, 1780, Joseph Reed wrote to Washington: "In my opinion we have miscalculated the abilities of the country, and entirely the disposition of the people to bear taxes in the necessary extent. The country not immediately the seat of either army is richer than when the war began, but the long disuse of taxes and their natural unpalatableness have embarrassed the business exceedingly; and tories, grumbling whigs, and party have all thrown in their aid to increase the discontent. . . . Our

[1] Steuben, 217. [2] Durand, 17.

country friends find their patriotism abate as their interests are affected by duties or taxes. I am inclined to think some stroke of adverse fortune necessary, and that lasting good may flow from it; for pretend what we may, the country is much recovered from the distress of the war, and really has the three great requisites of war, — men, provisions, and iron, if not in abundance, in sufficiency for all our wants. Our only difficulty is to draw them forth; and for this two things are essentially necessary, — namely, union among the States, generally and particularly." Party divisions in Congress have greatly weakened its influence, encouraged the tories, and discouraged the whigs.[1]

At the same time Marshall noted that there were great murmurings among the people on account of depreciation, heavy taxes, militia fines, enlistment, and dearness. Great importations had raised prices. "Wonder of wonders, never known before."[2] Grayson wrote to Smallwood: "America is full of resources, if properly called forth. If we fail in the present contest, it will not be for want of means. In fact, we shall die of the doctor."[3] We find in Jones's letters the following paragraph written in November, 1780: "The States never were blessed with greater plenty, or had it more in their power to lay up ample stores of provisions for the army than at present; and if the people will not lend them to the public and wait for future payment, they must be taken. But they should be so taken as to occasion as little disgust as possible, which a regular apportionment of specific articles may effect. Some vent should be found for the surplus of the earth's production, or I fear the collection of heavy taxes will be found oppressive and produce clamour and discontent, if their collection shall be found practicable at any rate.

[1] Reed's Reed, ii. 210. [2] Marshall's Diary, 248.
[3] Maryland Papers, 110.

Whether this can be effected by internal demand and consumption I doubt; and if it cannot, no other mode will answer but opening the ports."[1]

At the same time Pownall was telling the sovereigns of Europe: "North America has advanced, and is every day advancing to growth of state, with a steady and continually accelerating motion, of which there has never yet been any example in Europe."[2] In 1780 Peletiah Webster said that although the United States might borrow abroad to pay for importations, it was absurd to borrow abroad to pay for their own products. We are not weak in supply. Our country "is full of everything we want, clothing and military stores excepted; but the weakness of our councils and administrations, and that our domestic economy should be so bad that we should not be able to call into public use the very supplies in which the country abounds, is shameful." It will destroy our credit in Europe. He ridicules the plan of drawing bills when there are no funds, and they may come back "to the utter ruin and most laughable contempt of the credit of the States. They would doubtless have to be sold at twenty or thirty per cent discount. . . . Our country is richer, more full of men and stores necessary in war, than those of Europe in general. . . . Our country is not exhausted; it is full of supplies of every kind which are needed for public service."[3]

In December, 1780, Glover wrote that wheat was seventy-five cents a bushel in New York, and the army was starving.[4] Heath's Memoirs give a representation of comfort and plenty in the seaport towns in January, 1781.[5] In the spring of 1781 Reed wrote that trade was very flourishing in Philadelphia and New England.[6] In a letter to Jay,

[1] Jones's Letters, 41.
[2] Pownall's Memorial, 56.
[3] Webster, 63, 106, 153.
[4] Bancroft, x. 415.
[5] Heath's Memoirs, 271.
[6] Reed's Reed, ii. 296.

George Clinton said: "Our resources as a nation are, however, yet great. We abound in provision, and the prices in specie are nearly the same as at the commencement of the war."[1] Reed wrote to Washington in May that there was no scarcity, but abundance of flour in Philadelphia. Morris wrote the same thing, and attributed it to the repeal of the embargo.[2] Reed, however, asked Congress to lay an embargo, in order to get this flour into the government magazines.[3] In July Pickering wrote to his deputy in Virginia, from New York State: "All public credit is at an end here, as well as with you. Money is the universal cry. With that I can get anything, and at a cheap rate."[4]

In the year 1781 Virginia was the seat of war, and especial value attaches to the state of things there. February 12, 1781, Benjamin Harrison, being on a mission for the State at Philadelphia, reported to Governor Jefferson: "There is great abundance of clothing in this town, but it can't be procured without money or tobacco; nor will the latter do, unless the enemy leave our country [Virginia]." A week later he wrote again: "This town abounds with cloth, but the only way Congress can obtain it is on credit, and as I said before, theirs is at but a low ebb."[5] In June a deputy quartermaster wrote to the Speaker of the Assembly of Virginia, from Stanton, describing in strong terms the distress, and especially the need of wagons. "You must be well informed, sir, that there are wagons, provisions, and forage to be had in the country in the greatest plenty, so that nothing is wanted but ways and means to obtain them."[6] September 7, Colonel Carrington wrote to the Governor that Lafayette was in great distress for want of provisions. He had been

[1] Johnston's Jay, ii. 15, April 6, 1781.
[2] See vol. i. p. 272.
[3] Reed's Reed, ii. 300.
[4] Va. Papers, ii. 194.
[5] Ibid. i. 509, 527.
[6] Ibid. ii. 171.

obliged to borrow bread of the French army since it landed. "Amidst the most plentiful resources, our army is like to starve."[1] At the same time it was reported from Amherst County, Virginia: "Flour and grain are abundant; but unless the people are assured of payment, these articles cannot be procured;"[2] and from Prince William County, that it "can easily supply sixty thousand bushels of wheat."[3] Another quartermaster reports to the Governor that there are large quantities of beef in North Carolina, but it is mostly in the hands of individuals. He could not obtain it for the State.[4] Liquors and salt, which were especially wanted for the public service, were abundant on the eastern shore of Virginia.[5] Another officer in command of a detachment writes from Cumberland Old Court-House, that he does not know how to get provisions, although there are plenty in that county alone to support the post.[6] Another writes in October: "The resources of the State are ample, if effectual measures are pursued for obtaining them."[7] In December Colonel Armand, who was posted with his legion at Charlottesville, wrote that there was plenty of forage in that county, yet he was in the greatest necessity for want of it.[8] Colonel Febiger wrote, January 4, 1782, that he could not get supplies, and feared his troops would starve. "Although there is plenty of wheat in Amelia, Bedford, and Prince Edward Counties, it cannot be gotten except by impressment."[9] February 16, the head of the State War Department reported to the Governor: "The troops are entirely without food, although there is an abundance in the country." There is no one to collect and distribute the public beeves scattered over the counties.[10]

[1] Va. Papers, ii. 401. [2] Ibid. 406. [3] Ibid. 451.
[4] Ibid. 479. [5] Ibid. 454. [6] Ibid. 486.
[7] Ibid. 514. [8] Ibid. 648. [9] Ibid. iii. 7. [10] Ibid. 65.

Not only were these supplies in existence in the country in ample amount, but they could be obtained without difficulty if money was offered for them. In fact, this period proves, what is proved by so many others, that the time when people take into their heads the most extravagant superstition about gold is when they are forced to use paper.

The French in 1780 began to buy supplies with specie. This gave them command of the market, which Congress seemed to resent. June 5, 1780, they resolved that the public service would be best promoted if the same currency was used in obtaining supplies for the French army as for the American.[1]

In the next year, during the Yorktown campaign, this competition became most distinct. The State agent of Virginia reported to the Governor, that the French were buying supplies through the State. "The hard cash draws supplies to them from great distances." He thought that if the consul would employ an American agent, he could save twenty-five per cent. The agent evidently wanted to finger the specie. Another agent reported that the French agents were purchasing supplies with specie. "That infatuating metal will immediately have such influence that not an ounce of any kind of supplies will be furnished to the State agents. The people will go through thick and thin to get the crowns and louis d'or. I foresee the most dangerous consequences arising from these separate interests. The American army must infallibly suffer." The same day he writes again that there should be an understanding between the agents of the two armies. He has written to all the public officers: but it "all will avail nothing; the gold and silver will overset all." Quartermaster Young writes that the agents of the French

[1] Journ. Cong. vi. 58.

army buy with hard money; hence supplies cannot be obtained for certificates. All the supplies ought to pass through the Quartermaster's and Commissioner's hands. [This would mean that the French must buy provisions for both armies.] Major Claiborne complains of the fascination of the French crowns. Lieutenant-Governor Jameson writes to Governor Nelson that the agents can obtain no provision, because the French buy for specie. Colonel Davies reports to Governor Nelson that the hard money of the French engrosses the supplies. "It would be of great advantage could the purchases be made jointly. The hard money of the one would give credit to the other, as most people will readily receive certificates for one half, perhaps two thirds of their provisions, if they could have the remainder in hard money." Evidently they were all anxious to get the handling of the French money. M. de Tarle, the French agent, replied to Governor Nelson, that he would buy supplies for the French army of the Governor's agents when they had them, but would not consent to be restrained. "Experience has taught, and the world are convinced, that open markets and free liberty to individuals to sell, are the only sure means of supplying the army; and though temporary regulations may be at some times useful, in general, restraining the subject and preventing his disposing of his property in his own way causes a withholding, and often real scarcity. I am convinced that the markets will be well supplied when your Excellency shall make it known that the army of France will purchase with ready money such things as they want of those who bring them to market, and that no interruption will be given to them by impress or seizure." [1]

There is very little evidence of distress from the war. In Rhode Island, in 1776, we find it stated that women

[1] Va. Papers, ii. 450–565, September and October, 1781.

worked in the fields, which is supposed to mean that the men were absent in the army in such large numbers that the women had to do the work.[1] Anburey noted evidence of poverty and distress in central Massachusetts, in 1777, on the line of march of the Burgoyne prisoners from Albany to Cambridge.[2] That region, however, never was the seat of war at all, and the people there probably in the best of times might have made the same impression on him.

In July, 1778, just after the English evacuated Philadelphia, Gerard wrote that that town was reduced to a third of its inhabitants, three quarters of whom were tories; and that there was a similar state of things in New York, Boston, and other maritime cities.[3] The population of Philadelphia, in 1770, was, of whites, 39,765, and in 1779, 54,683.[4] During the British occupation it was, according to a census taken by Galloway, including all the territory within the British lines, 25,000.[5] The occupation produced only a temporary, although serious, interruption in the growth of the city. The same was true in other places. In 1781 Philadelphia was very prosperous.[6] In 1782 the English made their blockade very stringent, and succeeded in restricting commerce.[7] Reed said that the trade of Philadelphia was ruined.[8]

In his Report of 1785 Morris said: "The needy can never economize." The Americans of the Revolution, however, did not prove this proposition. Their case was one in which, by overwhelming evidence, ample means were unavailable, or were wasted because there was no system of administration. They proved another propo-

1 Vernon's Diary, 34, 44.

2 Anburey, ii. 37.

3 Doniol, iii. 272.

4 Poll lists cited by Brissot, ii. 92.

5 Galloway's Examination, 25.

6 See page 274.

7 See pages 40, 74, 88.

8 Reed's Reed, ii. 380.

sition, perhaps generally more true than that of Morris: Without method and discipline economy is impossible.

It must be noticed, however, that the strength and the weakness of the Americans lay in the same fact. It was because of the lack of social organization that it was impossible to conquer them. There was nothing which could be struck, a blow on which would be felt throughout the political body. The blows which were struck passed like those of a sword drawn through water.

If we turn to ask the question what was the military burden of the war upon the people, the following facts may be collected as bearing upon it: There was a current assertion that the colonies, in the Seven Years War, had 25,000 men on foot, and the assertion is met with that England had only 15,000 men in America.[1] In his examination before the House of Commons, on the repeal of the Stamp Act, Franklin put the number of white men in North America between sixteen and sixty years of age, at 300,000.[2] Kalb, in 1768, reported that there were reckoned to be 200,000 young men capable of bearing arms between Nova Scotia and South Carolina, without depriving agriculture of necessary labour.[3] Governor Penn, before the House of Commons in 1775, said that Pennsylvania had 60,000 militia, of whom 20,000 before he left had armed themselves at their own expense, and were receiving no pay; and Congress were making their own arms and cannon adequately for present and future needs. This statement was extremely exaggerated and incorrect in some points, and possibly in all.[4] Franklin put the white population of Pennsylvania at 160,000; of whom he thought one third were Quakers, and perhaps a third Germans. An anonymous writer, in a letter to Lord George Germain,

[1] Moore's Diary, i 231; Dip. Corr. Rev. ix. 257; Marshall's Washington, i. 403, 427.

[2] Franklin, iv. 165.

[3] Kalb, 290.

[4] Stedman, i. 161.

said that an American had calculated for him the fighting strength of America at 428,400; and he asserted that in the Seven Years War New York alone sent to sea forty-eight ships, with 675 guns and 5,530 men. Governor Tryon, in his report on New York in 1774, put the white population at 161,102. "The militia may be supposed to consist of about 32,000." [1] He evidently found the militia by dividing the population by five. Hamilton, in one of his youthful essays, taking the population as 3,000,000, calculated that there were 500,000 fighting men.[2] In 1781 he took the population as two and a half millions. The European rate was, he said, one soldier for a hundred souls. This would give 20,000 soldiers; but the United States had raised 30,000.[3] Galloway put the white men capable of bearing arms at half a million.[4]

The best calculation of the population at the beginning of the war is two million and a half. Upon the usual methods of calculation, this would give 450,000 adult males at least; and, if the bottom limit were taken at sixteen years, which was the custom for militia purposes, there must have been 500,000. These were not, of course, all able-bodied, and we have met with no calculation from that period in which the attempt is made to determine the proportion of able-bodied. Also an agricultural community, such as the United States then was, could not spare a large proportion of the adult male population for a standing army, unless it was under some militia system, allowing them to serve for limited periods at certain times of the year. Yet, certainly, a nation struggling for its independence might have put from one quarter to one third of its adult males under arms, as the maximum number, at a single period of greatest strain, before the military service could be said to be very heavy.

From all the statements made at the time, and from this

[1] Doc. Hist. N. Y. i. 517.
[2] Hamilton's Works, i. 158.
[3] Ibid. iii. 95.
[4] Galloway's Examination, 19.

general calculation, we are bound to infer that the United States should have raised an army of 100,000 men before the point of distress was approached.

In the Revolutionary army the numbers on paper were very different from the numbers in the field. In February, 1776, Washington wrote that, instead of 20,000 men, he had not half that, all included.[1] In July Reed wrote that the strength of the army was exaggerated in every way.[2] In June General Greene wrote: "I can assure you it is necessary to make great allowances in the calculation of our strength from the establishment, or else you will be greatly deceived." And in July he wrote: "The whole force we have does not amount to much above 9,000, if any. . . . Congress has never furnished the number of men voted by near one half, certainly by above a third."[3] This was just at the time of the battle of Long Island, and the preparation for it, when the English were obtaining a foothold on the continent. The Adjutant-general's return shows at that battle 7,389 men fit for duty.[4]

An official statement of the War Department in 1790 gives the following table, from which some indefinite reduction must be made for the difference between the paper returns and the facts:[5] —

	No. of men in Contin. pay.	Militia.	Estimated militia for a few months.	Quotas called for.
1775 . . .	27,443	27,443	10,180	
1776 . . .	46,891	26,060	16,700	
1777 . . .	34,820	10,100	23,800	75,760
1778 . . .	32,899	4,353	13,800	44,892
1779 . . .	27,699	5,135	12,350	41,760
1780 . . .	21,015	5,811	16,250	41,760
1781 . . .	13,292	7,298	8,750	33,408
1782 . . .	14,256		3,750	33,408

[1] Reed's Reed, i. 157.

[2] Ibid. 208.

[3] Greene against Bancroft, 16, 20, 21.

[4] 5th Series Am. Archives, vii. 1119.

[5] Report of 1790, 26.

It is certain that the military service never reached any excessive or distressing demand upon the population. In December, 1776, Washington had only about 3,000 soldiers left. At Valley Forge he had only about 5,000. It is very improbable that the number under arms at any one time ever reached 40,000, and much more likely that it never exceeded 30,000. If it is true that the colonies provided 25,000 for the Seven Years War, when their population was much under two million, the strain of the war of independence seems by comparison to have been very small.

Such statements as are met with in respect to the quality of the rank and file of the army forbid us to believe that it was recruited from the body of the independent class of the population.[1] It was made up of the social waste of the period, which, in an agricultural community, is always large in proportion to the total.

On the whole, if we compare the American war of independence with the struggle of the Dutch for independence, or with that of the Southern States in 1861, the sacrifices of the Revolutionary war must be considered trivial. It was not on account of either exhaustion of their resources, or general lack of means, or on account of the burden of military duty, that the people were not able to meet the financial demands which were made upon them.

The case was, as Hamilton expressed it with regard to New York: "There is no doubt that the State might have rendered more benefit to the common cause with less inconvenience to itself than by all its forced efforts; but there, as everywhere else, we have wanted experience and knowledge;"[2] and as Washington said: "The country does not lack resources, but we the means of drawing them forth."[3]

[1] See vol. i. p. 306.

[2] Hamilton's Works, viii. 64.

[3] Washington, vii. 338.

CHAPTER XXV.

THE NOTES OF ROBERT MORRIS.

WE have not been able to find a specimen of any note issued by Robert Morris, nor a citation anywhere of the tenour of those notes. The following is an attempt to learn from the incidental mention of these notes, which occurs in the printed record, what their character was.

In the Report of 1790 is given the following table, under the heading "Receipts and Expenditures of Public Moneys," "stated to show the annual or quarterly anticipation on the revenue which was supplied by Mr. Morris's notes *issued on the public credit*":[1] —

	Receipts.	Expenditures.	Balance in treasury.	Anticipations.
Feb. 20 to Dec. 31, 1781	1,054,215	747,590	306.624	
Quarter to Mar. 31, 1782	348,136	643,758	11,002	
" June 30,	436,208	467,824		20,613
" Sept. 30,	767,497	965,524		218,640
" Dec. 31,	1,393,918	1,555,638		380,360
" Mar. 31, 1783	1,092,882	1,290,153		577,630
" June 30,	774,725	1,021,709		824,614
" Sept. 30,	727,861	505,408		602,161
" Dec. 31,	781,470	409,312		230,002
" Mar. 31, 1784	164,838	118,505		183,670
" June 30,	290,215	224,890		118,345
" Nov. 1,	345,460	205,128	21,986	
	8,177,431	8,155,445		
Balance in the treasury		21,986		
		8,177,431		

[1] An abbreviation of the last two columns of this table constitutes the second column of the table on page 129.

This table is a table of the receipts and expenditures; and the deficiency, when there was one, is represented as having been met by an issue of notes, called "Morris's notes," but "*issued on the public credit.*" How much are these last words meant to affirm? Were they used with care and set intention or not? The current receipts and expenditures showed a surplus in this account in 1781, although there was a large floating debt. What, then, were the notes said to have been used in the Yorktown campaign? According to the representation here, there was a surplus at the beginning of 1782. It was cash, and would consist of the paper and specie which were current at that time. In the second quarter of 1782 there was a deficiency, which we understand was met by printing notes and paying them out to such an extent as was necessary to supply current demands. When things turned better and the deficiency decreased, it was by the in-payment of these notes which could be destroyed, or of other currency with which these notes could be bought. When a surplus appeared again, it must have consisted of other currency again; but it would not be possible that so large an amount of paper, put afloat in that way, could be brought in to the last note. The table is not, strictly speaking, an account of the outstanding notes. It is an account of the cash on hand or wanting.

Chastellux's translator says: "On the strength of his office as Financier-general he [Morris] circulated *his own notes of Robert Morris* as cash throughout the continent, and even had the address to get some Assemblies, that of Virginia in particular, to pass Acts to make them current in payment of taxes. What purchases of tobacco, what profits of every kind, might not a man of Mr. Morris's abilities make with such powerful advantages?"[1] It can

[1] Chastellux, i. 200, note.

hardly be understood that he refers to notes bearing the signature of Robert Morris as Superintendent of Finance, and issued as evidences of indebtedness of the United States. Upon the authority of a person who was a clerk of Morris, it is stated that his private notes were called "Long Bobs" and "Short Bobs," according to the periods of their maturity.[1] We infer, therefore, that they were post notes or "anticipations," as he called them, having different lengths of time to run. When Washington was preparing for the Yorktown expedition, a supply of guns and munitions is said to have been obtained for him by Morris's notes to the amount of $1,400,000.[2] We have not been able to find proof of an issue so large as that at any time in any kind of notes; but if the statement is correct with regard to the character of the paper, we must suppose that the notes were signed by Morris in his public and not in his private capacity. We note that this was in August, 1781. The report made by Morris of the issues of the notes on the credit of the United States in November, 1783, began no further back than December 26, 1782.[3]

In May, 1782, Timothy Pickering wrote to Washington with regard to the purchase of ox-teams with which he had been charged: "The sum I received for those purchases was in Mr. Morris's notes, and amounted only to about three fifths of the sum requisite for that service; and whether any purchases could be made with them at the eastward was a matter of uncertainty, from which no information from my deputies there has relieved me. But if they have succeeded, it is in such a way as forbids the Financier giving any more of them; for these notes are not received there as cash, but only as pledges, which are

[1] Phelps and Gorham Purchase, 242.
[2] See vol. i. p. 308.
[3] See pages 107, 110.

bought up by speculators who make a run upon the funds assigned for their redemption." [1]

On the 8th of July, 1782, Comfort Sands wrote to Hamilton, who was the Receiver of continental taxes in New York, that he was buying flour with drafts on Philadelphia; that the farmers would not take bank-notes.[2]

In July, 1782, General Greene wrote to Governor Harrison of Virginia: "Nothing has given me more pain than the opposition I hear was given in your House of Assembly to the plans of the Financier to give credit to public measures with the people. Upon what principle the circulation of his notes was opposed, I cannot imagine." [3]

In October, however, he wrote again: "It affords me the highest satisfaction to hear Mr. Morris's notes are in such demand with you, as I consider the business of finance the first object of the consideration of the United States, and their establishment inseparably connected with it." [4]

In the accounts we find an entry, February 11, 1782, of a payment to Hall and Sellers for printing "Cash Notes;" and December 16, a payment to Mark Wilcox for "Subsistence Paper."

March 2, 1782, Livingston wrote that taxes were being collected in notes of the bank. Whether this remark is entitled to any special weight, it is impossible to say. It is not probable that he meant to testify, of his own knowledge, on a controverted point, that that was the currency in which taxes were paid and in no other.[5]

The agent of Morris with the Southern army said that he had specie with which to redeem Morris's "notes or those

[1] Letters to Washington, iii. 512.

[2] State Dep. MSS., Hamilton Papers, xix. 33.

[3] Va. Papers, iii. 23c. [4] Ibid. 354.

[5] Dip. Corr. Rev. viii. 329.

of his bank."[1] This again is evidently inaccurate. Morris never had any responsibility for redeeming the notes of the bank, and surely never provided for it. What weight then can be given to the rest of the statement?

September 11, 1782, the contractors for the Northern army wrote to Morris a long memorial. The sub-contractors will hold them liable for the difference between specie and Morris's notes. The receivers do not receive money from taxes in sufficient amount to pay Morris's drafts. Those drafts are given out to quartermasters and commissaries as well as to contractors, and are paid out by the former below par. When the writers made their contract, they placed more dependence on Morris's personal than on his official character. They throw up their contract unless they can have monthly payments in specie or a guarantee against loss.[2]

In his bank speech of 1786 Morris said that he had been obliged to indorse notes given to contractors before they could get them discounted.[3]

October 5, 1782, Morris wrote to Hamilton that his notes, when first issued, depreciated ten to fifteen per cent in the Eastern States. If he had not stopped issuance in that quarter, they would have totally lost credit, at least for a time. From his mode of speaking here, as well as from the passage in Pickering's letter just quoted, we get the impression that the notes he is speaking of had been issued shortly before the time of writing (perhaps in the spring of 1782), and not that they were notes which he had issued from the time of taking office, a year before. The following passage from the same letter shows that the notes were receivable for taxes: "Whatever fine, plausi-

[1] Johnson's Greene, ii. 371.

[2] State Dep. MSS. 137, i. 834. See page 62.

[3] Carey's Debates, 50.

ble speeches may be made on this subject, the farmers will not give full credit to money merely because it will pay taxes, for that is an object they are not very violently devoted to; but that money that goes freely at the store and the tavern will be sought after as greedily as those things which the store and the tavern contain."

These notes were given to the contractors for the supply of the army, and they were to be redeemed by the receivers of taxes. The contractors presented them for redemption at once; in regard to which Morris writes: "This I expected, because much of that paper is not fit for other purposes. Some of it, however, which is payable to the bearer, is calculated for circulation, which you observe is not so general as otherwise it might have been by reason of the largeness of the sums expressed in the note." The motive of this paper was to provide currency for the payment of taxes to those who complained, though wrongly, that there was not currency enough, and therefore that taxation was unduly oppressive. Moreover there was a dislike of paper to be overcome. He prefers that his notes should be confined to merchants and large dealers. If they can use them for remittance, they will change them for other people. People do not generally trade for as large sums as $20. There is less danger of counterfeiting in the case of large notes used only by merchants.[1]

October 9, Hamilton wrote to Morris that he had received Morris's bills on Swanwick in favour of Sands & Co., half of them due in the next February. Sands exchanged them with the county treasurers for specie [that is, made the exchange of Morris's drafts for specie in the hands of the county treasurers before it had been paid over to Hamilton, and the Treasurer paid the taxes which had been collected in the Morris paper]. Hamilton tries

[1] State Dep. MSS., Hamilton Papers, xxii. 173.

to discourage this. He fears that people will discount Morris's bills and notes with the treasurers, and hurt the credit of them. Bank notes pass as cash, "with a manifest preference to your notes." [1]

It seems to have been expected that these notes and drafts, although only payable after a certain number of months, could circulate at par with specie. Hamilton wondered that Morris did not issue his notes for smaller sums, but he acknowledged the force of the reasons given by Morris in his letter of October 5.[2] From that letter we infer that the lowest denomination of these notes or drafts was $20.

When the Board of Treasury, in 1787, made contracts for supplying the army, they proposed a form of note in which payments should be made to the contractors, as follows: "Out of any moneys in your hands arising from requisitions of the United States in Congress assembled, passed previous to the first day of September last, pay to A. B. or bearer the sum of   specie dollars." Signed by the Board of Treasury and directed to the Receiver of taxes in some State. The Receivers were to take these at par. The contractors were to have five per cent allowance on all these notes, and six per cent interest for a year from the date of the note, the return of the Receivers to be the evidence of the negotiation.[3] We may infer that Morris's "drafts" in favour of the contractors in 1782 were of this general character; but there appear to have been notes besides, payable at a fixed limit of time, and each for a definite sum.

According to the report of a committee of Congress on the Department of Finance, June 17, 1783, the expenses of

[1] State Dep. MSS., Hamilton Papers, i. 130.

[2] Ibid., Hamilton Papers, xix. 37.

[3] Ibid., Reports of the Board of Treasury, 140, ii. 371.

the department exceeded its income, in 1782, by $404,713, which was supplied by Morris's notes.

In the summer of 1783 the United States notes, as they are called, were forged. Morris wrote to the governors, giving notice of this. "It happens well," he says, "that the true notes are struck upon paper made on purpose, and contain, in water mark, 'United States National Debt.'" He speaks of them as "these anticipations, which form our only support." These forgeries were committed at New York by a man from Massachusetts, named William May, who had been arrested with six others, against whom he informed, by the aid of Sir Guy Carleton. They had made preparations for counterfeiting notes of the different States. Nothing here shows whether these were the so-called Morris's notes or treasury notes, to be distinguished from them; but the Virginia delegates in Congress, reporting to the Governor the affair of the forgery, say that the men were arrested "on suspicion of forging the notes issued by the Superintendent of Finance." [1] Forgeries were also committed on the "United States notes" in Virginia.[2]

These notes were used as remittances. Rubsamen writes to Bland, in August, 1782, that if money can be got, it should be sent in Morris's notes, as the State Treasurer takes those for taxes.[3] Another case where they are used as a remittance occurs in April, 1783.[4] In December, 1782, Hamilton, applying to the Governor of New York for a remittance on his salary as member of Congress, asks for Morris's notes, if they have not more than a fortnight to run. He would like them still better if they were due.[5] Here again we see that these notes were post notes or exchequer bills, not bearing interest, so that they would be worth par at their maturity.

[1] Va. Papers, iii. 512, 515.
[2] Ibid. 519.
[3] Bland Papers, ii. 91.
[4] Ibid. 97.
[5] Hamilton's Works, viii. 92.

In the spring of 1783, when Morris agreed to issue notes for the payment of the army, we find mention in his diary which shows that the paper on which his notes were printed was of a special kind. In May he was trying to hasten the manufacture of this paper. There was a special mould for it, which was marked "U. S.," which he kept with care; and he speaks of intrusting it to Dudley, with a written commission to supervise the making of the paper, and to take precautions that none of it should fall into other hands. This Dudley was the expert coiner whom Morris hoped to employ if Congress should pass a law for the mint.[1]

In September, 1783, A. Lee moved for a return of all notes issued by Morris *on the credit of the United States.* Morris replied by a table of "Subsistence Notes," beginning in December, 1782, and coming down to October, 1783. The grand total is only $163,720.[2] We do not find notice of any cavil or objection by Lee, and he would have made cavil if he could. How is this return to be understood in connection with the table at the head of this chapter?

Waln says that, besides the notes of the Bank of North America, Morris issued his own notes, being treasury notes, payable out of the revenues of the United States and foreign subsidies.[3] The notes of the Bank of North America cannot have borne the name of Morris at all, as he never was an officer of the bank, nor connected with it otherwise than as a stockholder and borrower, either in his public or private capacity. Waln says that he set up "a kind of private bank," under the care of Mr. John Swanwick, to bolster up his first emission of notes. Swanwick had all the specie which could be borrowed from all his

[1] See page 43; Hist. Mag. for Jan. 1867. [2] See page 110.
[3] Waln, 301.

and Morris's friends set out in piles, where it could be seen. With this he redeemed the notes, and so produced a credit which brought the silver in again on deposit. Then it was returned to its owners.[1] There is an entry in the accounts, under date of June 30, 1784, of $225, expenses of the office of John Swanwick, "an appendage of the finance office."[2] That bureau was therefore in operation in 1783–84.

Morris wrote to Tilghman, April 30, 1784, that he was easy about *all his private and public notes.*[3]

Still there were notes of Morris's outstanding, when he left the treasury, which carried his personal responsibility; and in his advertisement of October 11, 1784, he pledged himself *personally* to the holders that the notes should be paid *at maturity.*[4] There seems good reason to believe that these notes, perhaps to an important amount, continued in circulation.

In the following March the money market became very stringent at Philadelphia. Morris wrote to Tilghman at Baltimore, with whom he had business relations, that there were big shipments of money, and that the managers of the Bank of North America seemed inclined to stop discount; also that the attack on the bank had caused it to curtail discounts. In April he wrote that discounts had been stopped at Boston, Philadelphia, and New York.[5] April 19, he wrote again to the same correspondent that he had a contract with the Farmers-general to provide tobacco. He thinks that raw adventurers have kept up the price of tobacco. He has a scheme to bear exchange, and so to prevent shipments of that commodity by remitters. The Farmers-general will not buy in Europe. He has prepared notes, with which he hopes to pay for tobacco

[1] Waln, 274.

[2] Cf. the story about the Bank of North America, page 34.

[3] Ford MSS. [4] Dip. Corr. Rev. xii. 502. [5] Ford MSS.

better than he could do so with coin. The notes are to be payable on demand in coin, or in sixty-day bills on Europe. The first thing to do is to give the notes a circulation. He will deposit money with Tilghman in order that he may redeem the notes, and will sell bills against gold for the current rates. Tilghman is to indorse the notes in blank, which will make them payable to bearer. The paper is to be manufactured for the purpose. The word "Commerce" is to be water-lined in it.

We therefore find that when he left office, in November, 1784, he had notes outstanding which in some way involved his personal credit, and that in April following he began to issue notes for his tobacco enterprise. It seems impossible to resist the conviction that he passed over from one of these issues to the other without any break; and if that is true, or if he could immediately float notes of his own, it seems that the notes issued by him while in office must some of them have been his personal notes, and not those of the Superintendent of Finance.

In a letter of January 19, 1786, we find the fullest explanation of what these later notes were, for he seems to be reorganizing the system of them. There are two kinds of them, as before, and Tilghman is to have money with which to redeem them, if people want it. He reissued them. The denominations mentioned are $100, $40, $20, $16, $15, $10, and $8. Morris drew promissory notes in favour of Tilghman, who endorsed them in blank. Notes redeemable in bills were to pass at "not less than five per cent advance." Virginia passed an act to prevent the circulation of private bank notes, and Maryland was considering the same plan. Thereupon, February 4, Morris wrote to his correspondent Tilghman: "I am unwilling to place myself in opposition to the laws of any country; and as I imagine these measures are levelled at me, I will be beforehand with them, and therefore request that you will not pass any of the notes you have by you, but send me an exact amount of them, and perhaps, after I have seen the Virginia law, I may order the whole to be returned to me. At any rate, you shall then hear from me fully respecting them." On the 15th, however, he wrote again that, on reflection, he did not see how the law could hinder him from giving his note to any one who would take it, and that he would go on using notes. July 9th was written the last letter which we possess in this series. Tilghman was dead, and a new firm was to be formed. Morris's notes are referred to as out and to be out.[1]

In 1796 "bills" or "notes" of Morris were mentioned as selling at a very low rate. Could these have been still some kind of circulating notes?[2]

The latest mention we have found of the use of Morris's notes as a remittance is from Virginia, April 23, 1787.[3]

The results of this investigation as to the kind and character of the notes issued bearing Morris's name are extremely unsatisfactory. It seems probable that he issued two kinds of paper. One of them, probably the earlier, which he began to issue in 1781, were certificates of indebtedness for irregular amounts, signed by the Superintendent of Finance, and binding the United States, not himself. The other kind he was probably led to issue later. In the state of public credit, his endorsement would add to the value of a note issued by the United States. The notes, if manufactured for regular and round sums, would have great advantages for purposes of circulation. The same would be true if they were made to fall due at a date. We still find it difficult to understand, however, in what way or to what extent he put his own name and credit into them.

[1] These letters to Tilghman are all in the Ford Collection.

[2] See pages 229, 282.

[3] Va. Papers, iv. 273.

The extreme difficulty of finding a specimen of any of Morris's notes of the period of the Revolution is a proof that they were all redeemed. Still they could not escape the accidents to which all paper issues are liable, and it is to be hoped that if attention is directed to the matter, a specimen may be found.

It seems very clear that Morris was seduced into the issue of notes in 1785 for the purchase of tobacco by the experience which he had had as a public financier. It must have given him a great sense of personal power and prestige to find that Robert Morris was really a greater personage than the Superintendent of Finance, and the suggestion lay near at hand: If he could circulate his personal notes for the purposes of the United States government, why should he not circulate them for the purposes of Robert Morris? If he controlled the commerce in the most important export staple of the United States as Superintendent of Finance, in order to win profits for the United States, why should he not do it likewise to win profits for Robert Morris? If he had demeaned himself as Superintendent of Finance to the vulgar devices of paper-mongering and bill-kiting, why should he not do it for Robert Morris? We have seen ample evidence that he was a sanguine, enterprising, and energetic man. The species of flattery to which he had been subjected for years, when he was told that he was the one man in America who understood the mysteries of finance, was calculated to turn his head. It is sad to believe that the services he rendered his country should have had such a disastrous moral reaction upon himself, but it seems to be forced upon us as the most reasonable explanation of his career.

CHAPTER XXVI.

MORRIS'S BUSINESS ENTERPRISES AND LAWSUITS, 1783–1793.

WHEN Morris obtained leave of absence from Congress in November, 1778, he said that the house of Willing and Morris was about to be dissolved. In a letter to Jay, President of Congress, January 28, 1779, he speaks of the late house of Willing and Morris.[1] In a letter to Tilghman, September 15, 1783, he announces the death of Mr. Inglis. The house of Willing, Inglis, and Morris seems to have lasted from 1778 to 1783. In the same letter he says that Swanwick has been taken in, and the firm is to be Willing, Morris, and Swanwick.[2] In Appleton's Encyclopedia of Biography, it is stated that the firm of Willing and Morris was dissolved in 1793. In his "Account" of his own property, Morris stated his partnership account with Thomas Willing as still open. There had been no settlement for years. It appears that there were debts due to the firm which they could not settle.

Waln says that Morris despatched the ship "Empress," Captain Greene, from New York to Canton in 1784, "the first American vessel that ever appeared there, — and that he made the first attempt to effect an out of season passage to China by going around the southern cape of New Holland, so as to avoid the adverse winds of that period in

[1] State Dep. MSS. 137, App. 245.

[2] Ford Collection.

the China Sea.[1] In a letter to Tilghman, June 28, 1785, Morris says that he is going to try the China trade.

Holker was, according to Chastellux's translator, the son of an Englishman who was implicated in the rebellion of 1745, but escaped from prison and fled to France, where he was induced by the French court to establish the cotton manufacture. He busied himself very early with contracts, etc., for America.[2] He came to America with Deane, and with a verbal commission to report on the state of things in America.[3] On the 21st of June, 1778, the Committee of Foreign Affairs asked the Commissioners at Paris to find out what Holker's status and authority were. The answer was that he had nothing beyond a verbal authorization to report any information which would be useful. He was, however, afterward made Consul-general of France in America. Chastellux's translator asserts that "by means of his situation as consul, he had many opportunities of shipping flour, etc. under permission, for the French fleet, in the time of a general and strict embargo. He speculated largely too in paper money, with which he purchased for almost nothing a very handsome house at Philadelphia, and an elegant country house and estate a few miles from that city. . . . He had a difference with Mr. Morris (Robert, his partner), on settling their accounts, to a very large amount, which has detained him in America since the peace."[4]

In a letter to Tilghman, April 30, 1784, Morris complains that Holker has treated him ill. They have a quarrel about the depreciation of continental money. Morris has in consequence withdrawn from Turnbull, Marmie, & Co., and has insisted that Holker shall withdraw from Harrison, Jr., & Co., of Richmond. He will not deal with any

[1] Waln, 368.
[2] Stevens, 162, etc., in 1777.
[3] Ford's W. Lee, 352.
[4] Chastellux, i. 318–320, note.

one who has acted so. April 5, 1785, he writes, in connection with the attack on the bank and the suspension of discounting by the bank: "The party malevolence has been aimed at me personally, in one of their laws calculated to give Holker an unjust advantage over me." This refers to an act of the Pennsylvania Assembly, April 1, 1785, entitled "An Act to enable the agent or agents of His Most Christian Majesty to sue for and recover in a more speedy way any debt or demand that may be due to them in this State." It provided for a trial "without the usual delay or imparlances." Fourteen members signed a protest against it because it was unconstitutional, was aimed at an individual, and was passed at the request of the French Minister, although he made no allegation that justice was likely to be defeated or delayed.[1]

In July Morris writes that the suit of Wharton *v.* Willing, Inglis, and Morris has been decided. For some reason the plaintiff did not use the law which had been passed in his favour. Morris exulted in the decision in that case as a victory over Holker's lawyer, although Holker does not appear as a party in the suit.

The suit of Wharton and others against Morris and others is in 1 Dallas, 124. Willing, Morris, and Inglis gave a guarantee of a contract of Pleasants, Shore, & Co., of Virginia, to buy tobacco of the plaintiff, in March, 1778. The bond was payable September 30, 1782, in "lawful current money of Pennsylvania." The question was as to the depreciation. Judge McKean said that he did not know what "lawful current money of Pennsylvania" was, because the Legislature had defined none, but that Congress had made the continental paper lawful and current for the whole country. Therefore the contract must be referred to that currency, to be reduced by the jury to gold or

[1] Ninth Assembly, 269.

silver at the scale of depreciation, or that they might find for the value of the tobacco, with interest from the day of sale. They adopted the latter course, and found £3,600 damages, with sixpence costs. The plaintiff had demanded £12,000 Pennsylvania currency, in hard money, with interest. The decision adopted the propositions in regard to depreciation which Morris had made.

In October, 1785, Morris wrote that the suit brought against him by Holker in the name of the King of France had been decided in Morris's favour. He now wants to settle with Holker.

In the "Account" of 1800 Morris makes this entry: "Joseph Fauchet, minister of France; the balance of this account is $49,822.33. It is due by Mr. Nicholson and me jointly to the French Republic. Notes were given for it, and judgment has been obtained. We often lamented our inability to satisfy this debt, and that its amount had not been retained in France out of the cargoes we sent thither."

There is a letter from Morris to Nicholson in the Ford Collection, dated December 17, 1797, in which he mentions a suit between himself and the French Republic. We have not been able to find any record of such a suit, or of the suit with Holker.

In January, 1786, Holker closed with a proposition which Morris had made to him eighteen months before, and the proposition was sent to a referee appointed by the court. In April Morris was still so occupied with this affair with Holker that he could not go to Baltimore, although his correspondent and partner there, Tench Tilghman, was dead.[1]

Holker remained in America, married there, and died

[1] These letters to Tilghman are all in the Ford Collection.

in Virginia in 1822.[1] In his "Account" of his property, Morris says of him: "This gentleman took it into his head, after I had rendered him very essential and faithful services, that he could recover large sums of money of me, under pretence of depreciation of continental money, etc., and after contests in the law and arbitration, protracted by his obstinacy for several years, an award was finally given in my favour for £1,570 12*s.* 1¼*d.* Pennsylvania currency, for which judgment was given me against him, which judgment I have since assigned to Thomas Fitzsimmons, Esq., who is to credit what he has received or may receive from this source in deduction of his claim on me."

Some letters of Carter Braxton were intercepted in 1778, published at New York, and again in the "Pennsylvania Packet" of March 18, 1779.[2] They were written to John Ross. Carter Braxton, Robert Morris, and Samuel Beall of Williamsburg, Virginia, are mentioned as partners. The commodity in which they are interested is tobacco, which it is said has not risen as other things have. We find Morris writing from Richmond, June 10, 1786, in reference to a suit of Carter Braxton against himself, complaining that he is kept in Richmond by Braxton's neglect to file papers. Braxton claimed that his answer was filed, and charged that Morris had wronged him.[3]

We have a few domestic letters of Morris to his wife while he was in Virginia in 1787 and 1788.[4] He seems to imply that Gouverneur Morris was there with him.

We learn the facts of the business relations of Braxton and Morris and of their quarrel from a report of the case in 1795.

There was an agreement between Carter Braxton on the

[1] Boogher, March, 1883.

[2] See vol. i. p. 129.

[3] Hist. Mag., November, 1868.

[4] Penn. Mag. ii. 170.

one hand, and Willing, Morris, & Co., on the other, dated March 9, 1785. Distinct accounts were to be made out by date, and a tobacco account was to be made out showing purchases and sales and investments of money or other property in tobacco. As to the depreciation, it was stipulated that when moneys were paid or received for any of the parties in Virginia, the Virginia scale was to be used, and in like manner as to any other scale. When bills were drawn between Virginia and Pennsylvania, if the bill was for moneys of the drawer, in the hands of the drawee, the depreciation should be estimated at the time when the bill was paid; but when bills were drawn to raise money for the use of the drawer, he not having moneys in the hands of the drawee, the depreciation should be estimated at the time when the bill was drawn. "But a reasonable allowance of time shall be made for the investiture of money according to the circumstances of the case." Robert Morris was to stand charged on the 1st of January, 1780, with half of what Braxton then owed to Webb & Co. for military stores bought of them, in which adventure Morris agreed to be one half concerned. The commissioners to settle all these accounts closed the account of Braxton with Willing, Morris, & Co. and carried the balance into the account of Robert Morris. There were, however, several matters left unsettled. Braxton had a claim against Morris for half the purchase money and charges of an estate in England, which Braxton had undertaken to buy, but to which he had not obtained a complete title.

Braxton took a long list of exceptions, and obtained a decree in the county court, from which Willing, Morris, & Co. appealed to the High Court of Chancery. This court, after hearing statements from the Commissioner, in 1793, reversed the decree of the county court, and ordered Braxton to pay Morris £9,627, giving orders, however, how certain matters yet pending should be reckoned and decided. Braxton appealed to the Court of Appeals, where the case came on in 1795. This court went over the points in Braxton's exceptions to the report of the Commissioner, allowing some and disallowing others, and giving orders for the treatment of still others, and remanded the case to the Court of Chancery to have the proper inquiries made and proceedings executed, according to the principles now laid down. As this put the whole case back to its beginning, it is safe to assume that it was all lost in the flood of Morris's bankruptcy. Among the rest, however, it is worth noticing that the Court of Appeals disagreed with the Court of Chancery as to the application of depreciation, and ordered two different scales of depreciation to be applied to two items which the other court had paired together.[1]

Morris's note on this matter in 1800 was: "Carter Braxton: After a lawsuit of twelve years, I got judgment for upward of £20,000, Virginia money, although he, like Holker, claimed a large sum from me, and tried hard to get it, by pretence of depreciation, etc. He died insolvent."[2]

Morris seems to have been led by the transactions in tobacco which he made on behalf of the United States to a determination to enter into that commerce on his own account. Therefore, about a year before his resignation, he made a contract to provide the Farmers-general of France with tobacco. According to the statement of the matter which is given in the report of the subsequent lawsuit, however, the first overtures were made to Robert Morris, in 1783, by the Farmers-general of France, for a contract for tobacco. Delicacy prevented him from pursuing the subject, because he received information that

[1] Call's Reports, iv. 288.

[2] Account of Property, 63.

Jonathan Williams and his father-in-law, William Alexander, had made such a contract with the same persons. This information was not correct to its full extent, but it led Morris to associate himself with Williams and Alexander in a contract to deliver fifteen thousand hogsheads per annum for three years. Morris joined the partnership in March, 1784. He was to have one third of the gain or bear one third of the loss, but have nothing for labour or services. He now made a new contract with Le Normand, Receiver-general of the finances of France, to deliver sixty thousand hogsheads of tobacco in the years 1785, 1786, and 1787. He was to receive thirty-six livres per hundred weight, which was to be paid to the bankers Le Couteulx, two livres per hundred weight being retained up to the reimbursement of a million livres, which were to be advanced to Morris immediately.[1]

The full text of the contract is given elsewhere,[2] from which we learn that the Farmers-general also promised to make no purchases in America, and undertook to pay all taxes either of export or import.

Sometime during 1785 a loss was sustained on a shipment of two thousand hogsheads, on account of the high price in Virginia. On account of this, Le Normand allowed Morris an option of shipping twenty thousand hogsheads more than the sixty thousand within the three years. July 6, 1786, Morris and Alexander entered into a new agreement, under which Morris took the position of principal and Alexander that of agent, to whom Morris allowed, for his abilities in the conduct of the business, a dollar per hogshead for every hogshead which had been or should be shipped to France, in consequence of the contract. He also allowed him two and a half per cent on all tobacco purchased and not sent to France. Morris did not

[1] Call's Rep. iii. 79.

[2] Dip. Corr. U. S. iii. 64.

exercise his option upon the twenty thousand hogsheads. The sixty thousand were shipped by the end of 1787. Morris tried to have the option extended into 1788, but did not succeed. The business is spoken of as having been carried on almost entirely by "facilities" and not by specie. "In the few instances where specie was required and sent for, it was furnished. The detention of the messengers a few days only proves the difficulty of procuring, and Morris's anxiety to furnish, the specie. . . . The true cause of disappointment appears in Alexander's letters to have been at first the high price of tobacco, and afterward the scarcity of that commodity, of which his strong expressions, that it could not be procured by the aid of the best funds of heaven and earth, are the most conclusive evidence."[1]

From the very first this contract produced a clamour in Virginia, for which there was perhaps some justification. Writing to Tilghman, April 20, 1784, Morris says: "I cannot help smiling at the idea of a remonstrance against Alexander's contract. To whom is it to be addressed? To the Farmers-general? they are interested to support it. If to the King, he must support the Farmers, for they support him. If to the tobacco-planters, they will sell to those who want to buy and can pay. It will not do." In September he asked Tilghman to have a cargo of samples prepared, to be sent to France. He had hopes of a big contract for annual supplies.[2] In January, 1786, Morris writes to Tilghman that complaints have come back of the quality of the tobacco. This hurts Morris, both in pocket and reputation. In February there were complaints in Virginia of the low price of tobacco. "Some think this is owing to a contract with the Farmers-general, the fulfilment of which, we are told, rests with Robert Morris."[3]

[1] Call's Rep. iii. 79.

[2] Ford Collection.

[3] Jones's Letters, 148.

Jefferson wrote to the Governor of Virginia from Paris, in January of that year: "I have duly received the propositions of Messrs. Ross, Pleasants, & Co. for furnishing tobacco to the Farmers-general, but Mr. Morris had in the mean time obtained the contract. I have been fully sensible of the baneful influence on the commerce of France and America which this double monopoly will have. I have struck at its root here, and spared no pains to have the farm itself demolished, but it has been in vain. The persons interested in it are too powerful to be opposed, even by the interests of the whole country." [1]

In May Jefferson wrote to Jay that there was great complaint of the monopoly of tobacco in the farm. Jefferson was trying to get it abolished, and a committee had been formed by the French government to consider the case. Jefferson calls it the double monopoly, — one of the purchase in America in the hands of Morris, the other of the sale in France. The committee resolved that the contract with Morris could not be annulled, but no similar one should be made thereafter. While it lasted the Farmers should be obliged to buy twelve or fifteen thousand hogsheads in a year, besides what they buy of Morris, on the same terms as his contract.[2]

In July Jefferson wrote to Adams: "The monopoly of the purchase of tobacco for this country [France] which had been obtained by Robert Morris, had thrown the commerce of that article into agony. He had been able to reduce the price in America from forty shillings to twenty-two shillings and sixpence lawful a hundred weight; and all other merchants being deprived of that medium of remittance, the commerce between America and this country, so far as it depended on that article, which was very capitally, too, was absolutely ceasing. An order has been

[1] Va. Papers, iv. 84. [2] Dip. Corr. U. S. iii. 61, 69.

issued obliging the Farmers-general to purchase from such other merchants as shall offer, fifteen thousand hogsheads of tobacco at thirty-four, thirty-six, and thirty-eight livres the hundred, according to the quality, and to grant to the sellers in other respects the same terms as they have granted to Robert Morris. As the agreement with Morris is the basis of this order, I send you two copies of it, which I will thank you to give to any American (not British) merchants in London who may be in that line. During the year this contract has subsisted, Virginia and Maryland have lost £400,000 by the reduction of the price of their tobacco."[1]

We have seen above that the tobacco enterprise was not a success, because the price rose and the article became exceedingly scarce. Here, now, Morris is charged with depressing the price. What was the fact? Did tobacco rise or fall?

According to the quotations of Virginia tobacco in the official record, the price in May, 1784, ranged from thirty-eight to twenty-four shillings. In January, 1787, it was from twenty-three to eighteen, and in December, 1789, it was from twenty to thirteen and a half.[2]

These quotations would seem to indicate that there was a great and steady decline in tobacco which went on steadily after the time when Morris was said to have interfered with it. Gouverneur Morris said that Morris's tobacco contract was the only means of destroying the monopoly of tobacco in Virginia, which was in fact held by the Scotch factors.[3] In 1789 there were great complaints of the quality of the tobacco sent by Robert Morris. The Farmers-general were so dissatisfied that a suit at law resulted.[4]

In explanation, then, of the fact that Morris did not make profits on his tobacco contract although the price

[1] Adams, viii. 409.
[2] Va. Papers, iii. 589; iv. 229; v. 94.
[3] Morris's Morris, i. 352.
[4] Ibid. 89, 92.

fell, we think that it is necessary to recur to the fact that he issued notes, or, as the court called them, "facilities;" and that, by the plan of those notes, he involved himself in speculations on the exchange, and in attempts to control the exchange.[1] It was another of the miserable delusions in which his experience as Financier had educated him, to believe that he had power to do this. His enterprise was a singular anticipation of the cotton speculation of Nicholas Biddle. In his letters to Tilghman we find some traces of his difficulties. April 19, 1785, he wrote that he would exchange his notes for bills of exchange at 166⅔, which he calls par,[2] although they were sixty-day bills. He expects to win on the price of tobacco what he loses on exchange. He will sell bills for gold only, at the current rates, — 176½ for ninety days, 177½ for sixty days, and 180 for thirty days. June 29, he mentions that the bills with which he redeemed his notes were drawn on Paris payable in London. He evidently hoped to control the great export, and thereby to control exchange, and by holding his rate for gold higher than for his own notes to put the latter at a premium over specie in the purchase of tobacco. Therefore he writes in May: "The higher the exchange, the more valuable my notes are."

In November he wrote that there was a great demand on him for bills. In February, 1786, he ordered Tilghman to pay out specie notes and return to him notes redeemable in bills of exchange. This was a retreat from the enterprise so far as it involved control of the exchange.

The relations of Morris and Alexander were complicated by the fact that in March, 1786, Morris directed Alexander to lend to Griffin money of Morris which he held, on a security of certificates. On the 3d of May, 1788, Morris wrote to Alexander that Griffin's debt was discharged, and

[1] See page 157. [2] See page 37.

he directed Alexander to surrender the collateral. This Alexander did not do, alleging that he retained the certificates to cover certain accrued or equitable charges which he had against Morris. Thereupon proceedings ensued, in which Morris was successful. The court rejected all of Alexander's charges. In all, five suits grew out of these transactions, in all of which, in the Virginia High Court of Chancery, Morris was successful; but they were all appealed, and being regarded as interwoven, or all parts of one case, they were tried together before the Court of Appeals in 1801, when the result below was substantially reaffirmed.[1]

In November, 1786, Knox, the Secretary of War, tried to negotiate with Robert Morris and Jeremiah Wadsworth a contract to supply the army. He submitted to the Board of Treasury a contract which he thought they would agree to. Wadsworth would not make the contract without conferring with Morris. The Board, therefore, submitted the contract to Morris, subject to the approval of Congress. To this he replied that the contract offered too much profit. He is sorry that the United States must submit to such hard terms, and he is afraid to accept them. "Experience has taught me to be cautious, even in doing good." He proposes that the United States shall reserve the right to cancel the contract at any time if, on account of obtaining money from the States, they shall be able to do better. He will accept, if no one else can be found to undertake it.[2] An account with him as "contractor," in 1785, appears on the treasury books.[3]

In 1786 it is said that he offered to the State of Pennsylvania to farm the excise in that State. He offered

[1] Call's Reports, iii. 79. See further below, page 282.

[2] State Dep. MSS., Reports of Board Treas. 140, ii. 343, 355.

[3] See page 220.

£70,000 per annum for it. There was a great prejudice against the system of farming the revenue, and the proposition was rejected. The excise was scarcely collected at all under the system in use.[1]

In 1789 Gouverneur Morris went out to France as agent and partner of Robert Morris. April 1, 1789, he proposed to Castries that he would furnish France with tobacco, flour, rice, and provisions, to be paid for partly in money and partly in the debt of the United States to France.[2] Later in the year he did make a contract to import 30,000 barrels of flour from America. He said that everything was falling to pieces in France, and subsistence was necessary first of all.[3] He also discussed grand operations with Necker on the American debt. Necker wanted 10,000,000 livres a year for three years. Morris offered 300,000 a month, to go on until 24,000,000 were paid.[4] He also offered Necker as much French debt as would produce 1,600,000 francs, in return for the American debt, — that being the interest overdue on the latter. Necker wanted part in money, and the bargain was not made.[5] These attempts to speculate on the debt fell through in 1790, because it appeared that the Americans were about to pay, which Necker said would be the best way.[6] In all these propositions, we must no doubt understand that Gouverneur Morris expected to carry them out with the assistance and co-operation of Robert Morris.

Morris had a large property on the Delaware, exactly opposite Trenton, to which the name "Morrisville" was given. The earliest mention of his ownership there which we have found is in 1787; but the place was then well developed. The conjecture offers itself that he may have

[1] Findley, 30. [2] Morris's Morris, ii. 47. [3] Ibid. 197.
[4] Ibid. 206. [5] Ibid. 239. [6] Ibid. 293.

bought the property in connection with the earliest propositions to erect the federal city near there.[1]

Manasseh Cutler mentions seeing at Morrisville, near the falls of the Delaware, "several long buildings in the form of barracks, occupied by nailmakers," in 1787.[2] In 1794 Morris wrote to his son William, who was then in London, directing him to visit a Mr. Wood, who is said to be able to build a steam-engine. If he is competent to do so, William Morris is to urge him to come to America, and to advance him money, if necessary. An engine is wanted at the Delaware works. William is to be cautious, lest he attract the notice of government.[3] In a letter to Nicholson, Morris mentions a man named Patterson, who says that he can and will finish the steam-engine for Morris. In the "Account" of his property Morris mentions a quantity of materials intended for the steam-engine. "John Patterson attempted to steal them; and on being recovered, I think they were sent to the building erected for the steam-engine. Whether they have been kept together in preservation or suffered to be lost, stolen, or decayed to ruin, I do not know." In the same document he speaks very ill of Patterson, who, he says, committed murder and then hanged himself.

The Duc de Liancourt gives a description of Morrisville. Robert Morris owns the whole of it. He has iron works there. He tried other manufactures, but they failed. If he was not so absorbed in speculation, and if his affairs were not so embarrassed, he could give more attention to these things and make them pay.[4] In a schedule of the property of the Pennsylvania Property Co., Morrisville is described as containing twenty-five hundred acres. There are fourteen farms, a grist-mill, a slitting-mill, a rolling-mill,

[1] See page 237.
[2] Cutler's Cutler, i. 249.
[3] Mag. Amer. Hist. xiii. 580.
[4] Liancourt, iii. 270, in 1795.

a wire-mill, a snuff-mill, a plaster-mill, an iron-forge, a saw-mill, and a brewery. There is also a fine dwelling-house of Robert Morris, with outbuildings, and a stone-quarry. It is estimated to be worth $250,000. In the "Account" Morris says that it was subject to a first and second mortgage, and was sold by the sheriff.

CHAPTER XXVII.

THE BANK WAR OF 1785–1786.

WE have seen that specie came into the United States in large amounts in 1780 and 1781;[1] but the State issues of paper continued, and the notes of the Bank of North America and Morris's notes were also filling the circulation. It was impossible that the specie and paper could both be retained. Webster tells us that although the public treasury was so distressed, there was abundance of cash, and that bills on Europe were at from twenty to forty per cent discount.[2] Of course this produced large importations of merchandise and exportation of specie. According to the notions of the time this was a great public calamity, and those who handled the specie were held to blame for it, as if they had done a mischievous thing out of private greed. Webster thought that an import duty on the merchandise would be a remedy; and most people agreed with him.

On the return of peace there were great fluctuations and much confusion, as the inevitable consequence of all the follies and mishaps of the previous years. We may quote a summary description of the state of things from Hamilton:[3] "The general devastation of personal property occasioned by the late war naturally produced on the one hand a great demand for money, and on the other a great deficiency of it to answer the demand. Some injudicious

[1] See vol. i. p. 99.

[2] Webster, 267.

[3] Report on the United States Bank, December 13, 1790: Folio State Papers, Finance, i. 71.

laws which grew out of the public distresses, by impairing confidence, and causing a part of the inadequate sum in the country to be locked up, aggravated the evil. The dissipated habits contracted by many individuals during the war which, after the peace, plunged them into expenses beyond their income; the number of adventurers without capital, and in many instances without information, who at that epoch rushed into trade, and were obliged to make any sacrifices to support a transient credit; the employment of considerable sums in speculation upon the public debt, which from its unsettled state was incapable of becoming itself a substitute, — all these circumstances concurring, necessarily led to usurious borrowing, produced most of the inconveniences and were the true causes of most of the appearances which, where banks were established, have been by some erroneously placed to their account; a mistake which they might easily have avoided by turning their eyes toward places where there were none, and where, nevertheless, the same evils would have been perceived to exist, even in a greater degree than where those institutions had obtained."

There certainly are points in this paragraph, where the writer attempts to account for and criticise the situation, which cannot be accepted as correct; but the situation which he describes and the notions about the explanation of it, were matters of the greatest public interest at the time. We have seen above reason to believe that the Revolutionary War did not bear with any great severity on the people, and that the distress which was occasioned was due to inexperience, perversity, and folly in administration; but the social changes brought about by the war were very great. All who had remained loyal to Great Britain had suffered severely. Thousands of them had been banished or had emigrated.

On the other hand, whigs had suffered in the districts which had been occupied by the English.[1] Many persons who had been in affluent circumstances before the war were impoverished.[2] On the other hand, large fortunes had been made by privateering and what was called speculation.[3] There had not, however, been any great destruction of capital, and the destruction of capital which had taken place had been very generally distributed over the country. One State had had its period of distress as the seat of war in one year, and another in another year. Each thought that it had suffered the most, but it is remarkable how evenly the loss had been distributed.

There had certainly been no impoverishment of the people, or exhaustion of the country; but there had been great changes in the position of classes, and many individuals had been either enriched or impoverished. These changes, so far as they were bad, were chiefly due, not to the war itself, but to the mistaken methods adopted for carrying it on, and to the lack of method, of which we have seen so much above. As early as 1777, John Adams observed that prize cases and controversies had made the barrister's profession more lucrative than ever before.[4] Pelatiah Webster asserted, in 1785, that forty or fifty per cent more could be obtained for labour and country pro-

[1] Many whigs of Suffolk County, Long Island, who had abandoned their farms, became involved in debt, and at the peace returned poor. "They found their farms out of order, buildings dilapidated, fences gone, stock carried off, woodland cut off, churches deserted or torn down" (Onderdonk, Suffolk, and Kings, 110).

[2] Mrs. Livingston wrote to Jay: "You can have no idea of the sufferings of many who from affluence are reduced to the most abject poverty, and others who die in obscurity" (Johnston's Jay, ii. 299).

[3] Chastellux (ii. 246) mentions Tracy, of Newburyport, who at the end of 1777 had lost forty-one ships. In 1782 he was worth £120,000 sterling by privateering.

[4] Adams, iii. 89.

duce than in 1774.[1] Hamilton said that labour was much dearer in 1782 than before the war.[2] When Franklin came home, although he heard complaints of hard times, dulness of trade, scarcity of money, etc., he was astonished at the changes. "If we enter the cities we find that since the Revolution the owners of houses and lots of ground have had their interest vastly augmented in value; rents have risen to an astonishing height, and thence encouragement to increase building, which gives employment to an abundance of workmen, as does also the increased luxury and splendour of living of the inhabitants, thus made richer. These workmen all demand and obtain much higher wages than any other part of the world would afford them, and are paid in ready money."[3] He wrote to Jefferson: "I do not remember ever to have seen, during my long life, more signs of public felicity than appear at present throughout these States." The crops were good, the prices high, the wages high, real estate was advancing. The merchants complained; but it was because there were too many of them.[4]

On the other hand Webster, enumerating the woes of war, mentioned the effect of depreciation on debts, salaries, fees, etc.; "also the distresses and losses arising from the limitations of the market, the ruinous effects of which were innumerable, and in many instances shocking and almost tragical. . . . While we rejoice in the riches and strength of our country, we have reason to lament with tears of the deepest regret the most pernicious shift of property which the above-mentioned irregularities of our finances introduced, and the many thousands of fortunes which were ruined. The generous patriotic spirits suffered the injury; the avaricious and idle derived benefit from the said con-

[1] Webster, 293.

[2] Hamilton's Works, viii. 64; Letter to R. Morris.

[3] Franklin, ii. 462.

[4] Dip. Corr. U. S. iii. 75.

fusion."[1] He said that some bad men rose to positions of influence, as they do in all revolutions.

It was exactly this contrast, and especially the effect on debtors of the collapse of the paper currency, which produced the riots and rebellion in New Hampshire, Massachusetts, and elsewhere, and the almost universal demand for more paper money. Creditors suffered far more than debtors during the period of the Revolution, but they are not the class which makes riots.

We have had occasion also to comment on the doctrines of political philosophy and constitutional law which were popularly entertained. A conservative party had been formed, which embraced the men of education and wider knowledge of the world, who were struggling for union, public credit, and the dominion of law. They found themselves opposed to the great drift of popular opinion and feeling. The mass of the people were still, as in the colonial days, turbulent, self-willed, and lawless. "The fruits of our peace and independence do not at present wear so promising an appearance as I had fondly painted to my mind. The jealousies, the prejudices, and the turbulence of the people at times, almost stagger my confidence in our political establishment, and almost occasion me to think that they will show themselves unworthy the noble prize for which we have contended, and which I had pleased myself was so near our enjoyment."[2] "Among the extravagances with which these prolific times abound, we hear it often said that the Constitution, being the creature of the people, their sense with respect to any measure, if it even stand in opposition to the Constitution, will sanctify and make it right."[3]

[1] Webster, 93 fg.

[2] Governor Trumbull to Washington; April 20, 1784: Letters to Washington, iv. 68.

[3] Hamilton's Works, iii. 495.

The conservative party, in their exhortations and arguments, spoke a language which was hardly intelligible to the popular party. By what arguments will you convince a man of the value of a thing like public credit, the value of which is never understood by anybody except through knowledge of the world and experience of affairs? The leaders of the popular party never had anything to do but glide along with the course of things, encouraging the people in all their prejudices, and falling in with all their wishes. The conservative party had to struggle for union, for adequate constitutional institutions, for taxation and provision for the public debt, for the restriction of paper currency, and for an adequate federal establishment in order to give Americans security on the sea and in all international relations. They could only accomplish these ends by persistent and careful effort to bring about one step after another.

As soon as the war was really ended and its results in effect achieved, the union fell to pieces. The army was brushed aside as quickly as possible, and the popular temper showed itself in a warfare on the money power. The Bank of North America was the institution which represented the money power. In 1784 and 1785 it earned fourteen per cent. If it was judged by modern standards, its methods of banking would be open to severe animadversions, but the criticisms which were made upon it at the time were almost altogether social and political. In 1784 it enlarged its capital by issuing a thousand more shares at $500 each. This led to the foundation of a rival institution, which was on the point of being chartered, when the new subscription was extended to four thousand shares at $400 a share, and those who had already paid in $500 received $100 back with interest. On June 13 the capital amounted to $830,000.[1] In the list of sub-

[1] Hazard's Register, iv. 136.

scribers at this time appears the firm of Willing, Morris, and Swanwick.

Joseph Reed wrote from London, in regard to the proposed new bank, that the whig representation in it was not large enough, but that he hoped it would check the influence which was predominant. " Mr. Morris has had all the effective powers of government in his own hands, as it was easy to foresee he would have. It was the misfortune of the times, and even good men were obliged to concur in it as the lesser evil." [1]

We obtain some insight into the situation of things from a letter of William Seton, cashier of the Bank of New York, to Hamilton, written from Philadelphia, March 27, 1784. The bank, he says, is in great confusion. On account of the opposition of the new bank they were obliged to extend their loans and issues until they put themselves in a dangerous position. For the safety of the community, therefore, " it became absolutely necessary to drop the idea of a new bank, and to join hand in hand to relieve the old bank from the shock it had received. Gold and silver had been extracted in such amounts that discounting was stopped, and for this fortnight past not any business has been done at the bank in this way. The distress it has occasioned to those dependent on circulation and engaged in large speculations, is severe; and as if their crop of misery must overflow, by the last arrival from Europe intelligence is received that no less a sum than £60,000 sterling of Mr. Morris's bills, drawn for the Dutch loan, are under protest. It is well known that the bank, by some means or other, must provide for this sum. The child must not desert its parent in distress; and such is their connection that whatever is fatal to the one must be so to the other. . . . I have had several interviews with our

[1] Reed's Reed, ii. 413.

friend Gouverneur Morris. He is for making the Bank of New York a branch of the Bank of North America; but we differ widely in our ideas of the benefit that would result from the connection."[1]

In April Hamilton wrote to Gouverneur Morris: "Discrimination bills, partial taxes, schemes to engross public property in the hands of those who have present power, to banish the real wealth of the State and to substitute paper bubbles, are the only dishes that suit the public palate at this time."[2]

In March, 1785, "petitions from a considerable number of the inhabitants of Chester County were read, representing that the bank established at Philadelphia has fatal effects upon the community; that whilst men are enabled by means of the bank to receive near three times the rate of common interest, and at the same time to receive their money at very short warning whenever they have occasion for it, it will be impossible for the husbandman or mechanic to borrow on the former terms of legal interest and distant payment of the principal; that the best security will not enable the person to borrow; that experience clearly demonstrates the mischievous consequences of the institution to the fair trader; that impostors have been able to support themselves in a fictitious credit by means of a temporary punctuality at the bank, until they have drawn in their honest neighbours to trust them with their property or to pledge their credit as sureties, and have been finally involved in ruin and distress; that they have repeatedly seen the stopping of discounts at the bank operate on the trading part of the community with a degree of violence scarcely inferior to that of a stagnation of the blood in the human body, hurrying the wretched merchants who have debts to pay into the hands of griping

[1] Hamilton's Works, i. 417. [2] Ibid. 418.

usurers; that the directors of the bank may give such preference in trade by advances in money to their particular favourites as to destroy that equality which ought to prevail in a commercial country; that paper money has often proved beneficial to the State, but the bank forbids it, and the people must acquiesce. Therefore, and in order to restore public confidence and private security, they pray that a bill may be brought in and passed into a law for repealing the law for incorporating the bank."[1]

A committee was raised "to inquire whether the bank established at Philadelphia was compatible with the public safety, and that equality which ought ever to prevail between the individuals of a republic." The committee reported that the bank as then managed was in every way inconsistent with the public safety, and recommended that its charter be repealed.

The bill for the repeal went over the session, but was taken up on the first day of the autumn session of the same Assembly. Counsel of the bank were allowed to argue before the House; but on the 13th of September, 1785, the charter was repealed.

The bank now fell back on its federal charter, but there were so many doubts of its validity that the attempt was made to get another State charter. February 2, 1786, Delaware gave one, which was accepted; and it was determined, if necessary, to move to some city in Delaware.

A popular agitation of the question, bank or no bank, was however begun in Pennsylvania, in the course of which Gouverneur Morris wrote an address on behalf of the bank, which, considering the time at which it was written, contained some very strong and clear writing on currency and banking. On the above charges he commented as follows: "If it be true that the bank enables men to

[1] Ninth Assembly, 233.

overtrade themselves by the use of money at an easy rate, it cannot be true that it throws men into the hands of usurers who exact for the use of money an exorbitant rate. If it be true that foreigners will buy out the stockholders, even as is said, at fifty per cent advance, so as to become proprietors of the whole, it cannot be true that the money of our rich citizens will be vested in bank stock and none remain for loans. If it be true that the use of money obtained by discount at the bank ruins the trader, it cannot be true that the directors and their friends would gain any advantage by it. If it be true that the bank has a tendency to lock up in its vaults the money of rich citizens, it cannot be true that it facilitates the exportation of coin. If it be true that foreigners will continually bring in money to buy the principal of the stock, it cannot be true that the country will be continually drained of specie by paying the dividend on that principal. If it be true that the funds of the bank must finally vest in foreigners, it cannot be true that it is destructive of equality among the citizens."[1]

Nearly the only element in the popular discussion which could be called financial was that which grew out of the notion that there was not money enough. On this Gouverneur Morris wrote: "The surest way to render money plenty is to bear the evils of scarcity. To make it plenty, according to the desire of some, would be, as in the continental time, to make it no money at all. For when it can be obtained without labour and found without search, it is of no use to the possessor. Those nice politicians, therefore, who try to make money so plenty that people may get it for nothing, will find that their money is good for nothing. The scarcity constitutes the value, and when that scarcity is such that men will do a great

[1] Sparks's Morris, iii. 440.

deal for a little it will become plenty; for those will always have most money who will give most for it. The complaint that money is scarce is generally made by the idle or unfortunate, — by those who will not, or by those who cannot give anything in exchange for money, except bare promises, which they cannot or will not perform.

"Now, such men would suffer more from the want of cash in Amsterdam or London, where it is most plenty, than in any part of the State of Pennsylvania. If folks are idle, they must be relieved by labour; and if poor, by charity. Till this be done, the complaint that money is scarce will continue, and though loud will not be very just. There was, for instance, a grievous complaint of the want of money at the close of the war, and yet every man who had a bushel of wheat could get eight or nine shillings for it. People in general plunged into extravagance, and laid out their coins for foreign fripperies, and the merchants, unable to remit for payment of these things in produce, except on ruinous terms, sent away the coin; so that in two years there has been more money exported from this country, in which a scarcity was then complained of, than is necessary for a circulating medium. The several States are now issuing paper, that what little specie is left may also be exported, instead of the wheat, corn, rice, and tobacco. Flour has long been cheaper in London than in Philadelphia. We buy fine coats and handsome buckles and a thousand other handsome fine things in London, and then, when called on to pay, though our barns be full of wheat, we will not sell it as formerly, for five shillings a bushel, but sit down and cry because money is scarce."[1]

He very nearly reached the two great doctrines of currency: (1) that there never can be a scarcity of currency except when there is too much of it; (2) that if the

[1] Sparks's Morris, iii. 448.

currency is perfectly good, it has no effect whatever on contracts; hence, if contracts are affected by currency, the remedy is to make the currency better. Considering the present state of opinion on currency, including bimetallism, we must give Gouverneur Morris great credit for his attainments in monetary science. He must have been much more than a mere assistant to Robert Morris.

Thomas Paine was hired by Morris and other friends of the bank to write for it. Callender, in 1802, said that stratagems were practised on Paine, and that he was ruined with his friends. He added that the bankers in that bank knew nothing about banking; that all European banks, except the Bank of England, limit themselves to buying and selling bullion.[1]

In October, 1785, Robert Morris was elected a representative in the General Assembly of Pennsylvania. His object was to join in the battle about the Bank of North America, but he was very diligent in his attendance throughout the year. His name is in almost every division, and he was on all the most important committees. He was chairman of the Committee of Ways and Means; on a committee for revising the road system of the State, which was said to be very bad; also on a committee to revise the test laws of the State, and to extend to free male whites the privileges of citizenship, although they had not taken the test oath, if they now swear allegiance (which was carried); and on the committee for a bill to pardon the Connecticut settlers in Wyoming, if they give surety for good behaviour. He voted with the majority against a law forbidding all theatricals, voted to table a bill for licensing a regular theatre, and tried in vain to improve the tax system.

The Committee of Ways and Means reported a long and careful plan for reforming the finances of the State, which

[1] Letters to Hamilton, 36.

was adopted and acted on; but in February, 1786, the part of it which provided for paying the State's quota of interest on the federal debt was repealed, against Morris's urgent opposition. This was no doubt one of the parts of it which interested him the most. The measure for admitting the tories to citizenship aroused great opposition; and a remonstrance against it by the citizens of Dauphin County was handed in, couched in the strongest rhetoric of the pre-revolutionary period. They threatened to defend their liberties by force. The House refused to allow the remonstrance to lie on the table. Another similar remonstrance they refused to hear read.[1] The bill contained a limitation that the tories must take oath that they had not voluntarily aided the English since the Declaration of Independence. Morris tried in vain to have this stricken out.[2] He also signed a protest of the dissenting minority against a bill to redeem the bills of credit of 1781 by collecting the arrears of unpatented lands, located before 1776. The grounds of dissent were that it was a favour to the landholders whose quit-rents had been abolished, and who also had enjoyed other favours; that it would produce uncertainty and speculation, and would deprive the State of taxes.[3] He favoured a proposition that no one should vote who did not pay taxes; which was lost, sixty to ten.[4]

The great question, however, was the one of rechartering the bank. March 3, 1786, a memorial from six hundred and twenty-four citizens of Philadelphia in favour of the bank was presented, in order to bring the matter up again. The debates on this occasion were published by Matthew Carey, at the expense, it is said,[5] of Robert Morris, who took a prominent part in the debate.

Lollar, arguing against the bank, said: "The learned

[1] Tenth Assembly, 177.
[2] Ibid. 189.
[3] Ibid. 195.
[4] Ibid. 253.
[5] Mease, 237.

counsel who have pleaded the cause of the bank before the late Assembly have candidly and ingenuously admitted that when the balance of trade was against the country a bank was injurious." Smilie said that bank paper money and State paper money could not exist together, and that the question was which should prevail. Pelatiah Webster, in an essay on the "Bank of North America," explained this notion by saying that the State paper money men thought that they could not circulate such paper unless the bank would give it currency.[1] Findley expressed the fear of the democrats, — that in America no other institution existed or could exist to offset the bank. In fact, the whole debate is a strange anticipation in miniature of the war between the Jackson party and the Bank of the United States, as respects both the political and the financial ideas involved in it.

Morris, in his speech, said that the stockholders voted to try at law whether the charter could be repealed. He represented the action then going on as resting on outside petition, and not on the petition of the bank. He said that trade was not good, that exports were less than before the war. He had heard that opposition to the bank was opposition to himself, but he was quite indifferent whether the bank was abolished or not. If it was, he would set up a bank of his own, with or without partners, and he was sure that his enemies "will deal with me and trust me; not that I expect that they may like me better than now, but they have confidence in me, and for the sake of their own interests and convenience they will deal with me." He gave a history of the bank and of the assistance which it rendered to him during his administration of the treasury. He argued that the bank brought capital into the country; which was an advantage, because it was loaned here at six or

[1] Webster, 448.

eight per cent, and the borrower could make fifteen or twenty. Therefore the more was imported, the better. He compared the amount of the government stock in the bank with the amount of the government debts to the bank, and spoke of the merchants as borrowing from the bank the amount of their stock in it. This gives us an insight into the mode of the business. The stockholders of the bank were regarded as warranted in borrowing from it to the extent of their stock, which was regarded as the security. He spoke of the deposits in it as the loanable funds. He said that people were afraid to lend on bond and mortgage on account of the paper money and the tender laws. His speech is a good one, and shows that he was a good debater.

The proposed recharter of the bank was defeated in April.

Morris was re-elected to the eleventh General Assembly for the year 1786–87. At the opening of the November session a committee reported that some amendments in the charter of the bank would make it free from objection ; and the bank was rechartered March 17, 1787, for fourteen years. Its capital was limited to two millions of dollars.

Morris was re-elected to the eleventh General Assembly for 1786–87 ; but in March, 1786, he had been appointed on the committee to whom was referred the proposition of Virginia for a Convention to regulate commerce. He was appointed delegate to that Convention, which met in 1786, and also a member of the Constitutional Convention which met in May, 1787, so that he took very little part in the proceedings of the General Assembly of that year.

CHAPTER XXVIII.

THE COMMERCIAL CONVENTION AND THE CONSTITUTIONAL CONVENTION.

JUNE 14, 1782, the Virginia Assembly passed resolutions to co-operate with Maryland in the defence of the Chesapeake Bay. Joint action was proposed in regard to duties, etc.[1] This was the earliest attempt to deal with a difficulty, which increased during the following years and became the immediate moving cause of the adoption of the federal Constitution. The different elements which combined in this connection were the limitation of jurisdiction over waters which lay between two States, the regulation of commerce by navigation laws, the impost for federal revenue, and the attempt to act upon the development of industry by import duties.

January 4, 1786, the Secretary of Congress made a report on the action of the States with respect to the revenue system, which was adopted by Congress April 18, 1783. The proposed impost had been adopted by all but Rhode Island, Delaware, Maryland, New York, and Georgia. In 1785 Rhode Island enacted that the State should appoint the collectors by its General Assembly, and that they should be amenable to it. Congress had proposed that the States should appoint, but that they should be amenable to Congress. Hamilton, in his answer to the Rhode Island objections to the impost in December, 1782, had main-

[1] Va. Papers, iii. 192.

tained "that no federal Constitution can exist without powers that, in their exercise, affect the internal police of the component members. It is equally true that no government can exist without a right to appoint officers for those purposes which proceed from and concentre in itself."[1] We now know well that these propositions were strictly correct. They belong to the very foundation of our existing federal system. They therefore raised, in a very distinct form at that time, the issue of Union or no Union. The Rhode Island Act further provided that the State should retain from the revenue $8,000 to pay its share of the interest on the foreign debt, and that the remainder should be paid on the interest of the domestic debt held in that State. Maryland had complied with all but the provision about the appointment and amenability of the collectors. There was no official report for Delaware; but it was said to have complied. As to providing other revenues to make up the million and a half required, besides the impost, New Jersey, Pennsylvania, and North Carolina had complied. Rhode Island had laid a tax of one dollar in silver on every hundred acres, and on every male poll over twenty-one, and on every horse or mare two years old, in order to pay the interest on the domestic debt held in Rhode Island.

New York, New Jersey, Pennsylvania, Maryland, Virginia, North Carolina, and Connecticut had complied in full with the Act of April 26, 1784, giving Congress power to regulate commerce. New Hampshire, Massachusetts, and Rhode Island had complied with it in effect.

A proposition had also been submitted for amending the Articles of Confederation, so that the basis of apportionment of requisitions should be population, and not the assessed value of houses and land. To this New Hamp-

[1] Journ. Cong. viii. 153.

shire, Rhode Island, Delaware, South Carolina, and Georgia had not consented.[1]

A month later the Committee on Finance reported: Over fifteen millions and a half had been called for within the last four years, on which there had been paid less than two millions and a half. They speak of the country as "having in a great measure recovered from the calamities of the late war, being in possession of a free and extensive commerce, at peace with all nations, and the economy of our own government, thus circumstanced, only to attend to." Hence they think it would not raise their credit to ask for any more loans abroad. They therefore recur to the plan of April 18, 1783, the impost and the State taxes for a million and a half of dollars. It was proposed to urge Georgia and New York to come into the plan.

On the 15th of February, 1786, a committee reported on the acts passed by the several States to comply with that plan. Some had put in one restriction or condition, and some another. Seven had agreed in such a way that if the other six would agree, the plan would go into operation. Only two had accepted the system in all its parts, and four had not decided in favour of any part of it; yet the committee cannot find that any objections have been made to it. They say that the requisitions are not to be depended on as a resource. The interest to be paid in Europe in 1787 will exceed half a million of dollars, and from that time until 1797 the average annual sum of a million dollars will be necessary to meet the contracts for interest and instalments of the principal in Europe. From the 1st of November, 1781, to the 1st of January, 1786, the amount brought into the federal treasury was not quite two millions and a half of dollars, and during the last fourteen months the income had been at the rate of $371,052

[1] Dip. Corr. U S. iv. 409.

per annum, — that is, less than the current expenses of the government itself.[1]

Perhaps nothing more distinctly proves the low position to which the treasury had sunk in 1786, than the fact that the Board of Treasury wrote to the loan officer of Massachusetts, hearing that he had $67,197 of the old notes, of March, 1780, in his hands, to ask him to sell $25,000 of those notes for specie, on the best terms possible, and send the proceeds to them.[2]

As time went on in the years after the peace, the chances of obtaining the impost, instead of improving, declined; for as the pressure of necessity passed away, all the wild and impracticable notions were brought forward without restraint. R. H. Lee would not agree that Congress should fix the mode of taxation or the manner of collecting it. He wanted to discourage large importations, lest the balance of trade should become unfavourable.[3] Osgood favoured an impost by the States, collected by officers appointed by the State, and accountable only to the State; the proceeds to be placed to the credit of the State.[4]

The States also became more and more jealous of each other. The Governor of Massachusetts, in 1785, sent a circular to the governors explaining a resolution of the Massachusetts Legislature. One State had levied duties on goods imported from any of the United States, especially on the products of Massachusetts; while the same goods imported from foreign countries were free. He refers, without naming the State, to New York, which was trying to prevent an importation through Massachusetts which had become customary while New York City was occupied by the English. Massachusetts expostulated, and asked for the support of the other States.[5]

[1] Journ. Cong. xi. 18.
[2] Phillips, ii. 234.
[3] Lee's R. H. Lee, ii. 62.
[4] Mass. Hist. Soc. Proc. March, 1862.
[5] Va. Papers, iv. 60.

Virginia, however, was more interested in her own case with Maryland. January 13, 1786, the House of Delegates of Virginia passed resolutions concerning the joint commerce of Maryland and Virginia. Among the rest, they provided that duties on imports and exports, if laid, should be the same in both States, and that each State should appoint Commissioners to meet once a year to confer on the commercial policy of the two States. This contemplated joint action.[1] Virginia proposed a Convention of the States, to which the Pennsylvania Assembly responded by an Act of March 31, 1786. Five Commissioners were to be appointed, any three of whom might act, to meet Commissioners of the other States at a time and place to be agreed upon; to take into consideration the trade of the United States, and to report propositions for a uniform system of commercial regulation, which, if unanimously ratified, will enable Congress to provide for trade; also especially to confer with the Commissioners of Virginia and Maryland about the regulations of commerce and the duties proposed by each State.[2] April 11, Pennsylvania appointed Robert Morris, George Clymer, John Armstrong, Jr., Thomas Fitzsimmons, and Tench Coxe, Commissioners.[3]

The Act of the State of New York with regard to the impost called out special action by Congress. The Act was passed May 4, 1786. A committee of Congress reported on it July 27, 1786. They said that this act of New York reserves to that State the sole power of levying and collecting the same, according to an Act of that State of November 18, 1784, so that the other States which have passed the Act on condition of its being passed by all, would not be bound; that the State has retained jurisdiction of the collectors, and that the duties would be payable in bills of credit of New York. Hence they report a reso-

[1] Va. Papers, iv. 80. [2] Ibid. 117. [3] Penn. Archives, xi. 522.

lution that this is not a compliance with the request of Congress, and it was voted to appoint a committee who should draft an ordinance to carry the impost into effect as soon as it had been complied with by New York, and as soon as Pennsylvania and Delaware had amended their acts.[1]

August 11, 1786, it was resolved to request Pennsylvania to amend her Act so as to grant an impost without the condition that all the States should grant the supplementary funds; also to urge New York to convene the Legislature, so as to grant the impost. This was passed unanimously, except New York. On the 23d of August Congress took up the answer of the Governor of New York, saying that he declined to convene the Legislature for this purpose. The delegates from New York made this letter the basis of a motion that there should be no further appeal to New York; which Congress rejected, and reiterated their appeal.[2]

This brought the matter of the impost to a crisis. It seemed to be demonstrated that a unanimous action of the thirteen States could not be obtained. On the other hand, the fact had been developed with great distinctness that an import duty was by far the best system of revenue possible for the federal government. It was the only one which could be made to produce revenue consistently with the industrial organization and the prejudices and customs of the people. It has often been asserted that the chief reason why the federal Constitution was required was in order to provide for the regulation of commerce and the protection of home industry. Webster and Clay had a great debate on this point in 1824.

The desire of certain interests, and among the rest, of the shipbuilding interest and the carrying trade, to secure special advantages by the adjustment of import taxes, pro-

[1] Journ. Cong. xi. 111. [2] Ibid. 133.

duced an attempt to effect an entrance here for protective taxes under cover of the necessity of revenue. In the end that attempt succeeded, and this has been the position of protective taxes ever since; but the necessity of the situation in 1786 was for an adequate revenue for the support of the federal Union, and there was no other necessity, either political, industrial, or financial.

The geography of the Atlantic coast had a very important and perhaps a decisive influence in bringing about the Union, for if the geography had not presented exactly the features which do appear, subordinate groups of States would have made local arrangements with each other. The reason why Maryland and Virginia could not agree as to the control of the waters between them was that each of them touched on the other side upon other waters, which they held in common with other States, — North Carolina on the one side, and Pennsylvania and Delaware on the other; or, if the waters did not exactly touch the territory, they approached near enough for commercial purposes. If Pennsylvania and Delaware had joined Virginia and Maryland, they would have found difficulty with New Jersey, with which they shared the Delaware River and Bay. If New Jersey had joined them, she would have found new difficulty with New York and Connecticut. Then through Long Island Sound and Narragansett Bay, Rhode Island and Massachusetts must have been taken in. On the other side, the sounds and bays of North Carolina connected with those of South Carolina and Georgia in such a way that, with the possible exception of New Hampshire, the thirteen colonies were forced to have one system of duty and one line of policy for the regulation of commerce.

The Convention met at Annapolis in September. Virginia, New Jersey, Delaware, Pennsylvania, and New York were the only States represented. Those who were present determined to report to the Legislatures which appointed them that it was desirable that a Convention of all the States should be called. John Dickinson was the chairman of this meeting. The Address, however, was written by Hamilton.[1]

The Commissioners considered the federal government inefficient, and that further provisions should be devised to render it adequate to the exigencies of the Union. Hence they recommended to the States to send delegates to Philadelphia on the second Monday in May. New York interposed with a proposition for a Convention to propose amendments to Congress, which was defeated. New York had sent instructions to its delegates to this effect. Then, on the proposition of Massachusetts, that proposition was in effect agreed to. The Convention was to report to Congress and the several Legislatures such alterations as, when agreed to by Congress and confirmed by the States, should render the federal Constitution adequate to the exigencies of government.[2]

At the same time with this Address, Tench Coxe, Commissioner for Pennsylvania, addressed a communication to the Commissioners of Virginia. Before Virginia proposed a general Convention of the States, Pennsylvania was considering the assimilation of the commercial systems of the States. An examination of facts showed that some States had discriminating tonnage taxes against the ships of other States, sometimes as great as the tax on foreign ships, and discriminating taxes on goods imported in ships of other States. The import taxes in some cases were as high on goods from other States as if they came from foreign countries. He asks the Commissioners of Virginia to obtain power to deal with these matters. Pennsylvania treats

[1] Madison Papers, ii. 698.

[2] Journ. Cong. xii. 12.

the ships of other States as she does the ships of Pennsylvania, and puts the same taxes on goods imported in the ships of other States as on those imported in her own, and taxes no goods which are the gross product or manufacture of the United States.[1]

April 2, 1787, Edward Carrington, delegate from Virginia, wrote to Governor Randolph from New York, that the late law of Virginia had had a bad effect on trade. "This circumstance evinces the impossibility of managing the trade of America by State arrangement, and the necessity of vesting the federal head with full authority over that and every interest of like general nature. Until this is the case, State schemes will be pursued, with surreptitious views against each other, which must eventually destroy a source of revenue that might be immensely valuable to the whole Union; and every effort prohibiting of foreign articles will also be vain."[2]

In May one of the Commissioners to establish a basis of trade between Virginia and Maryland reported that the existing arrangement between those two States for the control of the waters was not feasible or expedient. "Some system of a general nature should pervade the whole Confederation."[3]

There had already been two cases of riot and mob interference with the administration of the joint law of Maryland and Virginia. In 1782 a Maryland schooner at Fredericksburg violated the Virginia duties. The sheriff seized it; but a mob was raised, which carried away the salt of which the cargo consisted, and frustrated his efforts. Another officer reported to the Governor the name of the person in whose warehouse the salt lay. Edmund Randolph, the Attorney-General, seemed afraid of the case,

[1] Va. Papers, iv. 168.

[2] Ibid. 264.

[3] Ibid. 280.

but said that he would inquire into the particulars of the riot.[1]

In June, 1787, a searcher in the customs service of Virginia reported to the Governor from Alexandria that an attempt had been made to land rum contrary to law. The officer was resisted by the captain and crew, and when the vessel was seized, citizens helped the captain to rescue it and make sail. They refused to help the officer on his demand, "and appeared more ready to assist the violators than the executor of the law." A fortnight later he reported that steps had been taken to fine the persons who refused him their assistance. He expected that the vessel would pass Alexandria in the night, which she did. A poor labourer, who was suspected of having given information against the vessel, was taken out of his house at night by the mob, beaten, cut, and stabbed so that he would probably not be able to earn his living any more. Another under like suspicion was also abused a few nights later. Both were innocent of giving information.[2] This story is exactly like the stories of resistance to the custom-house officers in the last years before the Revolution.[3]

In the attempt to prosecute the second case, the impracticability of the joint arrangement then existing between Virginia and Maryland was distinctly shown. The local officer, in a report to the Governor, stated that the shipowners considered that if they entered in one State, they were only bound to take care that they did not violate the commercial regulations of that State, and that the Potomac was free to both. The laws of Maryland allowed retail trade to small boats over the side, and it was impossible to tell to which State they belonged. As he quotes the compact, it provided both that the river should be free to both

[1] Va. Papers, iii. 247, 257. [2] Ibid. iv. 301 fg.

[3] See, for instance, Biddle, 64, 72.

parties, and that each should make its own regulations. He says that every ship ought to obey the laws of both States, which would mean that it must obey the laws of the one which was more rigid. Referring to the outrage on the two supposed informers, he says that they were further compelled by threats to leave town, lest they be murdered.[1]

In August, 1787, the Attorney-general of Virginia maintained that Virginia had power to enforce her laws over the whole breadth of the Potomac.[2]

In June, 1787, a new complaint was raised at Philadelphia that Virginia exacted a discriminating tonnage duty on Dutch vessels contrary to the treaty of commerce with the Netherlands.[3]

In Washington's diary of his journey to Philadelphia to attend the Convention of 1787, he says that he was pressed by Mr. and Mrs. Morris to lodge with them, and that he did so. On the 14th of May he says that he "dined in a family way at Mr. Morris's." The diary does not give the impression that he made his home with them.[4] It speaks frequently of visits at Morris's, which, however, may refer to the occasions on which he dined with them. Morris wrote to his son that Washington was his guest during the Convention.[5]

Morris was a member of the Convention. He had from the first been of the little group who had struggled to bring about a better union. In 1782 he wrote to Hamilton: "A firm, wise, manly system of federal government is what I once wished, what I now hope, what I dare not expect, but what I will not despair of." [6]

He did not, however, take any active part in the debates or on the committees of the Convention. It fell to his

[1] Va. Papers, iv. 317.
[2] Ibid. 326.
[3] Ibid. 298.
[4] Washington, ix. 539.
[5] Penn. Mag. ii. 170.
[6] Dip. Corr. Rev. xii. 250.

duty as leader of the Pennsylvania delegation to nominate Washington for President of the body, because the other prominent candidate was Franklin, from Pennsylvania. Madison mentions that Morris was called in to a conference with Gouverneur Morris and Washington in the crisis of the strife between the large and small State interests [1] He acted so completely in unison with Gouverneur Morris that he left the public activity to the latter.

The Federal Farmer [R. H. Lee] declared that there was a strong tendency to aristocracy in every part of the Constitution which was adopted. Pennsylvania appointed aristocrats, who seized the chance to change the government.[2]

There is at least some colour of truth in this. Robert undoubtedly cherished all the views which were uttered by Gouverneur in his speech on the Senate. He thought that the House would be democratic, changeable, extravagant, and precipitate. The Senate should be based on property, and constitute an aristocratic body as a check to the House. Senators should be chosen for life. This plan would also prevent the danger to be apprehended from rich men, who are likely to favour tyranny. Any attempt to check the due influence of wealth only leads to its corrupt influence. He favoured a strong government, but the influence of the rich should be duly guarded against.[3]

Washington offered the position of Secretary of the Treasury to Morris, who declined it and recommended Hamilton.[4]

[1] Elliot's Debates, i. 508.

[2] Ford's Pamphlets, 285.

[3] Elliot's Debates, i. 475.

[4] Custis, 349.

CHAPTER XXIX.

THE ACCOUNTS OF ROBERT MORRIS AS AGENT OF THE STATE OF PENNSYLVANIA, AS SUPERINTENDENT OF FINANCE, AND WITH THE OLD COMMITTEE OF COMMERCE.

I. *The Accounts of Robert Morris as Agent of the State of Pennsylvania.*[1]

IN 1782 Morris rendered to the State of Pennsylvania the account of his transactions as agent of that State in 1781, and he made a proposition to the State that the Comptroller-general and some other person to be appointed on behalf of the United States by the Superintendent of Finance should be a committee to commute the money of the State, which he had expended for the general service of the United States, into specific supplies due from the State, so that the State might have credit for the articles, instead of the money. Giving an account of this affair in a private letter to Tilghman in 1785, Morris said: "I named Mr. Milligan to this service. He and the Comptroller-general could not agree, and after my resignation Mr. Milligan declined to act longer, supposing his powers to end with mine. And now Mr. Nicholson [Comptroller of the State], instead of applying to Congress or the Treasury Board for a new arbitrator, has found that it will answer the purposes of his party to have me rather than the United States for the debtor. This malicious attack will

[1] See vol. i. pp. 270, 282.

appear in its true colours, and in the end will serve where it is intended to injure. We shall have it tried next month, and at any rate the United States must bear me harmless, as they have had the money."[1] The amount at issue was £36,000. Process had issued against Morris for this sum.

In the Report of 1785 he made the following statement of the transaction in question: —

"The Superintendent of Finance made sundry purchases of, and formed some contracts for supplies. The articles obtained and issued are charged to the State at the prices they cost and at the times of delivery. The moneys received from the State are credited in the treasury books at the times of the several receipts, and as the supplies were furnished before the moneys were obtained from the State Treasurer, the State is charged in the treasury of the United States with the interest arising on the balances, being the excess of the cost of those supplies beyond the moneys received from the State. And this is done because that excess was partly supplied by the moneys of the United States, and partly by the credit of their officer. But although the State stands charged only with the actual cost in the account of the purchase, she has credit for the supplies at the rates fixed by the resolutions of Congress, which are much higher; and as this credit is also given upon the times of delivery, she of course has credit for an interest greater than that which she is charged in proportion as the prices credited are higher. So far the State seems to have derived the sole advantage. But, as part of these supplies were obtained by contracts for rations, the United States gain by saving the expense of issue, and as another part was obtained by purchases on the spot where the articles were wanted, the United States also gain by saving the expense of transportation. Indeed, in this latter case,

[1] Ford Collection.

the State of Pennsylvania have likewise gained from this circumstance, that the purchases were made on cheaper terms than they could have been within the State. And with respect to the rations, the component articles were obtained as cheaply, perhaps more so, than they could have been purchased by Commissioners; with this advantage, also, that the State paid for no transportation, and the moneys and articles being both expended on the spot, facilitated the operations of taxing, and contributed to the convenience of her citizens. From this, which is the true state of that transaction, an argument might be drawn to show that an union of measures and views between the several States and the Union must prove beneficial to all and to every one of them."

In June, 1785, Morris wrote to the Board of Treasury, asking them to appoint a Commissioner to meet the Comptroller of the State and adjust this account. He also petitioned Congress to the same effect.[1] July 6, he took an appeal under the State from the settlement of his accounts by the Comptroller-general. The Council ordered the accounts and papers with reference to the purchase of specific supplies to be sent to the Protonotary of the Supreme Court.[2]

In September, on a report of the Board of Treasury, Congress appointed Commissioners, according to the petition of Robert Morris, to act with Commissioners of Pennsylvania, in commuting the cash received from their agent into specific supplies, in order to adjust the accounts of that State.[3] As the matter disappears from the records, we suppose that they succeeded in settling it.

1 State Dep. MSS., Memorials, 41, 341.

2 Col. Rec. Penn. xiv. 482, 488, 495.

3 Journ. Cong. xi. 155.

II. *The Accounts of the Superintendent of Finance.*

March 26, 1785, Morris sent to Congress a statement of the accounts during his administration of the Treasury. He had caused five hundred copies of it to be printed, apparently at his own expense; and he offered to Congress as many copies thereof as they might deem necessary for distribution. This is the "Report of 1785." A committee of Congress reported on this letter that the accounts had not been examined and adjusted by any person duly authorized, which step is necessary. They therefore propose that Commissioners be appointed to "examine and adjust."[1] June 20, such Commissioners were appointed to inquire into the receipts and expenditures of public money during the administration of Morris, and to settle the accounts between him and the United States.[2] June 28, he wrote to Congress that he was very glad of the step they had taken, and wished that it had been done when he resigned, for he then had the papers at hand and could have explained.[3] June 27, he wrote to Tilghman: "You will see that Congress have appointed Commissioners to examine the receipts and expenditures during my administration. This is a very proper measure, and ought to have been adopted at the time I resigned. I am, however, very glad it is now done, as by this means I shall have an opportunity of stopping the malicious and envious who are fond of insinuating suspicions which they dare not charge. But I shall get the better of all these sons of darkness in the end, and oblige them to acknowledge the services they try to traduce."[4]

The matter now rested until after the federal government

[1] State Dep. MSS. 137, App. 381, and Reports of Committees, iv. 442.

[2] Journn. Cong. x. 151.

[3] State Dep. MSS. 137, App. 385.

[4] Ford Collection.

was organized under the new Constitution. Morris then presented a memorial to Congress, in which he complained of the resolution of June 20, 1785, as giving the impression that he had some accounts outstanding which were intricate and confused, yet that no action was taken. The accounts of Willing, Morris, & Co. with the United States before he was Financier are another thing. Imputations had been made against him on account of the delay. He said that in October, 1788, he went to New York to try to get a settlement, but there was no quorum of Congress. February, 1789, he went again, and made a beginning toward a settlement of the old accounts of Willing and Morris; but the new government coming in, the Commissioners were not willing to go on. He now asked for Commissioners to settle the account.[1] We may without hesitation suppose that the presence of Arthur Lee and Samuel Osgood in the Board of Treasury made it extremely disagreeable for him to do any business with that body, for we have seen what their personal feeling was toward him.[1] Commissioners were appointed, as he requested.

His colleague, Maclay, made the following comments on these accounts, and on Morris's behaviour in regard to them, while they were in the Senate together.

January 28, 1790, Morris told him that he was engaged in settling his accounts, and should not be regular in his attendance. "The business is a necessary one; indeed, I think it is highly so to him, if he regards his reputation, and in my opinion, he has left it too long at stake already." The next day Morris told him that he found Hamilton "damned sharp," with a keen eye.

February 8, Morris's petition for Commissioners to examine his accounts was handed in. "I am really puzzled with this conduct of my honourable colleague. The charges

[1] Annals of Congress, ii. 2, 168.

against him are not as Financier, but as chairman of the Secret Committee of Congress, and for money received as a merchant in the beginning of the business. It seems admitted that he rendered important service as a Financier, and if I can penetrate his design, it is to cloak his faults in the Secret Committee with his meritorious conduct as Financier." Next day this memorial was referred to Izard, Henry, and Ellsworth as a committee. "I am still more and more at a loss to know what he would be at. It seems as if he wanted to make a noise, to get Commissioners appointed on that part of his conduct which he can defend, and thus mislead the public. I find the old resolve of Congress, the 20th of June, 1785, was brought in by a committee appointed on a letter of his own. He represented this resolve of Congress to have been the act of his malevolent enemies and persecutors."

February 23, "Mr. Morris got on the subject of the difficulties he laboured under in the settlement of his account; told me that he had to send again to Philadelphia for a receipt book, in which were some trifling accounts for money paid to the extent of forty shillings and such small sums; but concluded, 'I will have everything settled, and the most ample receipt and certificate for the account being closed.'"

May 15, "Mr. Morris entertained me with a long detail of the difficulties he met with in the settlement of his accounts. I believe the clamours against him make the officers inspect everything with a jealous eye. . . . I must be on my guard with respect to my colleague. Hamilton, unhappily, has him in his power with respect to these old accounts, which are still before the treasury."[1]

We have not been able to find any report of the Commissioners, or any record of the closing of this account, or

[1] Maclay, 188, 193, 203, 265, 302.

any later reference to it. We must assume that it was settled as it appears in Nourse's Report.[1]

III. *Robert Morris's Accounts with the Committee of Commerce of the old Congress.*

From references which have just been cited from Maclay it will be noticed that these were the accounts upon which his enemies attacked him. It will be seen by the dates at the end of this section, when compared with the date of Maclay's remarks, that he had in mind the charges of "Centinel."

In a public letter, in January, 1779, in answer to Paine's reflections on him, Morris said that he had twice settled the accounts of Willing, Morris, & Co. with the Committee of Commerce. The last time was in May, 1778. The accounts outstanding were still open, on account of various matters, which it was not yet possible to liquidate.[2] On the 12th of August, 1783, Morris wrote to Congress that it was very important that the accounts of the Secret Committee should be settled. They were entangled with other accounts, especially with those of the Marine Committee.[3] In October he sent to a committee of Congress the copy of the contract under which Deane was sent to Europe. He stated that he had himself had advances of money, for which he exported cargoes on public account, "and have long since accounted for." Money was advanced to others in New York and Connecticut, whose accounts had not yet been closed. The risks becoming great, that plan was abandoned.[4]

In September, 1783, he sent to a committee of Congress a statement about the Secret Committee, in which he said

[1] Report of 1790. See page 128. [2] See vol. i. pp. 209, 223–225, 229.

[3] State Dep. MSS. 137, ii. 780.

[4] Ibid. 54, Papers and Accounts of S Deane, etc., 13.

that the members were often changed, and the accounts were unsettled. " Nor can they (from their number and intricacy) be settled but by some person specially authorized for the purpose, who must seek information from the minutes and papers of the Committee." As he was a member of the Committee, he refrained from saying anything about their transactions.[1] There is a letter of the same month to Arthur Lee about the transactions of the Secret Committee. "Money was granted to various persons to ship cargoes to Europe, the accounts of which are not yet settled, under the old Secret and Commercial Committees. Some shipments arrived, some were taken, some were detained by the enemy's naval power, so that the plan had to be abandoned. Deane was sent to Europe under this plan; but when it was abandoned he carried the amount of those remittances into his general account. Deane must produce the contract to which he refers to support his claim. Barclay is trying to settle those old accounts."[2]

Morris wrote also to the President of Congress, January 13, 1784: An investigation of some of the accounts of the old Commercial and Secret Committee "has not only discovered some balances due to the United States, but has reported other matters which show in a strange point of light the necessity of examining and settling those accounts."[3]

May 25, 1784, Joseph Pennell, Commissioner of Accounts for the Marine Department, reported that there were $5,307 unaccounted for in the accounts of the Naval Committee of Congress. It was impossible to tell what member of the Committee was responsible, as they had all handled money on public account, more or less. On the next day Morris transmitted this report to Congress, and pointed out the

[1] State Dep. MSS. 137, iii. 411.
[2] Dip. Corr. Rev. xii. 418.
[3] Ibid. 442.

danger of doing business by executive committees, and the need of investigation.[1]

We find no further mention of this matter until 1787; but Arthur Lee, who was one of Morris's most pertinacious enemies, was now one of the members of the Board of Treasury, and they had evidently taken this matter in hand. July 12, 1787, the Board of Treasury informed Congress that they were trying to settle the accounts of the Secret Committee, and needed all the resolutions there were in the Secret Journal of Congress concerning that Committee.[2] August 14, they addressed an inquiry to the Secretary of Congress whether "previous to the 27th day of September, 1775, there is among the papers of your office any trace of a contract made by Congress or any of their members with Messrs. Willing and Morris."[3] June 25, 1788, in connection with a memorial of Col. Samuel Nicholson, they reported that Thomas Morris's papers had been given to Robert Morris, and that he had not yet settled Thomas's accounts with the United States. They urged that these accounts should be settled, and proposed that Congress pass a resolution "requiring" Robert Morris to transmit to the treasury all accounts and vouchers of the public transactions of the deceased.[4] Such a resolution was passed July 2.[5]

The books and papers of Thomas Morris are mentioned in the inventory of the things which were in Robert Morris's room in the debtor's prison in 1800.[6]

A committee of Congress reported on the unsettled accounts in 1788, that during the late war, and especially in the early periods of it, many millions of dollars were advanced by the United States to sundry persons, of the ex-

[1] State Dep. MSS. 137, iii. 655, 651.

[2] Ibid., Reports Board Treas 140, ii. 427.

[3] Ibid. 443.

[4] Ibid. 138, ii. 207.

[5] Journ. Cong. xiii. 38.

[6] Account of Morris's Property, 25.

penditure of which proper accounts had not been rendered, nor had vouchers been offered, although often called for. Some accounts have been partially settled, and in some cases payments made, although it does not appear that the proper statements were made, or vouchers made of the articles which composed those accounts. "That from a general view of this subject the Committee are induced to think and believe that the United States have already suffered very great inconveniences by inexcusable negligence and unauthorized delays in persons entrusted with public money, in not rendering and settling their accounts, and that it has become highly expedient that decisive measures be speedily adopted for closing all the unsettled accounts of the late war." They therefore propose that suits be brought against all persons who do not within three months comply with the requirement to settle their accounts.[1]

September 30, 1788, a fuller report was made by the Committee of Finance: "No less a sum than $2,102,600 has been advanced to the Secret Committee of Congress before the 2d of August, 1777, and a considerable part of this money remains to be accounted for otherwise than by contracts made with individuals of their own body, while those individuals neglect to account. . . . Considerable sums have been paid out of the treasury, of which no appropriation is to be found on the public journal of Congress. Several of them remain to be accounted for. Of the accounts which have been partially settled or settled without authority or without proper vouchers, two or three, by reason of their magnitude, have claimed the particular attention of your Committee. Their amount is little short of a half a million of dollars specie; and though by the Acts of June 14th and 10th, 1781, and April 10th, 1783, those accounts appear to

[1] Journ. Cong. xiii. 22.

have claimed the attention of Congress, your Committee find that it remains very doubtful to this day whether many of the charges against the United States which are stated in those accounts have any solid foundation. . . . The total amount received in France was 47,111,859 livres. Of this there was drawn and spent in America 26,246,727 livres; salaries of foreign ministers, 1,160,183 livres; leaving 19,704,949 livres unaccounted for, so far as documents have been presented at the treasury. If such documents exist, they must be in France." [1]

This report fell in the midst of the contest over the ratification of the federal Constitution, which was exceedingly bitter in Pennsylvania, being complicated there with the contest of the old parties in Pennsylvania about the State Constitution. The supporters of the State Constitution were the popular party, and the opponents of the new federal Constitution. The leading writer on the side of the opponents was "Centinel," who called Morris: "Robert the Cofferer." He declared that Morris wanted the new Constitution adopted in the hope that debts to the old government would be cancelled.[2] The earlier letters of "Centinel" were dignified in manner and argument, so that they might even rank with the Federalist; but in the course of the writing, they became more virulent and personal, and Morris was singled out for a personal attack. "There were several members [of the Constitutional Convention of 1787] in the deputation from the State of Pennsylvania, who have long standing and immense accounts to settle, and millions perhaps to refund. The late Financier alone, in the capacity of chairman of the Commercial Committee of Congress early in the late war, was entrusted

[1] Journ. Cong xiii. 111, 113

[2] McMaster and Stone, xii. 631. "Centinel" was Samuel Bryan. Ibid. 6, note.

with millions of public money which to this day remain unaccounted for. Nor has he settled his accounts as Financier. The others may also find it a convenient method to balance accounts with the public. They are sufficiently known, and therefore need not be designated. This will account for the zealous attachment of such characters to the new Constitution, and their dread of investigation and discussion." [1]

In the next number he returned to the charge that the Constitution was wanted in order to cancel old debts of "defaulters" to the United States. It has been asserted, he says, that Morris's accounts were settled in November, 1784, although, June 20, 1785, Congress appointed three Commissioners to settle them." [This referred to his accounts as Financier.] "When we consider the immense sums of money taken up by Mr. M——s as commercial agent to import military supplies, and even to trade in behalf of the United States, at a time when the risk was so great that individuals would not venture their property; that all these transactions were conducted under the private firm of W——g and M——s, which afforded unrestrained scope to peculation and embezzlement of the public property, by enabling Mr. M——s to throw the loss of all captures by the enemy at that hazardous period on the public, and converting most of the safe arrivals (which were consequently very valuable) into his private property; and when we add to these considerations the principles of the Man, his bankrupt situation at the commencement of the late war, and the immense wealth he has dazzled the world with since, can it be thought unreasonable to conclude that the principal source of his affluence was the commercial agency of the United States during the war? — not that I

[1] McMaster and Stone, xii, 658; no. xvi. of "Centinel," February 26, 1788.

would derogate from his successful ingenuity in his numerous speculations in the paper moneys, Havana monopoly and job, or in the sphere of financiering."

Morris replied to these attacks in the "Independent Gazetteer" of April 8, 1788, the letter being dated at Richmond, March 21. He says that neither in the Committee of Commerce nor as Financier did he touch a penny of public money. He received money as a contractor to export commodities and put funds in Europe, and that he did it; but that the accounts are unsettled. Some of the papers were lost at sea. No duplicates have yet been obtained, and receipts are lacking for goods delivered at various places in America. He thinks that there is a balance due him. As Financier he touched no money. It went out from the treasury by warrant, of which there are full accounts on the treasury books. The statement which he prepared in 1785, about his administration, was intended for Congress to send to the States if they saw fit. A newspaper is no place to settle accounts.

"Centinel," however, continued his attacks. The tender laws are said to be disastrous and cruel. In order to recriminate, he would begin with the "Cofferer," the head of the other party, and trace his character through the numerous speculations on the public, from his appointment to the C——l A——y of the United States, to his resignation as F——r." He says that Morris admits, in his letter of April 8, that his accounts with the Committee of Commerce are not settled. "Centinel" now had before him the report above quoted, of the 30th of September, 1788, from which he quotes the part about two million dollars unaccounted for. By a report of a committee of February 11, 1779, it appears that the Secret Committee charged Robert Morris with all business of commerce and exchange. "Centinel," therefore, asks as to the two million dollars:

"Is it not more than probable that he has converted the public money to his own property, and that, fearful of detection and reluctant to refund, he has and will, as long as he is able, avoid an investigation and settlement of these long-standing accounts?"[1]

In the "Independent Gazetteer" of November 22, Morris responds again. He has lately been in New York and put his accounts in train of settlement. The large sums handled by him only prove his zeal for the public, and the confidence which is felt in him. "Centinel's" No. 24 and final paper is almost entirely about Morris, in reply to this letter of November 22. It refers to Morris's retirement to Manheim to con the accounts of the Secret Committee in 1777 and 1778, and affirms that Morris has prevented any commission from being appointed under the resolution of June 21, 1785. He now promises to settle the accounts because the election is coming on.

In the "Account of Robert Morris's Property," prepared by himself in 1800, is a series of notes on all the open accounts in his books. One of these is with John Ross, upon which he comments as follows: "Mr. Ross and Willing, Morris, & Co., made certain contracts, and the latter transacted much business for the old Congress, and upon the settlement of the accounts by officers who meant fairness, but who, I ever thought, did not truly understand mercantile method and principle, and who, by charging depreciation which I objected to, upon principles that I thought right, although overruled by them, brought a balance in favour of the United States, to which at last I submitted and gave security on land which, proving deficient, I have now assigned all my claims on Mr. Ross to the Comptroller of the Treasury and his successor in office, in additional security for the debt that may be ultimately

[1] McMaster and Stone, 693.

found due, for the former balance will be considerably reduced by objects of credit I have discovered that were not at the former settlement brought into view. As this debt to the United States, whatever it may prove to be, is in fact due in part by John Ross, and after that part shall be ascertained, the remainder is equally due by Thomas Willing, Esq., and myself, that is, each one half, I have therefore assigned also all my claim on the said Thomas Willing to the Comptroller of the Treasury, and his successor in office, in additional security for the balance that ultimately may be due to the United States, reserving in both cases any surplus that may arise in my favour to my heirs and assigns. From the examinations I have lately made into the state of matters between Mr. Willing and me, and with Mr. Ross, I expect there will, from these two sources, be sufficient to extinguish that debt to the United States, my part as well as theirs."[1]

On the books of the United States Treasury Department there is an account, dated June 29, 1796, on the debtor side of which is a summary of three accounts, Morris, Deane, & Co.,[2] Willing, Morris, & Co., and Morris & Ross. It is balanced on the credit side by two accounts of Willing, Morris, & Co., and by a new account of Robert Morris. Then follows another account bearing the same date. The entry on the debtor side is Robert Morris, Old Account, balanced on the other side, July 13, by Robert Morris h/a of bonds. Then follows a third account, July 13, of "Robert Morris, Esquire, of Philadelphia, h/a of bonds." On the debtor side of this stands an entry of $93,312.63, being the balance of the first of

1 Account of Morris's Property, 29.

2 No firm of this name is met with elsewhere. The connection of Deane and Morris here is interesting and important.

the three accounts described. There is no entry on the credit side.[1]

Here, therefore, after all, his enemies triumphed over him, or might have done so if they had known the facts, at the end of his life; and, as he alleges, it was all a matter of depreciation.

[1] Other accounts with Robert Morris on the treasury books, which are closed, are as follows: In October, 1776, an account with him, James Wilson, and George Ross; two items, aggregating $1,500. In 1781 there is an account for bills of exchange. In 1785 there is an account with him, in which he is called the contractor. In 1787 an account of specie was settled, which has entries of 1778 and 1779. In 1788 there is an account with him as late Superintendent of Finance, in which he is debtor to sundries, closed and paid. In October, 1795, is an account of receipts and expenditures by Robert Morris, admitted and certified by Tench Coxe, Commissioner of the Revenue, and R. Harrison, Auditor of the Treasury. The sum is over $75,000. The account is balanced and closed on the same day, and it is said to be "for transactions with the late Commercial Committees of Congress."

CHAPTER XXX.

MORRIS'S SOCIAL POSITION AND RELATIONS.

IN 1780, on account of the British raids in New Jersey, Mrs. Morris invited Miss Catherine Livingston, daughter of the Governor of New Jersey, and younger sister of Mrs. John Jay, to take refuge with her.[1]

In 1781 Robert Morris sent his two sons, Robert and Thomas, then twelve and ten years of age, to Europe for their education, because education here was then broken up by the war. They were under the care of Mr. Matthew Ridley, who went to France as commercial agent of Maryland.[2] He afterward married the Miss Livingston just mentioned. The boys were at Geneva five years and at Leipsic two years, and returned in 1788.[3]

Morris wrote to Jay upon this occasion, as follows: "Many considerations which it is needless to enumerate induce me to this measure, which my judgment approves, but which, now that it is to be carried into execution, awakens all the tender feelings of a father. Your and Mrs. Jay's sensibility will disclose the situation of Mrs. Morris and myself when I tell you that these two good and well-beloved boys leave us to-morrow. They are tractable, good boys. I hope they will make good men, for that is essential. Perhaps they may become useful to their country, which is very desirable; and if they have genius and judgment, the educa-

[1] Boogher, March, 1883.

[2] Va. Papers, ii. 552.

[3] Boogher, March, 1883; Penn. Mag ii. 168.

tion they will receive may be the foundation for them to become learned or great men ; but this is of most consequence to themselves. Should it fall in your way to notice them, I am sure you will do it. I expect they will be fixed at the schools in Geneva. This parting reminds me, my good friend, that we are but too much the slaves of ambition and vanity to permit the enjoyment of that happiness which is in our power. I need not part with my children, but —"[1]

Jay replied that he disapproved of educating the boys of a free country in Europe.

Mrs. Jay, writing to Mrs. Morris on this occasion, pays a very high compliment to Robert Morris. She says that when things go wrong with Robert, Jr., she asks him what his father would say upon such an occasion, telling him that that would be sure to be right.[2]

In Morris's books appears an entry of the expenses of these boys in Europe: £9,766 Penn.

Chastellux, describing a ball at the house of the French Ambassador, says : "On passing into the dining-room, the Chevalier de la Luzerne presented his hand to Mrs. Morris, and gave her the precedence, — an honour pretty generally bestowed upon her, as she is the richest woman in the city ; and, all ranks here being equal, men follow their natural bent by giving the preference to riches.[3] . . . Mr. Morris is a large man, very simple in his manners ; but his mind is subtle and acute, his head perfectly well organized, and he is as well versed in public affairs as in his own. He was a member of Congress in 1776, and ought to be reckoned among those personages who have had the

[1] Johnston's Jay, ii. 134.

[2] Boogher, March, 1883.

[3] Chastellux, i. 278. In Smith's "Historical Curiosities," ii. pl. lvii., is a facsimile of a dinner invitation card issued by Robert Morris to Mr. Jenifer, November 12, 1781.

greatest influence in the Revolution of America. He is the friend of Dr. Franklin, and the decided enemy of Mr. Reed. His house is handsome, resembling perfectly the houses in London. He lives there without ostentation, but not without expense; for he spares nothing which can contribute to his happiness and that of Mrs. Morris, to whom he is much attached. A zealous republican and an epicurean philosopher, he has always played a distinguished part at table and in business." [1]

On this passage the translator remarks: "The house the Marquis speaks of, in which Mr. Morris lives, belonged formerly to Mr. Richard Penn. The Financier has made great additions to it, and is the first who has introduced the luxury of hot-houses and ice-houses on the continent. He has likewise purchased the elegant country-house formerly occupied by the traitor Arnold; nor is his luxury to be outdone by any commercial voluptuary of London. This gentleman is a native of Manchester in England, is at the head of the aristocratical party in Pennsylvania, and has eventually been instrumental in the Revolution. In private life he is much esteemed by a very numerous acquaintance." [2]

On the 19th of May, 1782, the Prince de Broglie sailed, with a company of young nobles and officers, on board of "La Gloire" from Brest, but was forced to return on account of a storm. They were delayed until July 15, and then had to stop at the Azores. The excursion seems to have been a frolic, or an excursion of pleasure rather than one of war. On the 13th of September the gentlemen were put on shore on the banks of the Delaware; fortunately, for the ships were captured by the English immediately afterward. The Prince, in his diary, says that he reached Philadelphia August 13; but the other dates in

[1] Chastellux, i. 199. [2] Ibid. 200.

the context would make it September. He writes: "This is the capital, already celebrated, of a new State. M. de la Luzerne conducted me to the house of Mrs. Morris to take tea. She is the wife of the Financier of the United States. The house is simple, but neat and proper. The doors and tables are of superb mahogany, carefully treated. The locks and trimmings are of copper, charmingly neat. The cups were arranged symmetrically. The mistress of the house appeared well. Her costume was largely of white. I got some excellent tea, and I think that I should still have taken more, if the ambassador had not charitably warned me, when I had taken the twelfth cup, that I must put my spoon across my cup whenever I wanted this species of torture by hot water to stop; 'since,' said he to me, 'it is almost as bad manners to refuse a cup of tea when it is offered to you as it would be indiscreet for the master of the house to offer you some more when the ceremony of the spoon has shown what your intentions are in respect to this matter.' Mr. Morris is a large man, who has a reputation for honourableness and intelligence. It is certain that he has great credit at least, and that he has been clever enough, while appearing often to make advances of his own funds for the service of the Republic, to accumulate a great fortune, and to gain several millions since the Revolution began. He appears to have much good sense. He talks well, so far as I could judge; and his large head seems as well adapted for governing a great empire as that of most men."[1]

We have also a description of a visit to Morris in 1783, by Mr. Lowell of Boston, and H. G. Otis, his attendant who wrote the account. They dined with thirty persons at Morris's, "in a style of sumptuous magnificence which

[1] Balch, Français en Amer. 199.

I have never seen equalled." He says that Morris was esteemed next to Washington.[1]

In 1784, when the Chevalier de la Luzerne, who seems to have been intimate at Morris's house, returned home, the latter wrote: "Mr. and Mrs. Morris have more sincere good wishes for the Chevalier de la Luzerne's health, happiness, and safe arrival than can be expressed on this paper." Luzerne carried with him a shoe of Mrs. Morris, in order that he might send from Paris "six pairs of fashionable shoes to the size of the old pair." [2]

In the same year the Morrises extended hospitalities and kindness to Jefferson's daughter, for which Jefferson made hearty acknowledgment.[3]

In 1785 Morris became involved in a somewhat ridiculous quarrel with Marbois. The latter was about to leave Philadelphia. He had in his posssesion portraits of the King and Queen of France, which had been sent to Congress; but he had not been able to deliver them, because Congress had no abiding-place. He now asked Morris to take charge of them until they could be brought to New York. Morris consented, but preparations were made to unpack them. To this Marbois objected in writing. Morris wrote back in some irritation, as if he resented the suspicion that he was making an idle display of vanity by putting up the portraits in his own house. He said that he meant to lock them up. In a letter to Jay of the same date he shows that he was not on good terms with Marbois. The latter, however, replied courteously, repudiating the suspicion which had been ascribed to him, and proposing to deliver the pictures to Congress himself.[4]

In 1795 John Adams wrote to his wife that he had had

[1] Hist. Mag. i. 262. [2] Boogher, March, 1883.

[3] State Dep. MSS. Hamilton Papers, xx. 69.

[4] Dip. Corr. U. S. i. 184.

a big dinner with Robert Morris, "whose hospitality is always precious."[1]

Morris wrote to his wife from New York, April 22, 1790, about the news of the death of Franklin. He said that Franklin delighted to make as many people happy as he could.[2]

Through the Secret Committee and the Marine Committee Morris became acquainted with Paul Jones, and interested in him.[3] In 1777 the Marine Committee gave Jones a commission as captain. He was sent out in command of the "Ranger," but expected to have "L'Indien." This ship, however, belonged to the King of France. In 1780 Jones was in command of the "Alliance," and was to bring her to America; but Landais, with the approval of Arthur Lee, ran away with that ship. On the voyage Landais behaved in such a way as to raise doubts of his sanity, and was deposed from the command. Jones appealed to Morris, although he was not then in Congress or in any office, probably because he thought him a powerful friend. He attributed Lee's animosity to the fact that Jones adhered to Franklin, and he said that stores had been left behind which he, Jones, had obtained.[4] Landais had a claim for money which Morris would not pay. In April, 1782, in Morris's office, Landais threatened violence.[5] In that year Jones was here, and was promised command of the "America." That ship was given to the King of France to replace the "Magnifique," sunk in Boston harbour; but really, at Morris's suggestion, because there were no funds with which to finish her. It fell to Morris's lot to inform Jones of this new disappointment. He bore it so well that Morris wrote again to express his sympathy

[1] Adams's Letters to his Wife, ii. 176.
[2] Hist. Mag. Oct. 1858.
[3] 5th Ser. Am. Arch. ii. 172, 1105.
[4] Franklin, viii. 484.
[5] State Dep. MSS. 137, i. 419.

and esteem.[1] July 18, 1792, at Paris, Jones was dying. He sent for Gouverneur Morris, who made his will for him. Jones wanted the two Morrises to be his executors. Gouverneur excused himself, but Robert was named.[2] Jones bequeathed to Robert Morris the sword which had been given to him by Louis XVI. Morris gave it to the oldest commander in the navy in succession.[3]

Manasseh Cutler mentions Morris's country-seat on the Schuylkill ("The Hills") in 1787. It was then unfinished. He said that it would be very grand.[4] This spot is now in the Fairmount Park, just above the old water-works. When it was in the country, it must have been an extremely beautiful spot. Morris bought it in 1770. He called it "The Hills," but it was later called "Lemon Hill." It was afterward owned by the second Bank of the United States, and was bought by the city from the assignees in 1844 for $75,000, which was less than one third of the value at which it was held by the bank.[5] In the schedule of the Pennsylvania Property Company an estate of Morris is mentioned called the Trout Springs estate, in Upper Merion, in Montgomery County. It was about twenty miles from Philadelphia, and two and a half from Swede's Ford, on the Schuylkill. In the "Account" of his property he mentions an estate called Springetsbury.[6] We are informed that there were two manors of Springetsbury in Pennsylvania, — one in York County; the other lay between the city of Philadelphia and "The Hills." [7]

During the Revolution Robert Morris lived on Front Street, below Dock. In August, 1785, he bought some land on High Street east of Sixth, with the ruins of the

[1] Paul Jones, i. 289.

[2] Morris's Morris, i. 555; ii. 45.

[3] Homes's Sketch, 15.

[4] Cutler's Cutler, i. 257.

[5] Westcott, 380.

[6] See vol. i. p. 303.

[7] See Westcott, 367.

Penn house, which had been burned in 1780. He rebuilt the house. It was the finest in Philadelphia at the time, of brick, three stories high. The main part was forty-five and one-half feet by fifty-two, and there was an addition twenty by fifty-five. There was stabling for twelve horses, and a garden around it. When the federal government moved to Philadelphia, he gave up this house, which was taken by the city of Philadelphia as a residence for General Washington. Washington complained that it was not big enough, and was very scrupulous not to accept anything in the way of gift from the Morrises in the transfer.[1]

In 1791 Morris took the house which formerly belonged to Galloway, on the corner of Sixth and Market Streets.

In 1795 he bought the square of land bounded by Chestnut, Walnut, Seventh, and Eighth Streets, except a lot fifty by two hundred and fifty, on the corner of Seventh. The land cost £10,000.[2] The ground was then ten or fifteen feet above the present level. He employed Major L'Enfant, one of the engineers then employed at the city of Washington, to build him a large mansion on this piece of ground. The house was begun in 1795, and work was continued on it until 1800. There is a picture of it in Watson's Annals, and in Westcott. The house is represented with the roof finished and the windows boarded up. It never was finished, but was torn down and the materials were sold. The land was bought by William Sansom.

There are very many extravagant and contradictory legends about this house, which came to be known as "Morris's Folly." The account which seems most trustworthy states that the house was of brick with window and door trimmings of a pale blue stone. It was between

[1] Penn. Mag. ii. 173; Rush's Washington, xvi. There is a cut of this house in the Mag. Amer. Hist. xvii. 365.

[2] Simpson, 711.

eighty and one hundred feet by between forty and sixty. The total amount expended on it, according to Morris's books, was £6,138 5*s.* 10*d.*, say $16,369.[1]

In 1796 Callender published the following reference to the new house: "A person is just now building, at an enormous expense, a palace in Philadelphia. His bills have long been in the market at eighteen pence or a shilling per pound. This is the condition of our laws for the recovery of millions. At the same time the prison at Philadelphia is crowded with tenants, many of whom are indebted only in petty sums."[2] Lossing states, perhaps on the same authority, that Morris went on selling his notes at twenty cents on the dollar, when building his house.[3]

In the "Account" of his property, when speaking about his Chestnut Street lot, Morris writes: "Upon which Major L'Enfant was erecting for me a much more magnificent house than I ever intended to have built." When he comes to L'Enfant's account in the same document, he notes that that gentleman was a creditor for services rendered, although he had not rendered an account. "Various circumstances render me little solicitous on the score of his services, but he lent me thirteen shares of bank stock disinterestedly, and on this point I feel the greatest anxiety that he should get the same number of shares, with the dividends, for want of which he has suffered great distress." He is put into the Genesee assignment.

[1] Westcott, 360.

[2] Annual Register, 1796, 279.

[3] Am. Hist. Rec. ii. 305.

CHAPTER XXXI.

MORRIS IN THE SENATE OF THE UNITED STATES.

MORRIS and Maclay were elected the first Senators from Pennsylvania. Morris drew the long term, from 1789 to 1795. He was present on the 4th of March, 1789. We are chiefly indebted to Maclay's diary for our knowledge of him during the first two years of his service in the Senate. It is probable that he scarcely attended during the last two or three years, when he became occupied in building the city of Washington.

He objected to the title for the President of the United States, "Highness and Protector of the Rights of America." He opposed the discriminating duties against non-treaty nations, but wanted a discriminating duty to favour our own ships in the tea trade. He argued that a dollar sent to Europe for East India goods would not import more than half a dollar sent to the East Indies. He was by no means bitten with the protectionist mania. He held that the manufacturers of Pennsylvania would be better off under seven and a half per cent than under twelve and a half. He said that the manufacture of paper was in the most flourishing condition, and that paper was largely exported. He seems to have defeated the proposition to raise the whole seven and a half per cent class to ten per cent; but he favoured ten per cent on scythes, axes, spades, and hardware. He gave great dissatisfaction to his colleague, who held all the old notions in their narrowest and most rigid form. Morris was only half emancipated from them ; but that sufficed to irritate Maclay, who said, "His weight in our Senate is great on commercial subjects."

There were very few of his colleagues, or of the executive officers of the time, who succeeded in pleasing Maclay. There were two things that he wanted, — protective taxes on Pennsylvania industries, and the seat of the federal government at Harrisburg, where he owned some land. The only times when he was satisfied with the rest were when they were supporting those measures. He was also sustaining the character of a "rigid republican," which was no small burden in those days. It forced him to be on his guard against General Washington when that gentleman invited him to dinner and treated him with courtesy. He was a Jeffersonian before Jefferson.

Morris wanted the Senators paid $8 a day. He "almost raged ; and in his reply to me, said he cared not for the arts people used to ingratiate themselves with the public." He "likewise paid himself some compliments on his manner and conduct of life ; his disregard of money and the little respect he paid to the common opinions of people. . . . I answered Mr. Morris in a way that gave him a bone to chaw."

In the debate on the pay of Senators, "the doctrine seemed to be that all worth was wealth, and all dignity of character consisted in expensive living." He mentions Morris as one who led in this view. Carroll of Maryland, although the richest man in the United States, did not agree with it.

Maclay had a horror of Hamilton, and of funding and assumption. He thought that it was all corrupt, and that Morris was deep in it.

He thinks that Hamilton's recommendation to fund the certificates of the debt will " damn the character of Hamilton as a minister forever. . . . It appears that a system of speculation for the engrossing of certificates has been carrying on for some time. Whispers of this kind come from every quarter. Dr. Elmer told me that Mr. Morris must be deep in it, for his partner, Mr. Constable, of this place, had one contract for $40,000 worth. The Speaker hinted to me that General Heyster had brought over a sum of money from Mr. Morris for this business. He said the Boston people were concerned in it. Indeed, there is no room to doubt but a connection is spread over the whole continent on this villainous business. . . . I call not at a single house or go into any company but traces of speculation in certificates appear. Mr. Langdon, the old and intimate friend of Mr. Morris, lodges with Mr. Hazard. Mr. Hazard has followed buying certificates for some time past. He told me he had made a business of it ; it is easy to guess for whom. I told him 'You are, then, among the happy few who have been let into the secret.' He seemed abashed, and I checked by my forwardness much more information which he seemed disposed to give."

A North Carolina member said that he met two expresses with money on the way to North Carolina, to speculate in certificates. "Wadsworth has sent off two small vessels for the Southern States, on the errand of buying up certificates."

Butler and Izard of South Carolina manifested antipathy to Morris. January 21, 1790, Maclay reached the point where all confidence between him and Morris was at an end. "There never was any between me and any of the Philadelphians." Morris was one of those who treated the proposed amendments to the Constitution contemptuously. He insisted on a rate of six per cent for the whole domestic and assumed debt, otherwise he said that he would vote against the whole. He thought the State boundaries inconvenient, and favoured the proposition in the excise bill to make excise districts independent of State boundaries. This also alarmed Maclay, who said: "Annihilation of State government is undoubtedly the object of these people." Morris expressed himself very strongly against the doctrine of instructions. "We were Senators of the United States, and had nothing to do with one State more than another."

He often talked with Maclay about the settlement of his accounts, which led Maclay to this comment: "Mr. Morris chatted with great freedom with me to-day on his private affairs, explained some of the difficulties he had met with in the settlement of his accounts; says the balance will be in his favour; declares he will soon have done, and put to silence his adversaries. Justice says plainly this ought to be the case, if he has been injured. He is very full of the affair between him and me [about land purchases in western Pennsylvania]. His countenance speaks the language of sincerity and candour. Interest, however, the great anchor to secure any man, lies at the bottom.

Maclay detested New York. Although he does not seem to have been fond of company, he complained of inhospitality. "These Yorkers are the vilest of people; their vices have not the palliation of being manly." He mentions their caricatures in ridicule of the Pennsylvanians, no doubt referring to those against Morris. One of these represented Bobby marching off with the federal ark on his shoulders, the devil being represented on the Jersey City ferry-house, calling to him, "This way, Bobby."[1]

At a meeting of the Pennsylvania delegation in 1790 the question was raised who should be next Governor of Pennsylvania. Morris was one of the chief candidates.[2] Morris,

[1] Mag. Amer. Hist. xvii. 370. [2] Maclay, 200, 255.

as one of the leaders of the republicans, supported General St. Clair against Mifflin.[1]

Maclay left all the social duties, especially that of attending levees, to Morris, but in Morris's absence was forced to undertake it.[2] Mrs. Morris went from Philadelphia to New York with Mrs. Washington.[3] Maclay mentions a dinner at the former's house. She talked a great deal after dinner, but gracefully enough. She is considered the second lady at court. As to taste, etiquette, etc., she is certainly the first. She seemed to like New York; but he disliked it so much that he may have misjudged. She told a story of having some cream at the President's table which was stale and rancid, but Mrs. Washington ate much of it. She said that General Washington had declared in favour of generous salaries. Maclay thought this might be the effect of the high-toned manners of the pompous people of New York.

[1] Biddle, 244. [2] Maclay, 227. [3] Penn. Mag. ii. 172.

CHAPTER XXXII.

THE FEDERAL CAPITAL.

APRIL 10, 1783, the delegates of Virginia informed the Governor of that State that New York had offered to Congress a tract of land in the township of Kingston, or Esopus, with privileges of jurisdiction in civil matters. They propose that Virginia and Maryland shall offer a small tract on the Potomac, near Georgetown, granting wider jurisdiction than that offered by New York. They think that the position would be more central and more agreeable.[1]

June 4, Congress sent to the States the offer of Maryland to cede Annapolis, and of New York to cede Kingston, for a federal capital, with notice that said offers would be considered on the 1st of October.[2] On account of the behaviour of the government of Pennsylvania during the mutiny in June, Congress moved away from Philadelphia, under a strong feeling of resentment and unwillingness to sit there again. They believed that the mutiny had proved that Congress might be overawed by a mob in that place, and would have no protection. In October they determined to take the question in what State the public buildings should be erected, by beginning with New Hampshire and voting through the list. The result proved that there was no agreement at all.[3]

[1] Va. Papers, iii. 467. [2] Journ. Cong. viii. 199. [3] Ibid. 286.

October 7, it was voted that the buildings for the use of Congress should be erected near the falls of the Delaware if a site could be obtained, and if the necessary jurisdiction could be vested in Congress. A committee was appointed, to examine the site.[1] This vote caused great dissatisfaction, and on the 20th they voted that a second federal city should be built near the falls of the Potomac, with an amendment on the 21st that, until buildings were erected on the Delaware and the Potomac, the residence should be alternately, at equal periods of not more than a year, and not less than six months, in Trenton and Annapolis.

At the beginning of 1784 Osgood, who represented well the State rights party, was opposed to placing the capital in a large city for fear of intrigues, and favoured two alternate capitals as a device to prevent intrigues.[2]

In April, 1784, various motions to build buildings at the two proposed federal capitals failed, and on the 26th it was voted that the President of Congress should convene that body on the 30th of October following at Trenton.[3]

In May the accounts show entries of the expenses of committees who visited the proposed sites on the Delaware and the Potomac, — $46 for the former, and $61 for the latter.

December 10, 1784, a motion was made that Congress ought to adjourn from their present residence, — Trenton, — but it was lost. On the 20th they voted that it was inexpedient to erect buildings at more than one place. On the 21st they resolved that it was expedient to determine on one place at which they would sit until proper buildings were erected. On the 23d the battle opened between the site on the Potomac and the site on the Delaware ; but Virginia alone voted to put it at Georgetown exclusively. There was a great majority against continuing at Trenton.

[1] Journ. Cong. viii. 295.

[2] Mass. Hist. Soc. Proc. March, 1862, 466.

[3] Journ. Cong. ix. 115.

A motion to go to Philadelphia was lost, — five to four. Newport got only the vote of Rhode Island. They then voted to go to New York, Pennsylvania alone in the negative; and they appointed a commission to lay out a federal town on the Delaware, purchase the land, and contract for buildings.[1]

February 10, 1785, Philip Schuyler, Philemon Dickinson, and Robert Morris were elected Commissioners under the resolution for building a federal city on the Delaware. Schuyler declined, and John Brown was elected in March.[2]

Morris accepted the position. On the 2d of May he wrote to Congress from New York that part of the Commissioners were there, but that Brown had not come. They were arranging for buildings to accommodate Congress at New York.[3]

May 10, 1787, a resolution to meet at Philadelphia was lost, and a proposition to erect buildings at Georgetown was lost.[4]

Hamilton wrote to William Livingston, August 29, 1788, that the Northern States did not want to strengthen Pennsylvania by establishing the federal city at Philadelphia. If the capital was placed there, it would stay there. It might be placed on the Delaware, in New Jersey, at least temporarily, if it could be kept away from Philadelphia.[5]

Maclay says that he and Dr. Rush brought Adams forward for Vice-President, and puffed him in the newspapers, in order to play on his vanity and use him among the New England men, in their scheme of bringing Congress to Philadelphia.[6]

On the 25th of August, 1789, in the new federal Con-

[1] Journ. Cong. x. 14.

[2] Ibid. 37, 39, 58.

[3] State Dep. MSS. 137, App. 377 and 389.

[4] Journ. Cong. xii. 51.

[5] Hamilton's Works, viii. 195.

[6] Maclay, 86.

gress, Morris proposed the falls of the Delaware for the federal city. He owned a large tract of land at Morrisville, opposite Trenton.[1] Maclay proposed Lancaster and six other places in Pennsylvania, including Harrisburg, near which place he owned two hundred acres.[2] Morris declared that he would not vote for a site on the Susquehanna. August 29, Maclay heard a story that the Virginians and Pennsylvanians had made a bargain to fix a temporary residence at Philadelphia, and the permanent one on the Potomac. His diary shows the intrigue and dicker about the permanent capital. The Pennsylvanians were dickering with the Virginians on the one side and the New Englanders on the other, and they divided into two sets, — one of which was trying to carry the Virginia bargain, and the other the New England bargain; while Morris was working for his own situation on the Delaware, and others for other places in which they were interested. Maclay says that the Virginia terms seemed to be, " Give us the permanent residence, and we will give Philadelphia the temporary residence." September 3, 1789, Goodhugh moved in the House that the city should be on the Susquehanna, as the sense of the Eastern States without New York.[3]

September 3, 1789, Morris was working against the Susquehanna. He had said that the capital ought to be at Philadelphia or New York, as Maclay thinks, on account of commerce. September 4, Goodhugh's motion was carried, at which Morris was greatly chagrined. " It has long been alleged in this place that Mr. Morris governed the Pennsylvania delegation, and I believe this idea has procured Mr. Morris uncommon attention. This delusion must now vanish. . . . He mentions with apparent regret some rich lands in the Conestoga Manor, which he

[1] See page 175. [2] Maclay, 88, 134. [3] Ibid. 145.

had exchanged with John Musser for lands on the Delaware." [1]

September 7, the Susquehanna site was carried in the House. Maclay maintained that nothing would come to the Atlantic rivers from the western waters. "If it should the Susquehanna has the advantage in the double connection by Juniata and the west branch." September 16, he finds that Germantown is the place to be played against the Susquehanna. The Marylanders now insisted, as a condition, that Pennsylvania and Maryland should consent to the satisfaction of the President, that the navigation of the Susquehanna should be cleared. The Philadelphians opposed this, believing that it would build up Baltimore. Hence they opposed the capital on the Susquehanna.[2]

September 23, the Pennsylvania delegation had reached the point of voting for the Susquehanna site, if they could do it without agreeing that the navigation of the rivers should be improved; but if not, then they would abandon the Susquehanna and try for the falls of the Delaware and Germantown. Morris was very angry against the proviso. He said that Pennsylvania would allow the Susquehanna to be opened if Maryland would agree to a canal between the Chesapeake and Delaware bays, although Maclay showed him that there was a law of Pennsylvania for opening the river, with no condition in it. Maclay now became very angry with the Philadelphians. They never have been earnest for the Susquehanna. "Thus barefacedly to drive away Congress from the State, rather than a few barrels of flour shall pass by the Philadelphia market, in descending the Susquehanna; and rather than the inhabitants of this river should enjoy the natural advantages of opening the navigation of it." On the 24th of September Morris voted against the Susquehanna; so did all the

[1] Maclay, 147. [2] Ibid. 150.

New England men except Johnson. "Mr. Morris's vote alone would have fixed us on the Susquehanna forever." Morris offered, in behalf of Pennsylvania, $100,000 to fix the capital at Germantown; and if the State would not give the money, he would raise it himself. "A vacant stare on this seemed to occupy the faces of the Senate." This was a proposition for a district ten miles square, including Germantown. Maclay voted against Germantown, on account of the unwarranted offer of money, which, he says, "knocked down the Susquehanna." Germantown was carried by the casting vote of the Vice-President in the Senate. It passed the House, but with a little amendment which sent it back to the Senate; and so it went over the session.[1]

Morris wrote to Peters, September 13, that he wanted the federal city as near Philadelphia as possible, and that if the State Convention had not excepted Philadelphia, he would have tried to make that the capital. He is determined to vote first for the Susquehanna, second for Germantown, third for the falls of the Delaware. If the members from North Carolina arrive, the Potomac will be chosen. If those from Rhode Island and Vermont arrive, New York will be the capital.[2]

In November Madison visited Morris at Philadelphia and found him dissatisfied with the existing arrangement about the federal capital. He did not want it at New York.[3]

December 10, the House of Delegates of Virginia transmitted to the Legislature of Maryland a copy of an Act to cede ten miles square on the Potomac to the United States. Virginia proposed joint action with Maryland, if land from both States would be more convenient, and

[1] Maclay, 159.

[2] Peters Papers.

[3] Letters to Washington, iv. 293.

declared that Virginia would give $120,000 for buildings, if Maryland would give three fifths as much.[1]

Morris came to the next session prepared to vote for a federal city on the Susquehanna.[2] In May, 1790, Maclay wrote that the Philadelphians were very indifferent about the question of permanent residence. May 20, the New England men made a proposition in favour of Trenton, which pleased Morris; but Maclay objected to the position of Pennsylvania, which forced her to bargain either with the East or with the South. On the 24th of May Morris proposed that the next session should be held in Philadelphia.[3] Maclay told the Senate that "Philadelphia was a place they never could get as a permanent residence. The government of Pennsylvania neither would nor could part with it. It was nearly equal to one third of the State in wealth and population. It was the only port belonging to the State."[4] As soon as the proposition for a federal capital took the shape of a cession of territory, to be held by the United States, outside of any State jurisdiction, the large cities, Philadelphia and New York, were both put out of the question. May 30, the Pennsylvanians told the New Englanders that they would agree to any other place whatsoever, rather than stay in New York. May 31, the House voted that the next session should be held in Philadelphia. Maclay complains that Morris was negligent and absent at the crisis of this business. He gave as an excuse that his accounts engaged him so closely. On June 8, 1790, this question came to a crisis in the Senate. Two sick men were brought in, one on a bed and one in a sedan chair, but all the motions were defeated without a result.[5]

June 11, the House of Representatives voted to fix the capital at Baltimore. On the 14th Tench Coxe, Assistant

[1] Va. Papers, v. 75. [2] Maclay, 192. [3] Ibid. 267, 269.
[4] Ibid. 274. [5] Ibid. 277.

Secretary of the Treasury, proposed to Maclay a bargain, that Pennsylvania should have the permanent residence on the Susquehanna, and vote for assumption. Morris told Maclay of this same proposition; but preferring to deal with the principals, Morris had written to Hamilton that he would walk in the morning on the Battery, and if Hamilton had anything to propose to him, Morris, he might meet him there, as if by accident. They met, and Hamilton said that he wanted one vote in the Senate and five in the House, and if he could get them, would agree to put the residence at Germantown or the Delaware. Morris agreed to consult the Pennsylvania delegation, but proposed that the temporary residence of Congress in Philadelphia should be the price. Next day, however, Hamilton sent him word that he could not negotiate about the temporary residence.[1]

June 15, "Mr. Morris called me aside and told me that he had a communication from Mr. Jefferson of a disposition of having the temporary residence fifteen years in Philadelphia, and the permanent residence at Georgetown on the Potomac, and that he, Mr. Morris, had called a meeting of the delegation at six o'clock this evening at our lodging on the business. . . . The delegation met at six. I was called out. However, when I came in, what passed was repeated to me. Hamilton proposed to give the permanent residence to Pennsylvania at Germantown or the falls of the Delaware, on condition of their voting for the assumption. In fact, it was the confidential story of yesterday all over again. Mr. Morris also repeated Mr. Jefferson's story; but I certainly had misunderstood Mr. Morris at the hall, for Jefferson vouched for nothing."[2]

June 18, "Never had a man a greater propensity for bargaining than Mr. Morris. Hamilton knows this, and is labouring to make a tool of him."[3]

[1] Maclay, 291. [2] Ibid. 294. [3] Ibid. 299.

June 25, Walker told Maclay that the Pennsylvania delegation had, in a general meeting, agreed to place the permanent residence on the Potomac, with the agreement that the temporary residence should remain ten years at Philadelphia. Morris said that he was satisfied with ten years.

June 28, in the Senate, a vote was carried for New York for temporary residence for ten years, but the whole resolution was defeated. On June 30 the temporary residence at Philadelphia passed the Senate. Maclay says: "I am fully convinced Philadelphia could do no better. The matter could not be longer delayed. It is, in fact, the interest of the President of the United States that pushes the Potomac. He, Washington, by means of Jefferson, Madison, Carroll, and others, urged the business; and if we had not closed with these terms, a bargain would have been made for the temporary residence in New York. They have offered to support the Potomac for three years' temporary residence, and I am very apprehensive they would have succeeded, if it had not been for the Pennsylvania threats that were thrown out of stopping all business, if an attempt was made to rob them of both temporary and permanent residence." [1]

Maclay is convinced that residence, assumption, and six per cent rate were all bargained and contracted for on the principle of mutual accommodation for private interest. "The President of the United States has, in my opinion, had a great influence in this business. The game was played by him and his adherents of Virginia and Maryland between New York and Philadelphia, to give one of those places the temporary residence, but the permanent residence on the Potomac. I found a demonstration that this was the case, and that New York would have accepted of the temporary residence if we did not; but I did not then

[1] Maclay, 305.

see so clearly that the abominations of the funding system and the assumption were so intimately connected with it. Alas that the affection, nay, almost adoration, of the people should meet so unworthy a return! Here are their best interests sacrificed to the vain whim of fixing Congress and a great commercial town, so opposite to the genius of the southern planter, on the Potomac; and the President has become, in the hands of Hamilton, the dish-clout of every dirty speculation, as his name goes to wipe away blame and silence all murmuring."[1]

A letter from Ames to Minot, June 23, 1790, is quoted, that a bargain was first made between the anti-assumptionists and the Philadelphians, that the capital should be at Philadelphia for fifteen years and then on the Potomac; but when the bill came up, this bargain being known, Philadelphia was stricken out and Baltimore put in. By the rules of the House, Philadelphia could not be again inserted. Then assumption was defeated, whereupon the New England men threatened to secede.[2]

July 16, the law was passed fixing the temporary residence for ten years at Philadelphia, and then the permanent residence at the falls of the Potomac.

Morris was very angry because the full six per cent rate was not provided on the whole domestic debt; but Maclay told him that since Philadelphia had won the temporary residence, they ought to "guard the Union and promote the strength of the Union by every means in our power; otherwise our prize would be a blank."[3] Maclay said that the "effect must be sensibly felt in Philadelphia should a great commercial town arise on the Potomac." He thought that the Philadelphians imagined that Congress would be so pleased at Philadelphia as never to leave it; but the allurements of New York were ten times as great as those

[1] Maclay, 328. [2] McMaster, i. 581. [3] Maclay, 329.

of Philadelphia. Philadelphia is unsocial, and the Quakers proscribe dress and amusements.[1]

Beckwith, the English agent, quotes some American as saying, in 1790, that the session just closed had lowered Congress in public opinion, partly on account of the bargain connected with the residence and the assumption of the debt. These bargains were well known at the time.[2]

In 1791 the proprietors of the land on which the city of Washington was to be laid out conveyed it to Thomas Beall and John M. Gaunt in trust, to be laid out in a city as the President should approve; and said trustees were to convey to the Commissioners for the federal city all lands laid out in streets, parks, etc., and such as were allotted to the use of the United States. Other lands in the trust were to be equitably shared, and a part was assigned to the public. This latter part was to be sold as the President should direct. The sum thus obtained was to be used, first, to pay the original proprietors for all that part, except the streets, which was assigned to the United States, at £25 per acre, and secondly, to be expended under the direction of the President for the purposes of the federal city.[3]

At the beginning of August, 1791, the Commissioners for the federal city, Johnson, Stewart, and Carroll, wrote to the Governor of Virginia that they were in embarrassment for want of money. The sum they needed was $6,000. During 1792 they were begging Virginia for driblets of the money which that State had promised for the federal city.[4]

[1] Maclay, 340.
[2] Canadian Archives, 1890, 151.

[3] Report of 1800. A description of Washington City from the Maryland "Journal" was given in the "New York Magazine" for November, 1791; and a map of the city, as subsequently laid out, was given in the same magazine for June, 1792.

[4] Va. Papers, v. 353, 356, 465, 572.

The Capitol was begun in September, 1792. On the 18th Washington laid the corner-stone.[1] Not many lots were sold until 1793, when Robert Morris and James Greenleaf bought 6,000 lots, averaging 5,265 square feet each, at eighty dollars each, payable in seven annual instalments, without interest, beginning May 1, 1794. They agreed to build annually twenty brick houses, two stories high, and covering 1,200 square feet each. They also agreed to sell no lots before January 1, 1796, except upon condition that one such house should be built on every third lot within four years from the time of sale. In 1794 John Nicholson took a share in this contract.[2]

The Duc de Liancourt says that Morris and his partners bought about as much more of private owners as from the Commissioners. The object of the Commissioners in the large sales to Morris and his partners was to interest men of large means; but no other big lots were sold. Morris and his partners sold half their lots to other rich speculators, obtaining at least $293 a lot, with obligation on the purchaser to build. In the first eighteen months Morris sold about 1,000 lots, of which Law bought 445. Law had just returned from India. Dickinson was another buyer in similar circumstances. Others who bought were Lee and Howard, and some Dutchmen. The land sold for five, six, eight, and even ten pence, Maryland currency, per foot, with a contract to build. Blodgett, of Philadelphia, was another speculator in Washington lots. He got up two lotteries. The first prize in the first was a tavern, valued at $50,000; in the second lottery the first three prizes were three houses, to be built near the Capitol, valued at $25,000, $15,000, and $10,000. He made profits by these lotteries.

[1] Elliot, District, 97.

[2] Report of 1800.

The speculators began to vie with each other in efforts each to draw the city to his own section, because all saw that it was too big. Morris, Nicholson, and Greenleaf were forced to mortgage their lots, and could not go on with the improvements. They tried to escape the building obligation; hence those who bought of them tried to do the same. Law, who was very rich, engaged his fortune in the enterprise.[1]

Greenleaf, Nicholson, and Morris held on equal shares. The total number of lots owned by them was 7,234. They sold 769 lots. On July 10, 1795, Morris and Nicholson bought Greenleaf's share in the residue, and also bought of him 1,316 lots, with a reservation to him of 25. Thus they had 7,756 lots. In 1800 Morris wrote: "On some of these lots there were erected between forty and fifty brick houses, some of which were finished and others nearly so; but many of them have suffered great damage by neglect, pillage, etc., so as to be now in a most ruinous situation. There were also several frame buildings, some of which were sold, others pulled to pieces and plundered, etc. It is not possible for me to delineate all the embarrassments that hang over this property, because there are several of which the particulars are not known to me."[2] He enumerates the mortgages which were placed on various portions of this land for the loans which he and Nicholson contracted, although the total amount mortgaged does not amount to half of what he says that they owned. Still he says that there were other incumbrances on behalf of Nicholson, the details of which he does not know, and also Nicholson and Morris conveyed all their interest in Washington in 1797 to the trustees of Greenleaf, to secure the payment of the obligations of Greenleaf, endorsed or accepted by Edward Fox to the amount of

[1] Liancourt, vi. 128, 132, 164.

[2] Account, 7.

seven or eight hundred thousand dollars. To secure the same notes, Greenleaf had conveyed to the same trustees property estimated at from four to six hundred thousand dollars. All this property was to revert to Nicholson and Morris on payment of the notes for which Fox was liable, and also the trustees were to give them back their own obligations which they had paid to Greenleaf, to the amount of a million and a quarter. This bargain was made in 1797, and this trust is called the "Aggregate Fund." Morris enumerates six "riders" on this agreement, securing the payment of about $145,000 to different persons out of the surplus, if there should be any. Still again Morris and Nicholson formed a company having 300,000 shares, in which each of them had an equal interest, for the reversion of the residuum in this trust. Out of his own half of these Robert Morris transferred to various persons as security for debt 53,650 shares, "or thereabouts." Besides the incumbrances on the Washington estate, already mentioned, there had been attachments, executions, sales, bills in chancery, etc., "the particulars of which I am not acquainted with, as verbal information is all I have had." [2]

The Committee of Congress of 1800 say that in 1795 the contractors failed to pay the instalments due, and discontinued the building of the Capitol, on which some unimportant work had been done. In 1796 Congress authorized a loan of $300,000 for the building; but that amount could not be borrowed. Finally Maryland lent the Commissioners $200,000 in United States six per cent stock, on the guarantee of Congress and the individual bond of the Commissioners. In 1798 Congress ordered $100,000 advanced to the Commissioners. In 1799 Maryland lent $50,000 in stock of the United States, to be re-

[1] See page 285. [2] Account, 8.

paid in 1802, all unsold land being given as security.[1] The Committee estimated the property of the United States in the district at $884,819. The debts due for land to the Commissioners amounted to $144,125. The debts of the Commissioners were $360,881. In this account Morris and Greenleaf stand debtors for $115,241, of which $80,000 is stated to be "doubtful and not expected to be received." It was due for lots purchased by them. Many of these lots had been sold by them on credit, the proceeds of which would be credited on the debt of Morris and Greenleaf.[2]

A Committee on Expenditure at Washington, in 1801, reported that the contract of Morris and Nicholson had thrown titles into doubt. Congress ought to resolve these doubts. The Commissioners have estimated the lots too highly, and the income from the sale of lots cannot be relied on as a resource to build the buildings.[3]

Callender, in 1796, derided the federal city. "The name of this city has produced more than half the patience with which its expenditures have been endured." He wanted the capital at Philadelphia. The monarchical party, in 1787, put into the Constitution, he said, the provision for exclusive jurisdiction over a district ten miles square.[4]

In 1804 the surveyor of public buildings reported that the Capitol was very poorly built, and very much out of

[1] It was stated in debate, in 1809, that the two loans of stock by Maryland were repaid to her with a premium on the stock of $79,512, although the stock had not been sold. (Amer. Reg. v. 73.)

[2] Report of the Committee of 1800.

[3] In the debate, in 1809, a Member of Congress said that a neighbour of his bought a lot in Washington for over $400. There was a tax due on it of ninety cents. It was sold for this, and brought sixty-five cents. (Amer. Reg. v. 57.)

[4] Hist. U. S., 285.

repair. Fifty thousand dollars had been spent on repairs. Within that year $57,665 more were spent in repairs on the Capitol and President's house. The latter was unfinished, and the roof was leaky.

In 1809 the "American Register" said that inquiry would show that the reason for the establishment of the capital at Washington was "the authority acquired by a single man. Among many reasons assigned for the situation of the present metropolis, the chief were the wishes of Washington. The name was intended as a monument of his glory. These considerations are now found to be of little or no weight with either side."[1]

After the second war with England, Charles Biddle wrote that Trenton would have been a much better place for the capital of the United States. "Washington, notwithstanding all that can be said in favour of it, I believe would never have been thought of for the seat of government but for the great and good man it was called after."[2]

In the first few years after the removal to Washington, there was great complaint of the place, on account of dearness, dirt, over-size, expense, and inconvenience. Philadelphia was eager to bring Congress back, and made offers of all the necessary accommodations. In 1809 a proposition to remove was brought forward, not so much by those who wanted to go as by those who thought that an expression should be drawn from Congress which would set at rest all talk of removal. It was stated in the debate that the population of Washington in 1804 was 4,000, and in 1807, 6,000.

[1] Amer. Reg. v. 34. [2] Biddle, 327.

CHAPTER XXXIII.

MORRIS'S LAND SPECULATIONS.

IN a letter to the President of Congress, July 29, 1782, Morris said that a large part of America was held by great land-owners, and that a land tax would have the salutary effect of an agrarian law, without the iniquity.[1] At that time he was not himself a great land-owner. In 1770 he and Willing had bought a plantation in Louisiana, but they abandoned it during the Revolution.[2] In 1781 Morris bought an eighty-fourth share in the Illinois and Wabash Company, which he still held in 1800.[3]

In 1785 he wrote to Tilghman: "I am no great friend to the purchase of confiscated estates; not that I think confiscation was wrong, but there are certain parts of the community who look with an evil eye at the possessors. I have one or two such estates notwithstanding these sentiments, but I should like them better if they had not been so circumstanced, and at any rate they ought to be purchased cheaper than other estates."

Morris appears to have taken a share in the Virginia Yazoo Company, in 1794. In December of that year Scott, the agent who was advocating the cause of the Company before the Georgia Legislature, wrote to Fitzsimmons that if he succeeded, he should draw for money to satisfy the conditions on Morris and the other share-

[1] Dip. Corr. Rev. xii. 228.

[2] Account of Morris's Property.

[3] Ibid. 19.

holders in Philadelphia. In July, 1795, the Company was about to begin suits against the holders under later sales by the State, which had repudiated the grant to the Company. Morris, "Nielson," Greenleaf, and Fitzsimmons are called upon to subscribe to a fund for expenses.[1]

It appears that Morris did not pay the assessment, and forfeited his interest; for in the "Account," in 1800, he said, in reference to that stock, that he supposed it lost because he had not answered the calls.

Morris's name does not appear among the shareholders in the Tennessee Company, in the public documents. In the Henry MSS. is a letter of Watkins, in 1794, in which it is stated that Morris and others have taken half that Company's purchase.[2]

There are several lawsuits in the books which show that Morris's methods of business in his land transactions involved loans, mortgages, and trusts in complicated and mischievous reiteration. He piled one form of credit upon another, and it is plain that he soon became entirely lost, so that he did not know the amount or forms of his liabilities.[3]

In 1781 New York promised recruits, each, six hundred acres of land. On the 25th of July, 1782, a district of land was laid off to satisfy the warrants for this bounty land, which included the present counties of Onondaga, Cayuga, Seneca, Cortlandt, Tompkins, and parts of Oswego and Wayne.[4]

June 3, 1784, Congress served notice on New York that Massachusetts had petitioned for Commissioners to settle the conflicting claims of those two States to land.[5] De-

[1] Folio State Papers, Land, i. 200, 202.

[2] Communicated by Professor Haskins.

[3] Yeates, ii. 518; iii. 104; Washington, Va. Cases. ii, 325.

[4] P. & G. Purchase, 119.

[5] Journ. Cong. ix. 222.

cember 8, the trial of the controversy between the two States was pened.[1] For over a year efforts were made to organize courts which had been appointed, without success. Hence the States petitioned to be allowed to proceed by negotiation with each other.[2] This they did, and reported their agreement to Congress. It was approved and filed, and the commission for the court was revoked.

By the bargain made between the Commissioners of the two States at Hartford, December 16, 1786,[3] New York yielded to Massachusetts the pre-emption of all the land west of a line drawn northerly, from the eighty-second milestone westward on the boundary of Pennsylvania, to Lake Ontario, except a strip one mile wide the length of the Niagara River on its eastern side; being about six million acres. This line, which was known as the pre-emption line, was the western boundary of the soldiers' land, and was the eastern boundary of the land in which we are now to be interested. It was as nearly as might be a north and south line through the Seneca Lake.

Massachusetts yielded the sovereignty and jurisdiction over all the land in dispute to New York.

In April, 1788, Massachusetts sold all this land to Nathaniel Gorham of Charlestown and Oliver Phelps of Granville for a million dollars, to be paid in three annual instalments in the scrip of Massachusetts known as consolidated securities, which were then much below par.[4]

In 1787 a company was formed called the New York Genesee Land Company, with a branch in Canada. As the law did not allow companies to buy of the Indians, they took a lease for nine hundred and ninety-nine years of all the lands of the Six Nations in the State of New York, for $20,000, and $2,000 a year rent. The govern-

[1] Journ. Cong. x. 11.
[2] Ibid. 254.
[3] Ibid. xii. 117.
[4] Turner, 326.

ment of the State of New York denounced this bargain, and the sheriff was ordered to dispossess intruders under it. The Company was granted a tract of land ten miles square in the old military reservation, by way of compromise and settlement; but this Company made trouble by its intrigues for many years afterward.[1] The Indians were in great misery after the Revolution. The years 1789 and 1790 were years of scarcity, during which the State had to feed them.[2]

Phelps was obliged to buy off the Canada Company before the Indians could be induced to cancel the Indian title.

In July, 1788, Phelps and Gorham extinguished the Indian title to the eastern part of their purchase, bounded westerly by a north and south line from the Pennsylvania boundary to the junction of the Canaseraga Creek with the Genesee River, then to a point two miles north of the present village of Avon, then due west twelve miles, then northeasterly so as to be twelve miles distant from the Genesee River to Lake Ontario. The eastern part of the original purchase between the pre-emption line and the line just described is what has since been known as the Phelps and Gorham purchase. They sold land, sometimes by whole townships, during the next two years.[3]

Adam Hoops, who had been aide to General Sullivan on his Genesee expedition, lived in Philadelphia and was intimate with Robert Morris. Phelps and Morris were also intimately acquainted, as Phelps had been an army contractor. It is supposed that Hoops drew the attention of Morris and Phelps to Genesee.[4] Behind Phelps and Gorham there was a syndicate of persons who had desired to speculate in the lands, but who, in order not to compete

[1] P. & G. Purchase, 106.

[2] Ibid. 121.

[3] Turner, 326, 372.

[4] P. & G. Purchase, 135.

with each other, had united and allowed those two to act for all. It is believed that Morris was one of these, and had an interest in the Phelps and Gorham purchase from the beginning.[1]

In 1788 the pre-emption line was surveyed, so that it ran about a mile and a quarter west of the town of Geneva. Doubts of the correctness of this survey having arisen, a new one was made under the direction of Robert Morris. The correct line fell about the same distance east of Geneva. The space between is the gore.[2]

In 1789, at the instance of Pennsylvania, the eastern line of the cession of New York and Massachusetts to the United States, that is, the western boundary of New York, was surveyed. It required that a meridian should be drawn through the western end of Lake Ontario. It was found to pass some twenty miles east of Presqu'Isle, the present city of Erie. Pennsylvania then bought the Erie triangle of the United States, in order to have a port on the Lake. The same old question about the claim of Massachusetts or Connecticut to the land beyond the western boundary of New York recurred. Maclay says that Gorham wanted to get the triangle away from Pennsylvania, or at least to settle New England men on it, and make a second Wyoming of it. Maclay thought it a great point for Pennsylvania that that State had purchased the Indian title to this land.[3]

[1] Oliver Phelps was born in Windsor, Conn. He moved to Canandaigua in March, 1802, and died there in 1809. In 1795 he thought himself worth a million, with debts of less than $85,000. He closed his life in the midst of great reverses, on account of investments in land in different parts of the United States. He was in Congress from 1803 to 1805. The State of Connecticut, being a creditor of his, had a mortgage on his land; but it was finally settled so that his heirs got a good estate. (P. & G. Purchase, 149; Turner, 328.)

[2] Turner, 370; P. & G. Purchase, 247.

[3] Maclay, 123.

The assumption of the State debts by the United States raised the Massachusetts notes to par. When Phelps and Gorham made their contract, these notes were worth only twenty cents on the dollar. As the price was now multiplied by five, they reconveyed to Massachusetts all except that of which they had extinguished the Indian title, and it was agreed that they should pay for that, which was about one third of their original contract, at the rate of their original purchase, scaled down to its specie value, twenty cents on the dollar.[1]

This left the Phelps and Gorham purchase as above stated; namely, the district between the pre-emption line and the line through the Genesee River. The date of this reconveyance is variously stated. The contract to make it seems to have been settled in 1790. Morris states that as the year in which he bought of Phelps and Gorham all which they retained of their original purchase, except what they had sold to others. "In the year 1790 I purchased of Messrs. Gorham and Phelps a tract of country in the Genesee district, warranted to contain not less than a million acres, and sold the whole of that purchase in the year 1791 in England to handsome profit, but which was reduced by discounts and other circumstances so as to close with less than I had first expected."

He was to pay £30,000 New York currency. His agent in London was William Temple Franklin, grandson of Benjamin Franklin, who negotiated the sale to Sir William Pultney and others almost immediately. The price was £35,000 sterling.[2] At the time of this transaction Morris wrote to Franklin: "All our public affairs go on well. This country is rushing into wealth and importance faster than ever was expected by the most sanguine of the sanguine." He speaks enthusiastically of the reports from

[1] Turner, 371.

[2] Ibid. 243. See, however, page 259.

Genesee; among others from Wadsworth, who had made a settlement there.[1] Liancourt says that when the Pultney tract turned out to contain 120,000 acres more than was supposed, Morris would not make any demand for it, saying that he had sold all there was. "He certainly would have had a fine chance to make objections to this gratuitous surrender if he had not had the liberality and generosity which he has shown in all his transactions, and which make one sincerely hope that he may extricate himself happily from the present embarrassment of his affairs."[2] In 1795 Morris stated that the agent of Pultney had sold, up to December 31, 1794, 463,017 acres, for $657,965. The price at the time of writing was $3 per acre. Before 1804 it would produce over three million dollars.[3]

Thus Morris became the owner of the eastern part of the original purchase, which Phelps and Gorham did not reconvey to Massachusetts, and he immediately sold it again.

Turner says that Phelps and Gorham settled with Massachusetts, March 10, 1791. March 12, Massachusetts agreed to sell to Samuel Ogden, acting for Robert Morris, all the Massachusetts land except the Phelps and Gorham purchase. The sale was executed, May 11, by five deeds for five sections of it, divided by meridians. One sixtieth was reserved to satisfy a previous contract with John Butler, but Morris afterward bought out Butler's right.[4]

Liancourt implies that Morris got the resolution to sell him the New York land at a low price, through the Massachusetts Legislature, by legislative finesse.

Morris's story of this purchase in the "Account" is: In 1791 he bought a tract of Massachusetts, for which he paid at different periods a hundred thousand pounds lawful money, equal to £125,000 Pennsylvania, with heavy interest,

[1] Turner, 244.
[2] Liancourt, i. 222.
[3] North Am. Land Co. 56.
[4] Turner, 396.

besides other sums connected therewith. Samuel Ogden was interested to the extent of 300,000 acres; Gouverneur Morris, "who was expected to have assisted in making sales in Europe," had an interest of 250,000 acres; R. Soderstrom, 100,000 acres; and William Constable, 50,000 acres. The whole was estimated at 4,000,000 acres, and turned out rather more. It was divided into five tracts, which he here defines. In 1791 he borrowed of W. S. Smith of New York, agent for Pultney and Horsby, $100,000 at six per cent, and mortgaged Tract No. 1. He also mortgaged 100,000 acres in this tract to Alexander Hamilton for the use of John B. Church, to secure $81,679.44, which mortgage is dated May 31, 1796.

He had now, therefore, bought all the rest of the tract which Phelps and Gorham had undertaken to buy for the syndicate in the first place.

Taking up the retrospect of his land transactions in 1800, Morris says: "I shall begin with the lands purchased in the Genesee country, acknowledging that if I had contented myself with those purchases, and employed my time and attention in disposing of the land to the best advantage, I have every reason to believe that at this day I should have been the wealthiest citizen of the United States. That things have gone otherwise I lament, more on account of others than on my own account, for God has blessed me with a disposition of mind that enables me to submit with patient resignation to His dispensations as they regard myself."

In the pamphlet on the North American Land Company, in 1795, he wrote: "In order to give one instance out of many of the advantages to be derived to the holders of shares in this land, it is not improper to state that one of the parties of the first part to this plan [himself] did actually sell in the year 1791, to certain capitalists in Europe, one million of acres of uncultivated American land for £75,000 sterling, or $333,333⅓." Evidently when he wrote this, he was much more enthusiastic and confident about his Genesee transaction than in 1800. His old clerk, James Reese, who settled in Geneva, said that Morris's reverses were due to his great success, in the first place, in the sale to Sir William Pultney, to which he refers in the passage just quoted.[1] This is a very reasonable opinion.

When Jefferson heard of the Morris purchase from Phelps and Gorham, he wrote to Washington: "In that case the similarity of interests will produce an alliance with the Yazoo Company." [2] In 1790 Maclay found Morris averse to lowering the price of land in western Pennsylvania. He was for what the speculators call "dodging;" that is, selling lands in Europe before they were bought in America.[3]

The agent of the Pultney estate, Charles Williams or Williamson, was naturalized, and took up his residence in the Genesee country in February, 1792.[4] In a report of 1794 he spoke of his great expenses and difficulties; said that Morris knew the sacrifice he was making when he sold the land, but that he will rejoice at the writer's success. He expressed himself greatly indebted for support from Morris and his son.[5]

The population of the entire Massachusetts cession in 1790 was one thousand and forty-seven, — consisting of five hundred and twenty-three males over sixteen, one hundred and ninety-two males under sixteen, three hundred and eighteen females, two free negroes, and eleven slaves.[6] The Quaker settlement at Crooked Lake was not included. The Quakers are put at two hundred and sixty

[1] P. & G. Purchase, 240.

[2] Letters to Washington, iv. 366, in 1791.

[3] Maclay, 216.

[4] P. & G. Purchase, 251.

[5] North Am. Land Co. 82.

[6] Doc. Hist. N. Y. iii. 648.

persons.[1] The settlers were enduring great misery and many privations. They were greatly afflicted with fever and ague. Phelps wrote to Gorham that they were nearly all sick.[2]

In 1792 and 1793 Morris sold to the Holland Company all the land owned by him in western New York west of the transit line; that is to say, west of the line drawn due north from a point on the Pennsylvania boundary, twelve miles west of the southwest corner of the Phelps and Gorham purchase. This line began on the Pennsylvania boundary, between the present towns of Bolivar and Alma. It ran between the towns of Elba and Byron and Bethany and Pavilion, there being a jog in the town of Stafford.[3] To the north it comes out between Carleton and Kendall.[4]

This left for Morris about half a million acres between the Phelps and Gorham purchase and the land of the Holland Company, which was called "Morris's Reserve." Morris was to extinguish the Indian title, in guarantee of which he left £35,000 sterling of the purchase money in the hands of the buyers. The Indians did not want to sell. August 25, 1796, Morris applied to Washington to appoint a commission to treat with the Senecas for their title in this purchase, saying that it was no longer possible to keep the squatters off.[5] Washington consented, on condition that the Indians must ask for the treaty. Jeremiah Wadsworth was appointed Commissioner.[6]

Morris had established his son Thomas at Canandaigua as his agent in 1791. In 1793 he gave him fifty-

[1] Turner, 331.

[2] P. & G. Purchase, 143, 259.

[3] This statement is in accordance with the maps in Turner, although the line is described as having been a meridian line.

[4] Turner, 574.

[5] Hist. Mag. June, 1869.

[6] P. & G. Purchase, 436.

one hundred and twenty acres, being half of Mount Morris.[1]

Thomas Morris obtained the consent of the Indians to a meeting which was held at Big Tree, now Geneseo. The Indians were reluctant, and in fact broke up the meeting. Thomas Morris then had recourse to the women, who were said by the Indians to have control of the matter by their customs. Morris told them that the money obtained for the land would free them from drudgery. The result was that the council was reopened, and the bargain was made. The price was $100,000, to be invested in stock of the Bank of the United States by the President of the United States as trustee. Reservations of about three hundred and fifty square miles were provided for.[2]

About 1793 or 1794 a colony of Germans was formed in the city of Hamburg, to settle in America. There were seventy families, but they were drawn from the urban and not from the rural population. They were consigned to Robert Morris, and were set at work to make the road from Northumberland to Genesee. In the days of the first settlement of Genesee, the connections with Philadelphia and Baltimore were far easier and more direct than those with New York. These people could do no work. They were settled on land with tools, stock, and provisions, but they did not prosper at all. The settlement ended in a riot. Many of the colonists were arrested and taken to Canandaigua. The settlement appears to have broken up.[3]

In the "Account," Morris wrote that the Holland Com-

[1] Account 3. Thomas settled up his father's affairs, and assisted in the contract with the Holland Company. He was the first Representative in Congress from the region west of Seneca Lake. He shared his father's reverses, and moved to New York City in 1803 or 1804. He died in 1848 (P. & G. Purchase, 173). An account of Robert Morris's affairs in western New York, by Thomas, is in the "Historical Magazine" for June, 1869.

[2] P & G. Purchase, 436.

[3] Ibid. 254.

pany claimed that he owed them $53,000, but he had counter claims. "I believe they have filed a bill in chancery, to which I drew an answer and sent it to Mr. Fitzsimmons, but I do not know that it has been filed. I believe not." [1]

The interests of the Genesee region were deeply involved in Jay's treaty. The settlers believed that the English were all the time stirring up the Indians. Oswego and Niagara were in the hands of the English until that treaty was made, and they objected to a settlement which the Americans had made at Sodus.

A search through the files of Niles's Register has produced a number of statements about the Holland Company or its lands. They are either plainly erroneous or so inaccurate that they have the character of hap-hazard statements, and are not worth citing here.

In 1890 a newspaper statement was afloat that the heirs of Robert Morris intended to reopen a foreclosure which was obtained by Willink and his associates of a mortgage on land in Ontario, Steuben, and Erie Counties. In one of these newspaper statements it is said that the Farmers' Loan and Trust Company closed up the affairs of the Holland Company in 1845. In general, the statements contain so many inaccuracies, and confuse the different parts of the property in such a way, that it is impossible to understand from them what the issue is which is raised.[2]

John Nicholson, who was Comptroller of Pennsylvania from 1782 to 1794, and who in that office produced the trouble for Morris about the settlement of his accounts with Pennsylvania,[3] became engaged in land speculation, and at one time owned 3,700,000 acres in Pennsylvania, where his bankruptcy produced a great entanglement of

[1] See pages 293, 300.

[2] New York Times, October 15 and 22, 1890. The New York Herald for June 27, 1891, contained a very remarkable story about Robert Morris.

[3] See page 205.

titles.[1] We cannot tell just at what time he and Morris became associated with each other, but between 1792 and 1794 the latter made large investments in land in Pennsylvania.[2]

Putting together the facts which have so far been stated, we find that Morris had owned and sold the whole of the State of New York west of Seneca Lake between 1790 and 1793, except a million acres in a strip north and south nearly through the centre of that region. This he retained; but his contracts with the Holland Company kept him still interested in their part of it. In 1793 he also engaged in his enterprise at Washington, and he had immense land interests in a half-dozen States besides.

In 1794 Morris and Nicholson formed the Asylum Company, to buy a million acres in Pennsylvania.[3] Of this enterprise, Liancourt, writing in 1795, says: Asylum is on the right bank of the Susquehanna. MM. Talon and De Noailles bought two hundred thousand acres in the Wyoming district. A part of their project was to provide for fugitives from San Domingo. In 1793 they bought a tract of Morris and Nicholson. The Frenchmen were obliged, however, to annul this contract, because they could not carry it out. Then they all joined in a Company which was to own a million acres. The Company took over all the buildings and improvements. Nicholson bought out the Frenchmen. At first the enterprise prospered, but afterward declined. However, at the time of writing it was by no means a failure. A town had been built with important improvements, and clearings had been made. Robert Morris was out of the enterprise. Nicholson had made a joint stock company of it.[4]

This settlement was in Bradford County. It is evident that its weakness came from the fact that there were too

[1] Blackman's Susquehanna Co., 486.

[2] Account.

[3] App to Maclay, 324.

[4] Liancourt, i. 151.

many gentlemen in the company, and not enough workers. It does not seem to be a correct statement that Morris was out of the Company in 1795. In the articles of agreement and association of the Asylum Company, of 1801, it is recited that Robert Morris and the late John Nicholson could not perform their agreement of 1794 and 1795, so that the subscribers have been forced to buy in the shares, and have bought all but seven hundred and thirty-nine shares. They now form a new Company. The seven hundred and thirty-nine shares outstanding are to be exchanged for shares of the new Company, of which there are two thousand in all. In 1819 the lands and stock of the Asylum Company were offered for sale under the articles of association.[1]

In 1793 a company of French emigrants came to New York, in order to form a colony in that State. They were, however, persons entirely unfit for the work of colonization. They visited Philadelphia; but state that Robert Morris received them "without ceremony, seeing that there was nothing to be made out of us." Jefferson received them still worse. They settled at Castorland, in the present towns of New Bremen and Croghan, in New York.[2]

Priestley's son preceded him to America, and bought land in Northumberland County, Pennsylvania, on which it was intended that a colony of Unitarians should be settled. Land was bought of Robert Morris. When the scheme failed, Morris "generously" took back the land.[3]

In February, 1795, Morris, Nicholson, and Greenleaf formed the North American Land Company. They deeded to this company land in Pennsylvania, Virginia, North Carolina, South Carolina, Georgia, and Kentucky. There were 6,000,000 acres in all, — of which 2,000,000 were in

1. Document in possession of the Pennsylvania Historical Society.

2 Mass. Hist. Soc. Proc. February, 1864.

3 Liancourt, i. 129.

Georgia. There were 30,000 shares, — making a capital of $3,000,000 ; the land being put in at fifty cents an acre. The title was vested in trustees, who were to convey to purchasers. The trustees were Thomas Willing [later Jared Ingersoll], John Nixon, and John Barclay. Morris was named President of the Board of Managers.

They published a little book as an advertisement of the Company, and to contradict misrepresentations of it which had been made in Europe. It contained several letters by Robert Goodloe Harper, which presented nothing but glowing descriptions of the lands, climate, productions, etc.; especially of the Southern States. The book is more important to show the ideas of the projectors at the time, than for any information about the lands. In the introduction, which was no doubt written by Morris, it is said that land in America has doubled in value within five or six years. Since interest is at six per cent and much of the land will pay £6 per acre per annum, it ought to be worth £100 per acre. "The proprietor of back lands gives himself no other trouble about them than to pay the taxes, which are inconsiderable. As Nature left them, so they lie till circumstances give them value. The proprietor is then sought out by the settler who has chanced to pitch upon them, or who has made any improvement thereon, and receives from him a price which fully repays his original advance, with great interest."

We have here, repeated in its most distinct form, the fallacy which has possessed the minds of all those who, from the first settlement of America, have tried to make fortunes out of wild land. It is the pecuniary form of the same fallacy about wild lands which we meet with in political philosophy and sociology, — namely, the idea that wild lands, in a state of nature, are a commodity, or an estate, or an asset, or a good presented to man as a "bounty of nature." Land in a state of nature is simply a chance for a human being to win means of subsistence by the expenditure of his labour. "The prairie value" of land is always zero, or a minus quantity. The difficulty of clearing it and reducing it to use is an obstacle which must be conquered by the human being who wants to win food from it. If he is on the agricultural stage of life, this difficulty is great, and constitutes the cost of the struggle for existence in its very first and simplest form. Whenever, therefore, we make abstraction of all the arts, sciences, and established customs of civilization, in order to come back to the position of a man face to face with an unlimited amount of land, untouched by human hands, we find that man, not in possession of a boon or gratuitous good of any kind whatever, but simply face to face with an enormous task. If he is strong enough to conquer the difficulties and execute the task, he will extort from Nature food, clothing, and shelter. Whatever he gets from her he may have and enjoy. Access to wild land is nothing more than a chance to begin this enterprise and effort.

What, then, can the actual settler give to the State for a title to the wild land? Certainly nothing more than a remuneration for surveying it in order to define and secure to the settler that land upon which he has spent his labour, and also a remuneration for defence and protection in the possession of it against others. What can he give, or why should he give anything, to another man who has simply secured a paper title to the land under the civil institutions which nominally extend over the unsettled territory? There is no reason why he should give anything. As long as the land is to be reached in unlimited amount, he can always pass by that which has been taken up, and find more. Why, then, should he pay for the privilege of going on that which has been covered by a paper title? If he finds that he has taken up land of which somebody else owns the paper title, instead of coming forward to pay the owner freely and cheerfully, as Morris expected, according to the above paragraph, he refuses to do it, and resists as long as he possibly can. Of this our history has given abundant illustration.[1]

The proprietors and grantees in the colonial days had made ample experience of the fallacy of the notion that a thousand acres of wild land is an estate, or possession, or useful thing in any sense whatever to the owner of the paper title; but they had never recognized the fallacy. It had been more thoroughly exposed in Pennsylvania than anywhere else. Charles II. was indebted to William Penn. He gave him a grant of an empire of wild land with which to repay himself the debt. Penn and his descendants quarrelled all the time with the actual settlers who took up the land and tilled it with their own hands. The proprietor wanted to obtain a net revenue. The settlers wanted him to invest capital for the defence and development of the Commonwealth. He could see no reason why the Commonwealth should exist under his proprietorship, except that he might recover an income from it. They could see no reason why that relation should exist, unless he did something for them. The historical form of the contest was that the settlers had the political organization in their hands, and tried to tax the proprietor's land. If they had done so, even under their claim that they were developing and protecting the Commonwealth and building it up for the future, the proprietor would never have obtained any income. The United States government has inherited exactly the same contest with the new States. If they could tax the land owned by the United States, it would have to support them. The

[1] See the case of Greene *v.* Biddle, Wheaton, viii. 1.

Penns undoubtedly made a very good bargain to sell out their province for the amount they received in cash from Pennsylvania and the English government.

Morris did propose that the North American Land Company should do something for the land besides holding the paper title until such time as the settlers chose to come and buy it. The land was to be surveyed, an agent was to go upon a tract, build houses, mills, outbuildings, and then report to the Company, which was to advertise for settlers. This would have been an investment of capital, and then would have come the question whether it was a good investment. In 1800 the Pultney Association had spent $1,374,470, and had received $147,974, besides which they owed $300,000.[1] Jeremiah Wadsworth, of Hartford, bought lands of Phelps and Gorham. Two young men, relatives of his, settled on this land, cultivating it themselves. They raised hemp and tobacco. In 1796 one of them went to Europe to try to sell land for himself and others who were at that time embarrassed. He found a very bad market. He adopted the plan of exchanging his new land for farms in New England, — that is to say, he facilitated emigration. It was not until the War of 1812 made a good demand for his produce that he began to escape from his embarrassment; but the Erie Canal finally brought him relief, — that is to say, the development of the land and the advancement of value was a question of transportation.[2] Robert Morris had perceived this, and had tried to promote the Erie Canal even in his time.[3]

Custis says that Morris asked Washington to go into the North American Land Company, as Washington was then buying land. He refused, and in his turn urged Morris not to go into these speculations at his age. Morris re-

[1] P. & G. Purchase, 274; but see page 257. [2] Ibid. 324.
[3] Turner, 357.

plied: "I can never do things in the small; I must be either a man or a mouse."[1] In 1794 Morris declined a proposition which Washington had made to him, that he should buy the latter's lands. The price was too high.[1]

It should be understood that in the last decade of the last century there was a very great disposition on the part of men of enterprise and capital to speculate in land. Morris was only one of the most prominent and eager in the enterprise, one of those who had the largest means and went into it on the largest scale. The enterprise, however, had never any solid business foundation, or any prospect or possibility of success. It was not an investment in a productive enterprise, but an attempt to exploit the monopoly of land under conditions where that monopoly had no value, because the amount of land in proportion to the number of settlers was in unlimited excess.

The Minister of France to the United States, Fauchet, published a letter in Paris, in 1794, warning Frenchmen against the representations of land speculators in America. Another letter was published, signed by Jonas Fauches, who, Morris said, kept a tippling-house in one of the western counties of Georgia. The letters were reprinted in America. The general allegations were that the land titles were not good, and that the lands were unfit to support settlers. Fauches also asserted that fraudulent land claims had been sold to Robert Morris. In the book about the North American Land Company Morris denied these assertions, and said that he would take back any uncultivated lands which he had sold, and give six per cent per annum advance on the price from the time of sale. He wanted to sue Fauches. Fauchet replied that Morris was mentioned in the letters only as a victim of cheating speculators. His, Fauchet's, business was only to transmit to France any

[1] Custis, 326. [2] Hist. Mag., November, 1868.

information which he obtained which he thought would be useful to Frenchmen. His letter had in fact been directed to the Foreign Minister of France.

In 1797 Morris formed the Pennsylvania Property Company. He deeded to James Biddle and William Bell, as trustees, land, houses, etc., in the State of Pennsylvania, which they were to reconvey to the Company when formed. The plan of association is in the Pennsylvania Historical Society Library.

In the "Account" Morris refers to the schedule of the Pennsylvania Property Company to show what its assets were, and mentions the "Hills" and the Trout Spring estate as having been in it. "The destructive operation of sheriff's sales has cut off the surpluses that were expected to arise to the Company from those estates, which might have been ensured under proper management." He says that two persons formed designs of plundering that Company, having made bargains with some of Morris's creditors. The property of the Pennsylvania Property Company was divided into ten thousand shares, out of which he transferred two thousand to the trustees, and twenty-three hundred and sixty to various other persons, either as payment or security for debt. From mention which is made of incumbrances on different pieces of this property, it is evident that the Company never owned anything but equities in it. No evidence has been met with that any shares in this Company were ever sold to outside parties. By means of the "shares" Morris tried to distribute the equities among his creditors.

CHAPTER XXXIV.

WAS ROBERT MORRIS EVER RICH?

WE have seen that Robert Morris inherited from his father nearly $7,000 in cash, besides real estate, when he was seventeen years old. Therefore by the time he was of age he was able to enter the firm of Willing and Morris with a very handsome capital for a man to begin life with in Philadelphia in those days. His wife also inherited property which Morris sold for $15,860.[1] When John Adams said of him, "He rose from nothing but a naked boy by his industry, ingenuity, and fidelity, to great business and credit as a merchant,"[2] he stated what was incorrect. On the contrary, Morris started with very exceptional advantages.

There is among the Peters papers a letter from Robert Morris, dated November 29, 1759, to some one who is named only John. Morris says that a certain person, whom he does not name, "has paid us a great deal of money, which reprieves us from jail one month more. Our damned creditors are hungry as the devil, and we tumble hogsheads of sugar, bills of exchange, and paper money down their throats every day. But all won't do unless a fresh supply comes soon."

A story obtained currency during the Revolutionary war that Morris had been on the verge of bankruptcy when the war broke out. William Lee wrote to R. H. Lee,

[1] See page 296. [2] Adams, ix. 609.

March 25, 1779: "The critical situation of Mr. R. Morris at the beginning of the American war was not only generally known in London and Holland, but in other places. What is it now?"[1] The argument, which was often repeated by a certain class of Morris's enemies, was: He is rich. How did he become sŏ? We do not know. Therefore he has stolen public funds. On the inside of the cover of William Lee's letter book is a note by the owner of the book abusive of Morris. "Mr. Morris long before the war between America and Great Britain, though supported by the large property and still larger credit of his partner, Mr. Willing, had brought the house of Willing, Morris, & Co. to a state that is called bankruptcy in every commercial country in Europe; and when the American war commenced, he had the address to get the direction of the expenditure of the greatest part of the paper money issued by Congress, till at length he brought the United States of America to a public bankruptcy, while he, at the same time, amassed an immense fortune for himself; and even after this, when the Congress paper money was driven out of circulation for the want of payment, Mr. Morris had influence enough in Congress to get himself appointed Financier-general of the United States of America, when nothing but gold and silver were allowed to be current; by which manœuvre Mr. Morris could secure to himself the payment of the immense quantity of the former Congress paper money that he had collected while it was current at a thousand and twelve hundred per cent under value."[2]

Whenever we meet with the assertion, in later years, that Morris was bankrupt in 1774, it seems to be clearly traceable back to William Lee. We meet with it in "Cen-

[1] Ford's W. Lee.

[2] A copy of this entry, which is undated, but was evidently written about 1783, has been communicated by Mr. W. C. Ford.

tinel,"[1] and in Callender, in the direct line of Lee and the Lee party tradition, constituting a part of their stock of vituperation. Having thus got into the literature, it obtained wider circulation. We find John Adams repeating it in 1809: "At the beginning of our Revolution his commerce was stagnated, and as he had overtraded, he was much embarrassed. He took advantage of the times, joined the whigs, came into Congress and united his credit, supported by my loans in Holland, and resources of the United States. By this means he supported his credit for many years, but at last grew extravagant, as all conquerors and extraordinary characters do, and died as he had lived, as I believe, all his days, worth very little solid capital."[2]

If he was bankrupt at that time, the suspicion at once suggests itself that he took the whig side, as so many others did, in the hope that in political uproar he might find pecuniary relief. That suspicion is, however, at once refuted by the fact that he resisted the declaration of independence, and took very sober views about reconciliation, if any reasonable grounds for it could be offered.[3] It is possible, of course, that he was embarrassed at the outbreak of the war; but Adams is not a witness to the fact of his own knowledge, and when we trace up any Revolutionary tradition to the Lees, especially if it is derogatory to Franklin, Morris, and their friends, we must reject it until it is corroborated by other evidence.

In 1777 or 1778 Wentworth understood that Morris had become very rich.[4]

From the statements which were made when Morris took office, by himself and others, it is evident that he was regarded as a very rich man, and that he claimed to be such. The most definite statement on this point which we pos-

[1] See page 216.

[2] Adams, ix. 609.

[3] See vol. i. pp. 194-197.

[4] Stevens, 486.

sess is in Chastellux, who also offers an explanation of the chances of acquiring wealth at the time: "I could easily form an idea of the commerce of Philadelphia from seeing above three hundred vessels in her harbour, though the English had not left a single bark in it in 1778. Two years' tranquillity and, above all, the diversion made by our squadron at Rhode Island, have sufficed to collect this great number of vessels, the success of which in privateering as well as in trade has filled the warehouses with goods, insomuch that purchasers alone are wanting." He says, however, that Pennsylvania is not well governed, and is more exposed to convulsions of credit and manœuvres of speculation than other parts of America.[1] "Very large fortunes were made from nothing during this period [1779–80], but this state of prosperity was not of long duration. In 1781 and 1782 so numerous were the King's cruisers and privateers that frequently not one vessel out of seven that left the Delaware escaped their vigilance. The profits on successful voyages were enormous, but it was no uncommon thing to see a man one day worth forty or fifty thousand pounds and the next day reduced to nothing. Indeed, these rapid transitions were so frequent that they almost ceased to affect either the comfort or the credit of the individual. Flour shipped on board at Philadelphia cost $5, and produced from $28 to $34 a barrel in specie at the Havana, which is generally but a short run; and the arrival of one European cargo out of three amply repaid the merchant. So that, notwithstanding the numerous captures, the stocks were continually full of new vessels to supply such as were lost or taken. In short, without having been upon the spot at that period, it is impossible to conceive the activity and perseverance of the Americans. There was scarcely a captain, or even com-

[1] Chastellux, i. 326.

mon sailor, who had not been taken six or seven times during the war, nor a merchant who had not been more than once rich and ruined.[1]

"It is scarcely to be credited that amidst the disasters of America Mr. Morris, the inhabitant of a town just emancipated from the hands of the English, should possess a fortune of a million and a half or two million dollars. It is, however, in the most critical time that great fortunes are acquired. The fortunate return of several ships, the still more successful cruises of his privateers, have increased his riches beyond his expectation if not beyond his wishes. He is in fact so accustomed to the success of his privateers that when he is observed on a Sunday to be more serious than usual, the conclusion is that no prize has arrived in the preceding week. This flourishing state of commerce at Philadelphia, as well as in Massachusetts Bay, is entirely owing to the arrival of the French squadron."[2]

To this the translator, who is an inferior authority and addicted to gossip, adds: "Mr. Morris has certainly enriched himself greatly by the war, but the house of Willing and Morris did a great deal of business and was well known in all the considerable trading towns of Europe previous to that period. Mr. Morris had various other means of acquiring wealth besides privateering; amongst others, by his own interest and his connections with Mr. Holker, then Consul-general of France at Philadelphia, he frequently obtained exclusive permission to ship cargoes of flour, etc., in the time of general embargoes, by which he gained immense profit. His situation gave him many similar opportunities, of which his capital, his credit, and abilities always enabled him to take advantage. On the strength of his office as Financier-general, he circulated his own notes of Robert Morris as cash throughout the

[1] Chastellux, 201, translator's note. [2] Ibid. 199.

continent, and even had the address to get some Assemblies, that of Virginia in particular, to pass acts to make them current in payment of taxes. What purchases of tobacco, what profits of every kind, might not a man of Mr. Morris's ability make with such powerful advantages?"[1]

In May, 1782, Morris said that he was poorer than a year before.[2]

We can see the following important chances of profit which Morris possessed during the war. He made commissions on the commercial transactions which he made on behalf of Congress, and he no doubt had the best of that business. He imported, on his own ventures, and sold to Congress, goods on which the profits were immense. Privateering was full of risk. He may have been fortunate at it. He had chances to win the information which was most essential for profitable operations in the currency. His control of the foreign exchange in 1781 must have given him great chances of profit.

If we ask the question in what Morris's wealth consisted after the peace, it is not easy to answer. He never owned much real estate in the city of Philadelphia, and was not a very large stockholder in the Bank of North America. At that time he did not own any great amount of land. His property must have consisted in ships and goods. The tobacco speculation and the China trade upon which he entered, would call for a large capital in those forms.

In April, 1784, Morris, writing to Tilghman, says that the bank has refused discounts for three weeks past. There is a terrible and general distress for want of money. Three weeks later he writes that he thinks the bank will resume discounts the next week. In July he wrote that there were some great failures at Philadelphia; and in No-

[1] Chastellux, 200.

[2] Dip. Corr. Rev. xii. 142.

vember he wrote again that the bank thought of making discounts.[1] At the end of January, 1785, he said that the bank was discounting at that time. He seems to have had some disagreeable experiences during the financial crisis; for after referring to the embarrassment caused by helping a man, he says that he will do it no more, having suffered from it all his life.

In March, 1785, he tells the same correspondent that he is not at ease in money matters. He was writing in reference to a proposition by Tilghman that they should purchase some "works." He said that some large debts due him kept him poor when he ought not to be so. This was the time of the tobacco contract.

In 1788 Madison referred to Robert Morris's affairs as still very much deranged.[2] In the same year one of the English agents in the United States reported to Lord Dorchester: "Generally speaking, the commercial character and credit are sunk to the lowest ebb. Bankruptcy has ceased to be disgraceful. Even Mr. Morris of Philadelphia has bills to a great amount returned protested from Europe, the payments of which are suspended, and his immediate prospects of retrieving his affairs depended upon the arrival of a large ship from China, which did arrive about the middle of September." [3]

In 1789 Gouverneur Morris speaks of the trouble of Robert Morris's affairs.[4] In 1790 he wrote that the last and most difficult task he had in Europe was, "your various debts and engagements. Here I have to perform the task of the Israelites in Egypt, — make bricks without straw." [5] April 4, 1790, Robert Morris wrote to Hamilton that he wanted to mortgage his Ten (or Ton) Alley estate,

[1] See page 184.

[2] Madison's Works, i. 443.

[3] Canadian Archives, 1890, 104.

[4] Morris's Morris, i. 146, 150.

[5] Ibid. 342.

and spoke of paying his debts as an object of effort, although at the same time he proposed a time contract for a large purchase of bank shares.[1] Simpson says that Morris was in a whirlpool of trouble from 1787 to 1798.[2] The Duc de Liancourt, in 1794 or 1795, spoke of Morris's affairs as embarrassed.[3] In the "Account," however, Morris refers two or three times to gifts which he made in 1792 as made at a time when he had as good a right to give as any man.[4] There is great reason to believe, although we have found no recorded evidence of it, that he made great profits out of the rise in the public debt in 1790 and 1791.[5] We have found no evidence that he was troubled at all by the financial crisis in 1792 in connection with the failure of Duer.

In his petition in bankruptcy Morris dated his misfortunes from the failure of two houses in London and Dublin in 1793.[6] Simpson expresses the opinion that Morris was carried away by the éclat of his own reputation.[7] Lossing thinks that he became mad with speculation and ambition.[8] We find ourselves driven to the same opinion. The habit of dealing with large sums on paper when he was public Financier, the glory of giving credit to the United States by his personal endorsement, the discovery that he could with facility circulate his personal notes as currency, and the prestige which he had enjoyed, were enough to turn the head of any man. They led him to that saddest of all human delusions, to which the most able and most fortunate are always most exposed, — namely, that although other men are fools, one's self is wise; that one is not subject to the same follies and weaknesses as they, but can with ease and confidence do what they dare not attempt.

[1] State Dep. MSS., Ham. Papers, xxii. 181. [2] Simpson, 713.
[3] Liancourt, iii. 270. [4] Account, 15, 42. [5] See page 232.
[6] Westcott, 364. [7] Simpson, 711. [8] Amer. Hist. Rec. ii. 305.

CHAPTER XXXV.

"CONFIDENCE HAS FURLED HER BANNERS, WHICH NO LONGER WAVE OVER THE HEADS OF M. AND N."

THE Pennsylvania Historical Society owns five account-books of Robert Morris, containing the record of his affairs between 1791 and 1801. We have not been able to give to these books more than the most superficial examination. They are kept by a complicated system of single entry which it would require time to master, and they do not present any tests of the state of his affairs at any moment which could be easily applied. The accounts, indeed, are suspended or abandoned at the end of 1796. He had spent all his capital on land which produced him no income, and there were no accounts to keep. When he was in prison he undertook to post up the books, and the last entries in them are in an aged and tremulous handwriting, which is in consonance with the pathetic effect which is produced by all the other evidence we have about his last years.

During his prison days, probably in 1800, he also wrote out a series of memoranda explaining his enterprises as well as he could, and especially explaining his open accounts. This document was printed in two pamphlets, probably in connection with the legal proceedings of 1860; but it bears no titlepage or date. It is often referred to in this book as the "Account."

In 1800 he referred to 1795 or 1796 as the beginning of his troubles.[1] The whole "Account" of this property shows that he had bought land all over the United States, but had scarcely kept track of it himself, and had mortgaged it and disposed of it in a reckless manner, without any plan as to what he expected to do or where he expected to come out. He had apparently seized upon any or every asset or chose in action, and mortgaged it to raise money or put off creditors, and all the assets that appear there are simply the equity, or contingent interest, that might ultimately be saved, if all the other transactions could be liquidated. At the same time he had complicated these other transactions to such an extent that their liquidation was impossible on account of the conflict of interests that would certainly arise.

In 1795 we find him trying to put off Hamilton, who was urging him to pay what he owed to Church, and it appears from the letters that the contract for the bank shares had been made, but that payment had not been made in full by Morris; still without the other half of the correspondence we cannot be sure. Later we find that Hamilton has written that Church wants a settlement and will take land. Morris offered land in Washington County, Pennsylvania, where cultivated land, he said, was worth from \$4 to \$12 an acre, and uncultivated land \$1 to \$3. He called his own worth \$2.[2] In Hamilton's directions to his executor, July 25, 1795, he states that he holds Morris's note for \$9,500, with bills of exchange as collateral for \$4,000 and for £500 sterling. These are for Church's money, which Hamilton had lent to Morris. It was at first \$10,000, but Morris had paid \$500.[3]

March 13, 1795, Morris wrote to Nicholson that a storm

[1] Account, 48. [2] State Dep. MSS., Ham. Papers, xxii. 185, 190.
[3] Hamilton's Works, viii. 353.

was rising and they must have a consultation. On the 24th he writes that there is "no end to trouble and disgrace." April 13, he agreed that Greenleaf might discount Morris's endorsement at two and a half per cent per month. May 22, he writes: "Remember poor Higby; I am distressed for him beyond measure." July 20, he wrote to Cranch, who was his agent at Washington, that he and Nicholson had bought out Greenleaf's share of Washington. They made a contract of division, which is in the Ford Collection. Morris and Nicholson each owed Greenleaf $127,514, payable in 1796, 1797, 1798, and 1799. In the same collection is an account of John Nicholson with the three partners for land bought, being an account of their joint land transaction. August 14, Morris wrote to Cranch that he could not raise money. Two and three per cent per month was the common rate. On the 17th he wrote that he was determined to finish the houses which had been begun in Washington. November 13, he writes to Cranch: "Hard, very hard is our fate, to be starving in the midst of plenty, for we have abundant property. Money, however, cannot be obtained for any part of it at present, but it will come by and by." Other letters to Cranch through 1795 repeat this complaint of money distress. There was in fact a commercial crisis in 1795 and 1796 coincident with that in England. In March, 1796, Morris wrote to Nicholson: "We must see General Stewart [one of the Commissioners for building Washington] this day, and if you will not attend, the city of Washington will go ——." April 9, he writes to Nicholson: "You must squeeze out $500 for the bearer. He has come far for it, and must not return without."

May 28, 1796, Morris and Nicholson bought out Greenleaf's share in the North American Land Company for $1,150,000, one half in Robert Morris's drafts on Nicholson accepted by the latter, and one half in Nicholson's drafts on Robert Morris accepted by him, at one, two, three, and four years.[1]

A suit between Alexander and Morris was mentioned above,[2] in which Morris obtained a decision in the Court of Chancery which left Alexander indebted to him. In 1796, when Morris and Nicholson made their cross-notes and endorsements, Alexander bought some of them, and tried to pay his debts to Morris with them at their face value. With regard to the making of these notes, the court say: "It is impossible to justify Morris, whether his conduct proceeded from his distress or an insatiable thirst for riches, in coining these millions of notes to circulate under a promise to redeem them at full specie value, which he must have known he would not be able to do, and that the world would be thereby deceived. According to his account, however, mankind was not wholly deceived. They got into circulation by his depositing them in heaps for money borrowed, and their value to him was what they would sell for, and those sales gave a tone to their depreciation from time to time, as a rate at which they were generally passed between individuals. Of these deposits and sales we have no account till 1796." Some were then used as collateral at ten cents on the dollar, and were sold in February, 1797, at 3.6 cents on the dollar. This was the rate at which Alexander obtained them, the transaction having been proved in court. The court held that he could deliver them in payment of a judgment which had been obtained against him, after ten years' litigation, only at the price at which he bought them. "It is believed that the widows and orphans spoken of, and all others holding Morris's notes would be glad to be so paid for them." [3]

[1] Wright's Rep. vii. 23. [2] See page 174. [3] Call's Reports, iii. 91.

These notes are also mentioned as having been used as collateral in Petersen *v.* Willing *et al.*[1]

At the end of the "Account" Morris wrote, in regard to these notes: "It is well known that Mr. Nicholson and myself owe a very large debt by notes drawn and endorsed by each. The issuing of these notes is the blamable part of our conduct, which we have both felt and acknowledged. But as no use can arise to the holders of such paper from any reflection I can now make, I will forbear any attempt to justify that business, although circumstances might be adduced that would at least soften the disposition to censure. I do not pretend to name the amount of notes out, as I have not a correct account of what was issued, nor what has been paid, or otherwise satisfied. Mr. Nicholson was to have kept a register thereof; but when I entered with him into an examination, it was found very inaccurate. Therefore the amount of these notes that are or may be proved before the Commissioners must be taken as the nominal amount that remained unsatisfied. As to the value received for them, I must be silent."

In June, 1796, Morris and Nicholson conveyed part of the Washington land to Greenleaf. All through that year Morris was in dire distress for money. In a letter to Nicholson, December 19, 1796, he says: "I have a dreadful time of it."[2] December 13, Chauncey Goodrich wrote to Oliver Wolcott, Sr.: "This place [Philadelphia] furnishes indication of great depravity. Bankruptcies are frequently happening. Mr. Morris is greatly embarrassed."[3]

In the same month Morris writes to Hamilton that Talbot and Allen threaten suit against him as endorser on a bill drawn in his favour by John Nicholson on Cazenove, Nephew, & Co. Morris says that he is only endorser, and

[1] Dallas, iii. 507. [2] Dreer Collection. [3] Gibbs, i. 410.

wants to fight this claim. He employs Hamilton as his lawyer.[1]

January 7, 1797, Morris had not fulfilled a contract with William Smith, and was under obligation to deliver to him $50,000 in six per cent stock.[2] He gave Smith's assignee a mortgage on Genesee land as security. He has now freed it by other securities. Succeeding letters show a tangle in regard to this matter, which he is eager to break.[3]

January 13, 1797, Morris to Cranch: "The scenes of distress are here so universal that it is hard to say who are worst off." February 7, to Nicholson: "I am daily undergoing the most mortifying and tormenting scenes that you can imagine."[4] February 17, to Cranch, he writes that his controversy with Greenleaf will be carried on in the counting-house and not in the public prints. This referred to a newspaper controversy which was going on. Morris always claimed that Greenleaf was dishonorable or dishonest, and chiefly to blame for Morris's calamities. April 27, he wrote to Nicholson: "I have bad news from the city of Washington, and wish to see you as soon as possible." April 17, Morris and Nicholson made an offer to the holders of their notes, who had been advertising them, of twenty-five cents on the dollar in four annual instalments, with land security. May 15, they prosecuted this negotiation with the assignees of Greenleaf, who were trying to sell these notes as assets of his estate. His debts were $720,000. Morris and Nicholson offered to pay this sum in five annual instalments, in order to release their notes. May 14, Morris wrote to Cranch that Washington City was not good security in Philadelphia; that there was little faith in it there. [It belonged to the creed of a good Philadelphian at the time to believe that the city of Wash-

[1] State Dep. MSS., Hamilton Papers, xxii. 196. [2] See page 278.

[3] Ibid. 202. [4] Dreer Collection.

ington never would be built, and that the capital would stay at Philadelphia.] June 12, as the negotiation with Greenleaf's assignees had not succeeded, Morris and Nicholson gave notice that they should dispute the claim against them, and they offered a compromise. On the 15th they explained that they had never received deeds from the trustees of the first owners of the site of the city of Washington. In July they entered into further explanations of the entanglement of their endorsements. The assignees evidently found themselves forced to come to terms. All the interests of Morris, Nicholson, and Greenleaf's assignees were pooled in the "Aggregate Fund," of which the assignees were made the trustees.

May 20, Morris writes to Hamilton that a man has not answered a letter of his. "I have known the time when he would have thought differently, and perhaps I may, notwithstanding present appearances, see that time again."[2] Three days later, "I am not in a situation to answer offhand, as was formerly the case, every claim on my justice." June 2, he writes to quiet Hamilton's uneasiness. He will pay principal and interest. "The nature of your debt ties me at all events, and it shall be paid." He tries to reassure Hamilton also as to Church's security. No doubt Hamilton was exceedingly uneasy because he had loaned Church's money, being Church's agent and lawyer. Morris goes on: "I am, to be sure, disagreeably situated, but my affairs are retrievable, if I could get the common aid of common times, and I will struggle hard. Keep all this to yourself."[3]

September 6, Morris wrote to Nicholson: "My Chestnut Street house and lot, these grounds [the "Hills"], and some ground rents are advertised by Mr. Baker for sale on the 15th instant." He cannot raise $500; feels great dis-

[1] See p. 248. [2] State Dep. MSS. Ham. Papers, xii. 206. [3] Ibid. 210.

tress for people who are petty creditors of his.[1] September 23, in writing to Nicholson, Morris speaks of a house in which they spent two days in the "early stages of hide and seek."[2] September 30, to the same, he writes that if their afflictions are like those of Job, they must be patient. As to his family, his "soul is wrung to the quick. Here I must stop. This subject comes home to my feelings, which are at this moment too strong to proceed, and I lay down the pen." October 2, he wrote expressing chagrin at Hamilton's fears of losing what Morris owed him. He gives assurance that he will pay.[3] November 1, he begs Hamilton to intervene with Church. "I would fain hope that he does not wish to take advantage of my necessities to obtain my property at less than its worth." December 21, he has heard that Hamilton has attached his property, and he begs Hamilton to explain what it is for.[4] There is in the State Department a statement of this account, dated November 27, 1797. The amount lent in the first place was $10,000. The balance now due is $6,002, which is turned over to Thomas Morris for the latter to pay.[5]

As this year 1797 draws to an end, Morris is sometimes grimly facetious and humorous, and then again bursts into these exclamations of grief and anxiety. October 25, to Nicholson: "By heaven, there is no bearing with these things. I believe I shall go mad. Every day brings forward scenes and troubles almost insupportable, and they seem to be accumulating so that at last they will like a torrent carry everything before them. God help us, for men will not."[6]

In spite of his troubles, in 1797, Morris found time to congratulate Pickering on his spirited answer to Yrujo.[7]

[1] Dreer Collection. All the letters which have been quoted from the beginning of 1795 to this point, without reference, are in the Ford Collection.

[2] Ford Coll. [3] State Dep., etc. 211. [4] Ibid. 213, 215.

[5] Ibid. 199. [6] Dreer Coll. [7] Pickering, iii. 408.

November 16, he wrote again to his partner about the hopeless entanglement of their affairs. He wanted to provide for those who had become entangled in his enterprises, for whom he was greatly distressed. His dogs, by barking, gave the alarm that there was somebody on the premises. He opened the window and found that it was a sheriff's officer, to whom he answered: "Have patience, and I will pay thee all."[1] December 2, he wrote: "I never stir out of the door."[2] December 5, to Cranch, he speaks of "that painful distress of mind which has become my constant companion."[3] On the 15th he writes to Nicholson that he has caused his gardeners to drive creditors off the premises. It appears that the creditors had besieged his house at the "Hills," and lighted watch-fires on the premises. Of one creditor he says: "I respect him; and I swear by all that is sacred that he never shall suffer one cent by R. Morris."[4]

The writ of arrest for Morris is given in full by Lossing.[5] It was a *ca. sa.* writ to satisfy Blair McClenahan for a bill of $16,017.71 and damages, on which judgment had been obtained. It was issued by Judge McKean on the 30th of December, 1797. He was not, however, imprisoned immediately. The first commitment issued against him was January 17, 1798, at the suit of John Ely.[6] It is stated elsewhere[7] that one of the first creditors to sue Morris was the Bank of Pennsylvania, which levied on a lot on Chestnut Street and sold it at a sacrifice.

December 21, Morris wrote to Nicholson that he wished Nicholson was with him. He has a good fire. "The night is so cold that the devil himself would not turn out to

[1] Hist. Mag. August, 1870.

[2] Dreer Collection.

[3] Ford Collection.

[4] Hist. Mag. July, 1864.

[5] Amer. Hist. Rec. ii. 229.

[6] Simpson, 713.

[7] App. to Maclay, 325.

catch you going home." His worst trouble is with Church and Hamilton of New York. "Good heavens, what vultures men are in regard to each other!"[1] January 11, to Nicholson: "Confidence has furled her banners, which no longer wave over the heads of M. and N."[2]

January 17, 1798, writing to Hamilton, he mentions that the latter has given indulgence to Thomas Morris for the debt of Robert Morris. It appears also that Hamilton's action against Morris was in Church's interest. Morris now writes: "I have frequently been without what was necessary for the market. . . . I am a martyr to the times." He complains of usury. No loans are to be got. His property has been "advertised, sold, sacrificed, and plundered." He has provided for Hamilton. "I am sensible that I have lost the confidence of the world as to my pecuniary abilities, but I believe not as to my honour or integrity."[3] In the "Account" he says that his son Thomas had satisfied his debt to Alexander Hamilton.

January 17, 1798, he writes to Nicholson that he expects that his estate of the "Hills" will be taken from him in March.[4] January 22: "There is a Frenchman intends to shoot me at the window if I do not pay a note he had protested on Saturday."[5] January 29, he calls the "Hills" "Castle Defiance."[6] January 31, he expresses great fear of prison: "I detest Prune Street more than ever."[7] February 3: If he cannot raise money his house and lot and the "Hills" estate will be sacrificed on Monday.[8] February 8: The punishment of his imprudence in the use of his name is, perhaps, just, — but his family! "I will try to see you before I go to prison."[9]

[1] Dreer Collection.
[2] Ford Collection.
[3] State Dep., etc., 217.
[4] Ford Collection.
[5] Dreer Collection.
[6] Ibid.
[7] Simpson, 713. The prison was in Prune Street.
[8] Ford Collection.
[9] Dreer Collection.

February 15, being under arrest, he sent back to Nicholson forty dollars which he had received of him, saying, "You want money as much if not more than I do." [1] He went to prison on the 16th. On the 24th he writes: "Starvation stares me in the face." February 27: "I have not money enough to buy bread for my family." [2] February 20, he wrote to Nicholson that he had no place in prison; was trying to hire a room at a high rent, and make himself comfortable.[3] Wood, an actor, who, when a very young man, was in prison at Philadelphia, reports that he met Robert Morris there. "His person was neat, although a little old-fashioned, adjusted with much care." He was cheerful, but silent. He carried pebbles in his hand, of which he dropped one at each round of the prison yard. He spoke to the boy with great kindness, and gave him good counsel. Greenleaf was then in the prison also.[4] In a letter of April 9, 1798, Morris says that he walks about the prison-yard fifty times every day. The pebbles were to keep his count.[5]

March 13, we find a letter in which he begins to show a certain grim and desperate reconciliation to facts. He drops into the most atrocious poetry, — for the only time, so far as we have found. The text of it, as it is given, would require emendation as to capitals and punctuation before it could be reprinted.[6] March 21, he tells Nicholson that he disapproves of the conduct of Law, but will not consent to a suit against him. "I think he has been a sufferer by his transactions with us, and I cannot add thereto unless I saw very strong and justifiable cause, which at present I do not." [7] Thomas Fitzsimmons stood by Robert Morris to the last. To him the latter wrote from jail that he had

[1] Homes's Sketch, 16. [2] Ibid. [3] Simpson, 713.
[4] Wood's Recollections. [5] Dreer Collection.
[6] Hist. Mag. July, 1864. [7] Ford Collection.

been trying to get a room to himself, but that the rents were high. He would soon get one, and be more comfortable. "I feel like an intruder everywhere; sleeping in other people's beds and sitting in other people's rooms. I am writing on other people's paper, with other people's ink, — the pen is my own; that and the clothes I wear are all I can claim as mine here. If my creditors were wise for their own sakes, they would not keep me idle here, when, if I had my liberty, I might work efficiently for their benefit."[1] May 15, he wrote to Nicholson: "I get frighted as I go through my memorandums at the number and amount of our notes. Then I leave off the work and lay the papers aside, not for them to cool, but that my mind may do it. I received your letter of yesterday, by which I see the prison scene has made its impression on your mind. You must come every Sunday; and it will grow so familiar that you will think little of it, so long as you keep out on weekdays."[2] He sent to Nicholson a facetious invitation to dine with him in the Prune Street prison on Sunday. He calls it "the hotel with grated doors."[3]

September 7, he wrote that his son William was ill with a slight cold. September 8, that William had a bilious fever. October 10, he refers to the loss of William.[4] The yellow fever was raging in the city at the time. Many of the prisoners had it. Morris's wife and daughter visited him daily. He said that he could not feel afraid of the disease for himself. His son William died, not of the epidemic, but of a bilious fever, at the age of twenty-seven.[5] October 15, Morris writes that the sick are all about him. He has no apprehension. On the 18th he writes to the same effect, but that he will move to another

[1] Lossing, Am. Hist. Rec. ii. 306.

[2] Smith's Curiosities, xxx. facsimile.

[3] Custis's Washington, 328.

[4] Dreer Collection.

[5] Penn. Mag. ii. 178.

room, on account of Mrs. Morris's terror.[1] November 26, he wrote to Charles Young: "I have just heard of an estate of mine worth $100,000 being sold for $800 to pay taxes. 'Such things are done.'"[2] December 15, evidently in answer to an appeal from Young, Morris says that he cannot help him to save his furniture; "for that furniture which was my own is selling by piecemeal, because I cannot raise money to save it."[3] Young was one of the victims of Morris's enterprise at Washington.

In 1798, when Washington was at Philadelphia as general of the army of the United States, he visited Robert Morris in prison.[4] In 1799 General and Mrs. Washington wrote a joint letter to Mrs. Morris, inviting her to Mount Vernon, and assuring her of their "affectionate regard" for her and her husband.[5] Custis says that Robert Morris was the one man to whom Washington unbent.[6] Washington certainly felt, to the end of his life, that Morris was one of the few who had given him essential aid and unswerving support to the best of their abilities, in the hardest crises which he had been obliged to meet. He therefore showed warm personal affection and regard for him.

January 30, 1799, Morris writes to Nicholson: "I am looking forward with fear and trembling to the 18th day of February, when another quarter's rent will be due and must be paid, or my sponsor will be called upon; and that would be worse than to be turned into the street. I am now laying plans to provide for the payment."[7] February 6, he writes that he has made a push for prison bounds; but if not obtained, "I will quit all and begin again, being now determined not to spend my life here for the sake of any property whatever."[8] April 24, he wrote that Gouverneur Morris had come to see him.[9] Of this visit Gouverneur

[1] Dreer Coll. [2] Penn. Hist. Soc. Coll. [3] Ibid.
[4] Custis, 327. [5] Simpson, 717. [6] Custis, 325.
[7] Ford Coll. [8] Hist. Mag. Nov. 1868. [9] Dreer Coll.

Morris writes: "I am strongly affected by the situation of my poor friend, and he seems equally so. Mrs. Morris, who is with him, puts on an air of firmness which she cannot support, and was wrong to assume." Next day he dined with them in prison. "Morris and his family are in high spirits, and I keep them so by a very lively strain of conversation; but see, with infinite concern, that his mind is more made up to his situation than I could have believed. Mr. Ross speaks to me of Robert Morris's situation, and says he behaved very ill. Mr. Fitzsimmons tells me that he is completely ruined by advances to Robert Morris. Another man has sunk his $80,000 in the vortex. Mr. Morris tells me that my share of the Genesee lands has swept off what I owed to him, without which I should have been considerably in his debt."[1]

April 29, Morris wrote to Nicholson again: "I enclose herein two pitiable letters, — one from poor Swanzey, dated the 30th of March, and the other from Robert James, dated 15th instant. I wish we could raise some money for the North American Land Company to pay these poor fellows."[2] April 2, he wrote a letter to the Trustees of the Aggregate Fund, on brown wrapping-paper.[3] In a letter of December 11, 1800, he asks his correspondent: "If you should find it necessary to write again, be good enough to pay the postage of your letters, for I have not a cent to spare from means of subsistence."[4] He mentions a broker in Boston who owed him $47.70, balance of account. "I wrote to request he would remit it, to help out subsistence, but got no answer."[5]

March 14, 1801, Gouverneur Morris visited him again.[6]

Morris was in jail from February 16, 1798, until August 26, 1801, — three years six months and ten days.[7]

[1] Morris's Morris, ii. 378. [2] Penn. Hist. Soc. Coll. [3] Ford Coll.
[4] Turner, 357. [5] Account, 40. [6] Morris's Morris, i. 406.
[7] Penn. Mag. ii. 176.

CHAPTER XXXVI.

MORRIS'S ACCOUNT OF HIS PROPERTY; HIS WIFE'S PENSION; HIS DEATH; HIS FAMILY; HIS ESTATE.

FROM Morris's Account of his Property we select the statements which are of the most general interest.

The oldest judgment against Morris in New York was by Talbot and Allen, "under which, as is said, all my rights and claims in the Genesee country have been executed and sold by the sheriff." Colonel Burr, as attorney for Levi Hollingsworth & Son, obtained a judgment for outlawry, "under which it was meditated, as I have been told, to sell the whole of my purchase," meaning the Genesee purchase. The Holland Company bought all the rights and claims in the Genesee tract of Robert Morris, "it is said," under the judgment of Talbot and Allen, as well as under that obtained by Colonel Burr.

Morris constituted a special trust of 110,000 acres, in the easternmost tract of the Genesee country, which he gave to Fitzsimmons, Higby, and R. Morris, Jr., "in trust to secure the payment of sundry debts in that deed enumerated, being debts arising from disinterested loans of money or name, or attended with circumstances that rendered them of superior claim upon my justice or integrity. This conveyance is dated February 14, 1798." He made the list of beneficiaries and their credits in round numbers, not having the books. "If any of my creditors are omitted, that upon the same principles ought to have been included, it is attributable to the absence of books and papers, and not to any desire to discriminate improperly."

He often mentions, in his notes on the open accounts, persons who had lent him money on endorsements, having great confidence in him, and sometimes persons to whom he had given assurances which had not been fulfilled, the means being swept away in the current of his disasters. Such a case was James Carey, of Baltimore. "The balance due to him appears to be $3,718, exclusive of interest. This debt is of the first class. It was a disinterested assumption to relieve me from distress, and is included in the Genesee security."

Thomas Fitzsimmons was a creditor for over $150,000, chiefly indorsements. Hence he was one of the trustees of the Genesee assignment.

Richard Soderstrom, Swedish consul, is Morris's debtor for more than $18,000, sums advanced for his subsistence, assumption of his debts, and loss on a ship which he sold to Morris, as it appears, fraudulently, not being the owner. Morris gave him 100,000 acres of Genesee land, in payment for services rendered, although he rendered none, being well intentioned, but incompetent. Morris credited him with the gain on this tract, leaving a balance as above. "Under all these circumstances, this man, in imitation probably of some others, circulated among his creditors that I had caused his ruin; and one of them actually called upon me last summer to ask if what Mr. Soderstrom said was really true, 'that he had lent me 100,000 guineas in cash.' My answer was that he never had had a guinea of his own to lend since I knew him."

Nicholson and Morris contracted with Charles Young for $100,000 worth of goods; and besides notes for that amount, they deposited notes to eight times the amount, with power to sell if they failed to pay. He did sell to a considerable amount, "but the notes having depreciated, at his request a loan to a large amount of notes was made, which he was to replace. These accounts have not been settled."

"James Greenleaf. This is an unsettled account, and I suppose ever will be so. Here commenced that ruin which has killed poor Nicholson, and brought me to the necessity of giving an account of my affairs. But I will forbear to say more, lest I should not know where or when to stop."[1]

George Harrison is a creditor; "but he has taken such ample satisfaction by unbounded abuse that I feel less on that score than otherwise I should."

"Gouverneur Morris, Esq. These accounts show that I am in his debt nearly $24,000, exclusive of what he paid in Europe on my account, the amount of which I do not exactly know."

John Nicholson, deceased. "A heavy balance will be found due to me on the accounts depending between this my fellow-sufferer and myself, probably upward of $600,000 specie, when all entries are made that the transactions require. With the purest intentions, he unfortunately laid a train that ended as it hath done. I here say he laid the train, because there are living witnesses that I opposed as soon as I knew it, although from infatuation, madness, or weakness, I gave way afterward."[2]

Gen. Henry Lee was a creditor for protested bills, $39,466, besides damages and interest. "I have greatly regretted that it has not been in my power to relieve the General in this affair."

[1] Nicholson died in 1800. Greenleaf lived until 1836.

[2] Upon the settlement of his accounts, in 1796, with the State of Pennsylvania, Nicholson was a debtor for $58,429. (Yeates, iv. 6; Smith *vs.* Nicholson.)

The following entries concern his family and his personal affairs.

There is an inventory of the articles found in his possession in the debtor's prison. The furniture was nearly all borrowed. Besides this there was a mass of papers, books, and letters.

In 1797 he conveyed his household furniture to Thomas Fitzsimmons. It was sold at public auction. "What is now in Mrs. Morris's use has been lent to her by Mr. Fitzsimmons principally, and some few articles by Mr. Marshall [his son-in-law], so that I do not recollect anything, and believe there is nothing in that house of my property except bedding, clothing, part of a quarter cask of wine, part of a barrel of flour, some coffee, a little sugar, etc., in the family use. There is some bottled wine which I do not consider as mine, but I choose to mention it that I may avoid suspicion or reproach. This wine is what remained in a quarter cask which I gave to my daughter Maria, at the same time that I gave one to her sister some years ago, destined to be used on a particular occasion. The cask leaked, and the remainder was bottled, put up in boxes, and Mrs. Morris has possession of it for her daughter."

"Mrs. Mary Morris, my wife. The sum at the credit of this account, $15,860.16, arose from the sale of two or three tracts of land or farms in Maryland, left to her by her father, the late Col. Thomas White, which I sold with great reluctance when necessity pressed and she urged me to it. I consider this as a sacred debt, but have made no provision for it (an assignment I made upon the Genesee property intended as a compensation for relinquishment of dower, being invalid and of no effect). Therefore it depends on my creditors whether any is to be made or not."

"Esther Morris, my daughter. In this account will be

found a credit for a legacy of a hundred pounds, left to her by her grandmother and received by me. As I gave her nothing on her marriage except clothes and some old wine, I thought it a duty to pay this legacy, and for that purpose I have assigned to her two quarter chests of tea which I sent to Alexandria for sale. I fear, however, that this will not amount to principal and interest." In his books there stands an entry of a debt to her of a balance for which he promised to buy her a share of bank stock. Her poor little legacy was lost no doubt in the great deluge of calamity.

His son-in-law, James M. Marshall, husband of Esther, just mentioned, was his creditor for more than £20,000 sterling, advanced to Robert Morris, Jr., in London, to take up Morris's bills. Morris tried to secure him by an assignment of North American Land Company's stock, and other things of the same sort.

Bishop White, his brother-in-law, was one of his creditors for some amount exceeding $3,000.

His son Robert was a debtor for sums of money spent in Europe, which his father considered large. Robert had presented no vouchers that these expenditures were for his father's account.

A tailor's bill for $144.94 "is for an account against my son Charles, when under age, contracted without my knowledge. It was owing to the facility of such credits that this son Charles of mine contracted habits I never could break him of afterward." Charles's shoemaker's bill, $24.50, follows.

"I have an old, worn-out gold watch that was my father's. He died in 1751. I have had it ever since, and do not want to part with it even now, if I can avoid it. I believe it will sell for very little." At his death he gave this watch to Robert, Jr.[1]

[1] Westcott, 375.

The "Account" is the product of an attempt on Morris's part to inform his creditors about his affairs, to save trouble to his children after his death, and, by setting off debts against credits and assets, to distribute the remnants of his property among his creditors as equitably as possible. It is a pathetic attempt, and awakens the pity of the reader. He still had faith in the big figures at which he had valued his land, when others had lost that faith; and he went on putting "riders" on the assignments already made so as to distribute a "surplus" which would never be realized.

Morris retained many of his friends; but, after 1796, his credit was gone. From the time that he and Nicholson issued their cross-bills, he was in the position of a wild and desperate bankrupt.

Those who have written about Morris and his career have almost always contrasted the end of his life with his services to the United States, and have expressed or implied blame on the country for neglect or ingratitude. A little reflection will show that there is no ground whatever for any imputation of the kind. Morris's enterprises were undertaken entirely on his own judgment and responsibility. He engaged in the ones which immediately caused his ruin ten years after he left office. He had a large salary and good opportunities, which he used while in office. He never gave anything to the public, nor lost anything by the public service. He died indebted to the United States for nearly $100,000. It cannot be said that the United States were bound to guarantee him against his own speculations for the rest of his life.

In 1800 Callender wrote, with reference to him: "It is likely that Morris cannot tell within five millions of dollars the extent of the sums for which he is indebted. They have been variously guessed at, from twelve millions of dollars to thirty millions. His bills would hardly bring fourpence per pound at auction, and perhaps nothing ; yet he lives in all the splendour that a prison can afford. It is supposed that he will transfer an ample fortune to some of his descendants. To this perfection has a federal Congress improved the laws of bankruptcy."[1] Morris was released under the federal bankruptcy law.

In the "Account" Morris gives the facts of one of his transactions to the following effect: He sold to Cazenove a million and a half of acres, with an option to the purchasers to make it a sale or a mortgage at a time fixed. They elected to make it a purchase, and later wanted deeds of confirmation. When these were submitted to lawyers, they informed Morris that he had an equal right with the purchasers to elect whether it be a sale or a mortgage, upon repayment of the consideration, — namely, £112,500 sterling. "And it was urged that as my affairs were then so deranged that I was obliged to keep close house, it became my duty to reserve this right to my creditors, and not to sign the deeds of confirmation. To this reasoning I submitted reluctantly; because I thought the sale a fair one, intended at the time by me to be positive, and which, if my affairs had been in such a situation as that no creditors could have been affected, I certainly would have signed a new deed without hesitation. That I did not do it was to me a matter of regret, under which I have never felt perfectly satisfied. By this detail my creditors are informed of this claim."

February 10, 1801, T. L. Ogden and Gouverneur Morris, the latter holding all the right which Robert Morris had in the year 1797 or subsequently under this transaction, made a conveyance to the purchasers or lenders, it being in controversy which they were. By these deeds all the entanglements of buyers from Robert Morris with his affairs

[1] Callender, Prospect before Us, 21.

were dissolved.[1] We have not been able to learn certainly whether it was in connection with this transaction or another that Gouverneur Morris obtained for Mrs. Morris from the Holland Company an annuity of $1,500 per annum. The statement which is made about it is that it was her dower right which had not been cancelled in some of the transactions.[2]

When Robert Morris came out of prison he went to live with his wife, in the home which she was enabled to provide by means of this annuity. It was in Twelfth Street, between Market and Chestnut. There he ended his days.[3]

January 14, 1803, Gouverneur Morris wrote in his diary that Robert Morris, in the last summer, "came to me lean, low-spirited, and as poor as a commission of bankruptcy can make a man whose effects will, it is said, not pay a shilling in the pound. Indeed, the assignees will not take the trouble of looking after them. I sent him home fat, sleek, in good spirits, and possessed of the means of living comfortably the rest of his days." [4]

Robert Morris died May 8, 1806. He was buried behind Christ Church, on Second Street, Philadelphia. The entrance to the vault is enclosed in an old-fashioned rectangular brick enclosure, with a slab lying horizontally upon it. The inscription on it reads: "The family vault of William White and Robert Morris. The latter, who was Financier of the United States during the Revolution, died the 8th of May, 1806, aged 73 years." Probably when he was buried there the vault was in the grass of the churchyard, with the blue sky and the bright sun above, even though there was a city about. Now the whole churchyard is covered with a brick pavement, and a school-

1 O'Reilly, 148.

2 Amer. Review, vi. 79; Penn. Mag. ii. 180. Cf. page 296.

3 Simpson, 713.

4 Morris's Morris, ii. 432.

room addition to the church has been built at the height of the second story above the grave. His resting-place is now, therefore, a damp and dark corner.

Sullivan wrote of him: "In his person (as now recollected) he was of nearly six feet in stature; of large, full, well-formed, vigorous frame; with clear, smooth, florid complexion. His loose, gray hair was unpowdered; his eyes were gray, of middle size, and uncommonly brilliant. He wore, as was common at that day, a full suit of broadcloth of the same color, and of light mixture. His manners were gracious and simple, and free from the formality which generally prevails. He was very affable, and mingled in common conversation, even with the young."[1] Hart says that he was a patron of the arts.[2] There are four portraits of him, one of which was engraved for the ten-dollar silver certificates of 1880.

Morris was rather a modern than an eighteenth-century man. John Adams said that he was a "frank, generous, and manly mortal."[3] He was energetic, enterprising, and sanguine. If he had lived in our day, it would have suited him far better than the time in which he lived. His portraits show that he had a sanguine temperament, and could sleep well even under heavy anxieties and responsibilities. In all his public career, and in the best part of his life, we find him constantly tugging against the sluggish habits of his contemporaries, and the slow and shiftless methods which then prevailed. Evidently his habit was to take the best and most hopeful view of things, and this led him sometimes to put a better face on them to other people than the facts would strictly warrant. He had the speculator's zeal, and the enthusiasm of an enterprising man to fire others with his own faith in what he had undertaken.

[1] Sullivan, Public Men, 141.
[2] Penn. Mag. ii. 182.
[3] Adams, ix. 609.

This sometimes makes him appear plausible and disingenuous. He showed this as much when these enterprises were in the discharge of public duty as when they were private. This gave people occasion sometimes to charge that he had misled them ; and we can often see now, when we read what he wrote, that he went beyond the facts.

In following his career we have repeatedly noticed that he entered upon a new undertaking with fire and enthusiasm, but seemed to tire of it later. The greatest virtue of that period was fortitude. By force of that virtue a man could bear up and persist against the disappointments, delays, shiftlessness, and negligence which were universal. It was this virtue which made George Washington great. Franklin and Hamilton also possessed it in a less degree. Morris did not possess it. He broke impatiently with the bonds he could not endure.

He had seven children, — five boys and two girls. Three boys and two girls survived him.

When Lafayette visited Philadelphia in 1824, the first private call which he made in that city was on Mrs. Morris. She died January 16, 1827.[1]

In the spring of 1801 sales of Morris's lands in eastern Pennsylvania were being made under execution.[2]

July 28, 1801, a commission in bankruptcy was issued against him in the eastern district of Pennsylvania, under the Act of Congress of April 4, 1800. Debts were proved to the amount of three million dollars. The Commissioners in bankruptcy assigned the assets to the assignees of the creditors. No action was taken until 1825, when Henry Morris, son of Robert, petitioned the district court to supersede the commission in bankruptcy, on the ground that Morris was dead and his estate was being wasted. In 1830 this petition was granted without opposition. After

[1] Penn. Mag. ii. 182.

[2] Wallace, Circ. Ct. Rep. 118.

due proceedings, land in Schuylkill County was sold to satisfy a judgment obtained in 1797, by Joshua Bond. In 1836 and 1838 attempts were made to revoke the supersedeas of the commission in bankruptcy, but without success.[1]

Robert Morris made a will June 13, 1804, by which he left all his property to his wife. She made a will, October 22, 1824, by which she left all her property to her daughter, Mary Nixon. The latter died September 11, 1852, having left all her property by will to her four daughters. June 13, 1853, the heirs of Robert Morris united in a deed to Robert Paschall. January 31, 1854, he conveyed it all to John Moss.[2]

Only two thirds of the six million acres which it was at first intended to put into the North American Company were transferred to the trustees. The best lands, being those in Pennsylvania, were kept out of it. Therefore only 22,365 shares were issued, of which each partner had one third. May 28, 1796, as above stated, Morris and Nicholson bought Greenleaf's interest, or made a contract to do so. Greenleaf was to keep the shares until they were paid for, and also the cross notes and indorsements which the other two gave him. The three had agreed to guarantee six per cent dividends on the stock, and had put one third of the shares issued in pledge to secure this guarantee.

September 30, 1796, Greenleaf created the "381 Trust" by transferring to George Simpson as trustee the shares and notes of the other two held by him. Morris and Nicholson paid the guaranteed dividend for two years.[3]

October 23, 1807, the shares which had been deposited to establish the guarantee were sold at seven cents each,

[1] Crabbe, 72.

[2] Pamphlet in the possession of the Pennsylvania Historical Society.

[3] Wright's Rep. vii. 23; P. F. Smith's Rep. x. 250.

and bought in by the managers. In 1856 the trustees of the North American Company held $92,071.87 to distribute. The auditor of this account made a report upon the distribution which was proposed, from which an appeal was taken. In 1862 the Supreme Court decided that the guarantee of the dividends was enduring, and barred out the Morris and Nicholson interest from any share in the amount.[1]

In 1862 and the following years, however, other proceedings took place upon the second accounting of the trustees, and in 1869 the previous decision was reversed. It was established that the shares were sold in 1807, not in order to pay dividends, but to buy in the shares and get control, and it was held that the guarantee was waived. A reconstruction of the Company took place at that time, to which the guarantors never assented.[2]

In 1870 the Auditor-general of the State issued a commission to the Deputy Escheator in the matter of an alleged escheat of the "381 Trust" and the "Aggregate Fund." The Pennsylvania Company for the Assurance of Lives applied for an injunction against the Escheator, that Company being the trustee of the money which was on hand for somebody, if it could be found out to whom it properly belonged. It was claimed by the State as the property of persons unknown for seven years or more. January 14, 1871, the Supreme Court in banc made the injunction perpetual, on the ground that the property was not a waif or stray, but in the hands of a trustee until the question of its ownership should be properly decided.[3]

An Auditor's report of 1880, on the administration of this estate, says that litigation in the affairs of the North American Land Company has been phenomenal. The

[1] Wright's Rep. vii. 23.

[2] P. F. Smith's, Rep. x. 247.

[3] Ibid. xiv. 195.

counsel for the Morris and Nicholson interests have pursued the funds for twenty-five years, seeking to obtain them from the trustees of the North American Company, the "381 Trust," and the "Aggregate Fund." After all counsel fees and expenses, the amount available for division to the Morris interest was $9,692.49.

LIST OF AUTHORITIES.

[*Full titles of books referred to in this volume, in the alphabetical order of the short designations by which they have been cited.*]

Account. Account of Robert Morris's Property, without titlepage or date, but apparently printed in connection with the legal proceedings of 1860.

Adams. Works of John Adams, with a Life and Notes by Charles Francis Adams. Boston, 1856.

Adams's Letters to his Wife. Letters of John Adams, Addressed to his Wife. Edited by C. F. Adams. Boston, 1841.

Almon. The Remembrancer; or, Impartial Repository of Public Events. J. Almon, London, Period of the Revolution.

Amer. Arch. American Archives, published by M. St. C. Clarke and Peter Force. 4th and 5th series. 9 vols. Washington, 1837–1853.

Amer. Reg. The American Register; or, General Repository of History, Politics, and Science. 1806–1812.

Amer. Rev. The American Review. A Whig Journal of Politics, Literature, Art, and Science. New York. From 1845.

Anburey. Journal d'un Voyage fait dans l'intérieur de l'Amérique septentrionale traduit de l'Anglais. [By Thomas Anburey.] Paris, 1793.

Anonym. Biog. of 1841. A Life of Robert Morris, the great Financier. With an engraving and description of the celebrated house partly erected in Chestnut Street, between 7th and 8th, south side. 1841.

Arnold's Court-Martial. Proceedings of a General Court-Martial for the Trial of Major-General Arnold. Privately printed. New York, 1865.

Balch's Français, etc. Les Français en Amérique pendant la Guerre de l'Indépendance des Etats Unis. 1773-1783. Par Thomas Balch. Paris, 1872.

Bancroft. Bancroft's History of the United States. Boston, 1874.

Bayley. The National Loans of the United States from July 4, 1776, to June 30, 1880. By R. A. Bayley, Treasury Department. 10th Census. Washington, 1882.

Belknap Papers. Collections of the Massachusetts Historical Society. Sixth series, vol. ix. 1891.

Biddle. Autobiography of Charles Biddle. Edited by J. S. Biddle. Privately printed. Philadelphia, 1883.

Blackman. History of Susquehanna County, Pennsylvania. By Emily C. Blackman. Philadelphia, 1873.

Bland Papers. The Bland Papers, being a selection from the MSS. of Col. Theodoric Bland, Jr. Edited by C. Campbell. Petersburg, Va., 1840.

Boogher. Boogher's Repository. Edited by H. W. Smith. Philadelphia, 1883.

Breck. Historical Sketch of Continental Paper Money. By Samuel Breck. Philadelphia, 1863.

Brissot. Nouveau Voyage dans les Etats Unis de l'Amérique septentrionale en 1788. Par J. P. Brissot [de Warville]. Paris, 1791.

Call. Reports of Cases Argued and Adjudged in the Court of Appeals of Virginia. By Daniel Call. Richmond, 1823.

Callender's History. A History of the United States for 1796. By J. T. Callender. Philadelphia, 1797.

Callender's Letters. Letters to Alexander Hamilton, King of the Feds. New York. Printed for the Hamilton Club. 1866.

Callender's Prospect. The Prospect before Us. By J. T. Callender. Richmond, 1890.

Canadian Archives. Report on Canadian Archives. 1890. By Douglas Brymner. Ottawa, 1891.

Carey's Debates. Debates and Proceedings of the General Assembly of Pennsylvania on the Memorials, Praying a Repeal or Suspension of the Law Annulling the Charter of the Bank. Edited by Matthew Carey. Philadelphia, 1786.

Chalmers' Opinions. Opinions on Interesting Subjects of Public Law and Commercial Policy arising from American Independence. By George Chalmers. London, 1784.

Chalmers' Revolt. An Introduction to the History of the Revolt of the American Colonies. By George Chalmers. Boston, 1845.

Chastellux. Travels in North America in the Years 1780, 1781, and 1782, by the Marquis de Chastellux. Translated from the French. London, 1787.

Cheetham's Narrative. A Narrative of the Suppression by Colonel Burr of the History of the Administration of John Adams, late President of the United States, written by John Wood. [By James Cheetham.] New York, 1802.

Circourt. Histoire de l'Action Commune de la France et de l'Amérique pour l'Indépendance des Etats Unis par George Bancroft; traduit et annoté par le Comte de Circourt. Paris, 1876.

The Civil War in America. The History of the Civil War in America, from 1775–1777. By an Officer of the Army. London, 1780.

Coll. State Papers. A Collection of State Papers relative to the First Acknowledgment of the Sovereignty of the United States of America and the Reception of their Minister Plenipotentiary by their High Mightinesses, the States-General of the United Netherlands, at the Hague. 1782.

Crabbe. Reports of Cases Argued and Adjudged in the District Court of the United States for the Eastern District of Pennsylvania. By William H. Crabbe. Philadelphia, 1853.

Custis. Recollections and Private Memoirs of Washington. By G. W. P. Custis. New York, 1860.

Cutler's Cutler. Life, Journals, and Correspondence of the Rev. Manasseh Cutler. Edited by W. P. and J. P. Cutler. Cincinnati, 1888.

Dallas. Reports of Cases Ruled and Adjudged in the Courts of Pennsylvania before and since the Revolution. By A. J. Dallas. Philadelphia, 1806.

Delaplaine. Delaplaine's Repository of the Lives and Portraits of Distinguished Americans. Philadelphia, 1818.

Deane's Address. An Address to the Free and Independent Citizens of the United States of North America. By Silas Deane. Hartford, 1784.

Deane's Narrative. In the Volume of Papers published for the Seventy-Six Society. Philadelphia, 1855.

Deane Papers. Papers in relation to the Case of Silas Deane. Printed for the Seventy-Six Society. Philadelphia, 1855.

Dialogue, etc. A Dialogue between a Southern Delegate and his Spouse, on his Return from the Grand Continental Congress. By Mary V. V. 1774.

Diary of the Rev. Diary of the American Revolution. By Frank Moore. New York, 1860.

Dip. Corr. Rev. The Diplomatic Correspondence of the American Revolution. Edited by Jared Sparks. Boston and New York, 1829.

Dip. Corr. U. S. The Diplomatic Correspondence of the United States, 1783–1789. [Edited by Jared Sparks.] Boston and New York. 1832, 1833.

Doc. Hist. N. Y. The Documentary History of the State of New York, Arranged under the Direction of C. Morgan, Secretary of State. By E. B. O'Callaghan. Albany, 1850.

Durand. New Materials for the History of the American Revolution. By John Durand. New York, 1889.

Elliot's Debates. The Debates in the Several State Conventions on the Adoption of the Federal Constitution. Collected and Revised by Jonathan Elliot. Philadelphia, 1866.

Elliot's District. Historical Sketches of the Ten Mile Square. By Jonathan Elliot. Washington, 1830.

Elliot's Funding. The Funding System of the United States and Great Britain. By Jonathan Elliot. Washington, Blair and Rives, 1845. 28th Congress, 1st Session, Executive Documents, Vol. II.

Ellis and Evans. History of Lancaster County, Pennsylvania. By F. Ellis and S. Evans. Philadelphia, 1883.

Findley. History of the Insurrection in the Four Western Counties of Pennsylvania in the Year 1794. By William Findley. Philadelphia, 1796.

Ford's Pamphlets. Pamphlets on the Constitution of the United States, Published during its Discussion by the People. 1787 and 1788. Edited with Notes and a Bibliography by P. L. Ford. Brooklyn, 1888.

Fox's Adventures. The Adventures of Ebenezer Fox in the Revolutionary War. Boston, 1838.

Franklin. The Works of Benjamin Franklin. By Jared Sparks. Boston, 1836.

Franklin in France. Franklin in France. By E. E. Hale and E. E. Hale, Jr. Boston, 1887.

Friendly Address. A Friendly Address to all Reasonable Americans on the Subject of our Political Confusions. [By Dr. Cooper.] New York, 1774.

Futhey and Cope. History of Chester County, Pennsylvania. By J. S. Futhey and Gilbert Cope. Philadelphia, 1881.

Gallatin's Writings. The Writings of Albert Gallatin. Edited by Henry Adams. Philadelphia, 1879.

Galloway's Exam. The Examination of Joseph Galloway, Esq., by a Committee of the House of Commons. Edited by Thomas Balch, Philadelphia. Printed for the Seventy-Six Society. 1855.

George III. The Correspondence of King George the Third with Lord North from 1768 to 1783. Edited by W. B. Donne. London, 1867.

Gibbes. Documentary History of the American Revolution, consisting of Letters and Papers relating to the Contest for Liberty, chiefly in South Carolina. 1776–1782. By R. W. Gibbes. New York, 1857.

Gordon. History of the Rise, Progress, and Establishment of Independence by the United States. By William Gordon. London, 1788.

Gouge. A Short History of Paper Money and Banking in the United States. By William M. Gouge. New York, 1835.

Graydon. Memoirs of his own Time, with Reminiscences of the Men and Events of the Revolution. By Alexander Graydon. Edited by J. S. Littell. Philadelphia, 1846. [First published in 1811.]

Greene against Bancroft. Nathaniel Greene: An Examination of some Statements concerning Major-General Greene, in the Ninth Volume of Bancroft's History of the United States. By G. W. Greene. Boston, 1866.

Hamilton. Alexander Hamilton. By W. G. Sumner. Makers of America Series. New York, 1890.

Hamilton's Republic. History of the Republic of the United States of America, as traced in the Writings of Alexander Hamilton and his Contemporaries. By J. C. Hamilton. New York, 1858.

Hamilton's Works. The Works of Alexander Hamilton. Edited by H. C. Lodge. New York, 1885.

Hazard's Annals. Annals of Philadelphia and Pennsylvania in the Olden Time. By W. P. Hazard. Philadelphia, 1879. [The 3d Volume of Watson's Annals.]

Hazard's Register. The Register of Pennsylvania. Edited by Samuel Hazard, from 1828. Philadelphia.

Heath's Memoirs. Memoirs of Major-General Heath. By himself. Boston, 1798.

Hinman. A Historical Collection from Official Records, Files, etc., of the Part sustained by Connecticut during the War of the Revolution. Compiled by Royal R. Hinman. Hartford, 1842.

Homes. Description and Analysis of the Remarkable Collection of Unpublished Manuscripts of Robert Morris. By H. A. Homes. Albany, 1876.

Hopkinson. Hopkinson's Judgments, in the Supplement to the Reports of Cases Adjudged in the District of South Carolina. By the Hon. Thomas Bee. Philadelphia, 1810.

Hough. Proceedings of a Convention of Delegates from several of the New England States, held at Boston, August 3-9, 1780. Edited by F. B. Hough. Albany, 1867.

Hutchinson's Letters. The Letters of Governor Hutchinson and Lieutenant-Governor Oliver, printed at Boston, and Remarks thereon, with the Assembly's Address and the Proceedings of the Lords Committee of Council, together with the Substance of Mr. Wedderburn's Speech. London, 1774.

Impartial History. An Impartial History of the War in America, between Great Britain and her Colonies, from its Commencement to the End of the Year 1779. London, 1780.

The Independent Gazetteer, or the Chronicle of Freedom. Philadelphia.

Jay's Jay. The Life of John Jay. By William Jay. New York, 1833.

Jefferson. The Writings of Thomas Jefferson. Edited by H. A. Washington. Washington, 1854.

Johnson's Greene. Sketches of the Life and Correspondence of Nathaniel Greene. By William Johnson. Charleston, 1822.

Johnston's Jay. Correspondence and Public Papers of John Jay. Edited by H. T. Johnston. New York, 1890.

Jones's Letters. Letters of Joseph Jones, of Virginia. Department of State, Washington. 1889.

Jones's New York. History of New York during the Revolutionary War. By Thomas Jones. Edited by E. F. De Lancey. Printed for the New York Historical Society. 1879.

Journ. Cong. Journals of Congress from Folwell's Press. Philadelphia, 1800.

Journal of the General Assembly of the Colony of New York, 1691-1743. New York, 1766.

Journal of the Legislative Council of the Colony of New York, 1743-1775. Albany, 1861.

Kalb. The Life of John Kalb. By F. Kapp. New York, 1884.

Laurens's Corr. In Materials for History, which see.

Leake's Lamb. Memoir of the Life and Times of General John Lamb. By Isaac Q. Leake. Albany, 1850.

Lee's A. Lee. Life of Arthur Lee. By R. H. Lee. Boston, 1829.

Lee's R. H. Lee. Life of Richard Henry Lee. By R. H. Lee. Philadelphia, 1825.

Lee on the Friendly Address. Strictures on a Pamphlet entitled "A Friendly Address to All Reasonable Americans, on the Subject of our Political Confusion," addressed to the People of America. [By Gen. Chas. Lee.] Philadelphia, 1774.

Lee Papers. Collections of the New York Historical Society, 1871–1874.

Letter to Lord G. Germain. A Letter to Lord George Germain. London, 1776.

Letters to R. Morris. In the Collections of the New York Historical Society for 1878.

Letters to Washington. Correspondence of the Revolution. Edited by Jared Sparks. Boston, 1853.

Lewis. A History of the Bank of North America. By Lawrence Lewis. Philadelphia, 1882.

Liancourt. Voyage dans les Etats Unis d'Amérique fait en 1795–1797. Par la Rochefoucauld-Liancourt. Paris, 1799.

Livingston and Smith. Laws of New York, 1752–1762. Edited by William Livingston and William Smith. New York, 1762.

Lloyd's Debates. Proceedings and Debates of the General Assembly of Pennsylvania, taken in Shorthand by Thomas Lloyd. 1787.

Lomenie. Beaumarchais et son Temps. Par Louis de Lomenie. Paris, 1873.

Lossing's Hist. Rec. The American Historical Record and Repertory of Notes and Queries. Edited by B. J. Lossing. Philadelphia, 1873.

Macaulay's Chatham. The Earl of Chatham. By Lord Macaulay. London, 1890.

Maclay. Journal of William Maclay. Edited by E. S. Maclay. Second Edition. New York, 1890.

Madison Papers. The Papers of James Madison. Edited by H. D. Gilpin. Washington, 1840.

Madison's Writings. Letters and other Writings of James Madison. Philadelphia, 1865.

Mag. Amer. Hist. The Magazine of American History. New York. From 1877.

Marshall's Diary. Extracts from the Diary of Christopher Marshall, kept in Philadelphia and Lancaster during the American Revolution, 1774–1781. Edited by William Duane. Albany, 1877.

Marshall's Washington. The Life of George Washington. By John Marshall. Philadelphia, 1805.

The Massachusetts Historical Society Collections.

Mass. Journ. The Journals of each Provincial Congress of Massachusetts in 1774 and 1775, and of the Committee of Safety. Boston, 1838.

Mass. Papers. Papers relating to Public Events in Massachusetts preceding the American Revolution. Printed for the Seventy-Six Society. Philadelphia, 1856.

Materials for History. By Frank Moore. Printed for the Zenger Club. New York, 1861.

McMaster and Stone. Pennsylvania and the Federal Constitution. By J. B. McMaster and F. D. Stone. Published by the Pennsylvania Historical Society. 1888.

Mease's Life of Morris. In the Portfolio, vol. xxix. 177, Hazard's Register, ii. 234, and the American Edition of the Edinburgh Encyclopedia, Philadelphia, 1832.

Morris's Morris. The Diary and Letters of Gouverneur Morris. Edited by A. C. Morris. New York, 1888.

N. Hamp. Prov. Papers. Documents and Records relating to the Province of New Hampshire, 1692 to 1722. Manchester, 1869.

Nassau la Teck. Brieven over de Noord Americaansche Onlusten, door Yonkheer Lodewijk Theodorus Grave van Nassau la Teck. Utrecht, 1777.

New Haven Historical Society Papers.

N. J. Corr. Selections from the Correspondence of the Executive of New Jersey, from 1776 to 1786. Newark, 1848.

N. J. Council of Safety. Minutes of the Council of Safety of the State of New Jersey. Jersey City, 1872.

N. J. Prov. Cong. Minutes of the Provincial Congress and the Committee of Safety of the State of New Jersey. Trenton, 1879.

N. Y. Journ. Journals of the Provincial Congress, Provincial Convention, Committee of Safety, and Council of Safety of the State of New York. Albany, 1842.

North Am. Co. Observations on the North American Land Company, lately Instituted in Philadelphia, to which are added Remarks on American Lands in General, in two Letters from Robert G. Harper, Esq., to a Gentleman in Philadelphia. [R. Morris.] London, 1796.

Nourse. Twentieth Congress, First Session, State Papers, No. 107.

Obras de Florida Blanca. Ed. Ferrer del Rio. Madrid, 1867. Biblioteca de Autores Españoles.

Onderdonk, Suffolk, and Kings. Revolutionary Incidents of Suffolk and Kings Counties. By H. Onderdonk. New York, 1849.

Onderdonk, Queens. Documents and Letters intended to illustrate the Revolutionary Incidents of Queens County. By H. Onderdonk. New York, 1846.

O'Reilly. Sketches of Rochester. By H. O'Reilly. Rochester, 1838.

Paine's Works. The Political Writings of Thomas Paine. Boston, 1859.

Paris Papers; or, Mr. Silas Deane's Late Intercepted Letters to his Brother and other Intimate Friends in America. New York.

Parliam. Hist. The Parliamentary History of England from the Earliest Period to the Year 1803. London, 1814.

Paul Jones. Memoirs of Paul Jones. [Mackenzie.] London, 1843.

Pellew's Jay. John Jay. By George Pellew. Boston, 1890.

Pennsylvania Archives. Philadelphia, 1854. Second Series. Harrisburg, 1876.

Penn. Col. Rec. Minutes of the Supreme Executive Council of Pennsylvania. Harrisburg, 1852.

Pennsylvania Historical Society Collections. Vol. I. Philadelphia, 1853.

Penn. Journ. Journals of the House of Representatives of the Commonwealth of Pennsylvania, beginning the 28th day of November, 1776, and ending the 2d day of October, 1781, with the Proceedings of the several Committees and Conventions before and at the Commencement of the American Revolution. Philadelphia, 1782.

The Pennsylvania Magazine of History and Biography.

The Pennsylvania Packet.

Penn. Papers. Letters and Papers relating chiefly to the Provincial History of Pennsylvania, with some Notice of the Writers. [Thomas Balch.] Philadelphia, 1855.

P. and G. Purchase. The History of the Pioneer Settlement of Phelps and Gorham's Purchase and Morris's Reserve. By O. Turner. Rochester, 1851.

Phillips. Historical Sketches of American Paper Currency. By Henry Phillips, Jr. Roxbury, Mass., 1866.

Pickering's Pickering. Life of Timothy Pickering. By O. Pickering and C. W. Upham. Boston, 1867–1873.

Pinkerton. A General Collection of the Best and most Entertaining Voyages and Travels in all Parts of the World. By John Pinkerton. Arthur Young in France, in Vol. IV.

Pownall, Admin. The Administration of the Colonies. By Thomas Pownall. London, 1766.

Pownall, Memoir. A Memorial most humbly Addressed to the Sovereigns of Europe, on the Present State of Affairs between the Old and New World. [Thomas Pownall.] London, 1780.

Prior Documents. A Collection of Papers relative to the Dispute between Great Britain and America. London, 1775.

Reed's Reed. Life and Correspondence of Joseph Reed. By William B. Reed. Philadelphia, 1847.

Report of 1785. A Statement of the Accounts of the United States during the Administration of the Superintendent of Finance, from February 20, 1781, to November 1, 1784. Philadelphia, 1785.

Report of 1790. Statements of the Receipts and Expenditures of Public Moneys during the Administration of the Finances by Robert Morris, Esquire, late Superintendent, with other Extracts and Accounts from the Public Records made out by the Register of the Treasury [Joseph Nourse] by Direction of the Committee of the House of Representatives, appointed by an Order of the House on the 19th of March, 1790, upon the Memorial of the late Superintendent of Finance. This Report is reprinted in the Bankers' Magazine, vol. xiv. p. 577.

Report of 1801. Report of the Committee appointed to inquire into the Expenditure of Money made by the Commissioners of the City of Washington, February 27, 1801.

Report of 1804. Message from the President of the United States, transmitting a Report of the Surveyor of the Public Buildings at the City of Washington, February 22, 1804.

R. I. Coll. Rec. Records of the Colony of Rhode Island and the Providence Plantations in New England. Edited by J. R. Bartlett. Providence, 1862.

Rogers's Smith. An Inquiry into the Nature and Causes of the Wealth of Nations. By Adam Smith. Edited by J. E. Thorold Rogers. Oxford, 1880.

Sabine. Loyalists of the American Revolution. By Lorenzo Sabine. Boston, 1864.

St. Clair Papers. The St. Clair Papers. Edited by William H. Smith. Cincinnati, 1882.

Schwab. History of the New York Property Tax. By J. C. Schwab. Baltimore, 1890.

Secret Journ. The Secret Journals of Acts and Proceedings of Congress, 1775–1788.

Sheffield. Observations on the Commerce of the American States. By John, Lord Sheffield. London, 1784.

Simpson. The Lives of Eminent Philadelphians. By Henry Simpson. Philadelphia, 1859. The Life of Robert Morris is by Brotherhead.

Smith's Curiosities. American Historical and Literary Curiosities. By J. J. Smith and J. F. Watson. Two Series. 1860 and 1861.

South Carolina Historical Society Collections. Charleston, 1857.

Sparks's Morris. The Life of Gouverneur Morris, with Selections from his Correspondence and Miscellaneous Papers. By Jared Sparks. Boston, 1832.

Staples. Rhode Island in the Continental Congress, 1765–1790. By W. R. Staples. Edited by R. A. Guild. Providence, 1870.

State Dep. MSS. The Manuscripts in the State Department about Robert Morris are No. 137, three volumes and an Appendix.

Steuart. An Inquiry into the Principles of Political Economy, being an Essay on the Science of Domestic Policy in Free Nations. By Sir James Steuart. London, 1767. Written in 1760.

Steuben. The Life of Frederick William von Steuben, by F. Kapp. New York, 1859.

Stevens. B. F. Stevens's Facsimiles of Manuscripts in European Archives relating to America, 1773–1783. To Subscribers. London.

Stille's Dickinson. The Life and Times of John Dickinson. By C. J. Stille. Philadelphia, 1891.

Sullivan. The Public Men of the Revolution. By W. Sullivan. Philadelphia, 1847.

Thomson Papers. The Papers of Charles Thomson, in the Collection of the New York Historical Society for 1878.

Treaties and Conventions concluded between the United States of America and other Powers since July 4, 1776. Washington, 1873.

Trumbull. Autobiography, Reminiscences, and Letters of John Trumbull from 1756 to 1841. New York, 1841.

Turner. Pioneer History of the Holland Purchase of Western New York. By O. Turner. Buffalo, 1850.

De Vayrac. Etat Présent de l'Espagne. Par Jean de Vayrac. Amsterdam, 1719.

Va. Papers. Calendar of Virginia State Papers and other Manuscripts preserved in the Capitol at Richmond. Richmond, 1875–1885.

Vernon. The Diary of Thomas Vernon, 1776. Rhode Island Historical Tracts, No. 13. Edited by Sidney S. Rider. Providence, 1881.

Votes and Proc. Votes and Proceedings of the House of Representatives of the Province of Pennsylvania, 1767–1776.

Van Schaack's Van Schaack. The Life of Peter Van Schaack, by his son, H. C. Van Schaack. New York, 1842.

Wallace. Reports of Cases Adjudged in the Circuit Court of the United States for the Third Circuit. Philadelphia, 1838.

Waln. Biography of the Signers of the Declaration of Independence. By John Sanderson. Philadelphia, 1823. Vol. V., the Life of Robert Morris, was written by Robert Waln, Jr. See Mass. Hist. Soc. Proceedings for 1876–77, p. 393.

Walpole's George III. Memoirs of the Reign of King George the Third. By Horace Walpole. Edited by Sir Denis le Marchant. Philadelphia, 1845.

Walpole's Last Journ. Journal of the Reign of King George the Third from 1771 to 1783, by Horace Walpole, edited by Dr. Doran. London, 1859.

Washington. The Writings of George Washington. By Jared Sparks. Boston, 1837.

Washington's Va. Cases. Reports of Cases Argued and Determined in the Court of Appeals of Virginia. By Bushrod Washington. Philadelphia, 1823.

Webster's Essays. Political Essays on the Nature and Operation of Money, Public Finances, and other Subjects. By Pelatiah Webster. Philadelphia, 1791.

Wells's S. Adams. The Life and Public Services of Samuel Adams. By William V. Wells. Boston, 1865.

Westcott. The Historic Mansions and Buildings of Philadelphia. By Thompson Westcott. Philadelphia, 1877.

Wilkinson's Memoirs. Memoirs of my own Time. By Gen. James Wilkinson. Philadelphia, 1816.

Wood. Personal Recollections of the Stage. By William B. Wood. Philadelphia, 1855.

Woodbury's Rep. 27th Congress, 3d Session, Senate Documents, vol. iv. no. 229.

Wright. The American Negotiator; or, The Various Currencies of the British Colonies in America. By J. Wright. London, 1765.

Yeates. Reports of Cases Adjudged in the Supreme Court of Pennsylvania. By the Honorable Jasper Yeates. Philadelphia, 1818.

INDEX.

ACCOUNTABILITY, i. 6, 7; ii. 105, 106, 110, 214.
Accounts, lack of, i. 285. Publication of, i. 287. Of the Financier, i. 267; ii. 116, 126-131; table, ii. 130, 208–211, 233, 241. Of the Committee of Commerce, i. 206, 209, 214, 223-225, 229; ii. 210, 216–220. Of the Agent of Pennsylvania, ii. 205–207, 262.
Act, of March 18, 1780 (on currency), i. 85, 286, 298, 307. Of April 18, 1783 (revenue project), ii. 66, 101, 193, 195. Of April 26, 1784 (regulation of commerce), ii. 194. The English Navigation, i. 110, 114. The American Navigation, ii. 193, 198–203. The English Restraining, i. 114, 115, 125.
Adams, John, i. 25, 87–91, 105, 176, 181, 186, 188, 194, 222, 250, 252, 274; ii. 13, 112, 117, 122, 130, 225, 237, 271, 273, 291. And the Lees, i. 177. His memorial, i. 253, 300. He helps Morris, ii. 114, 116, 132.
Adams, Sam., i. 261, 262, 266.
Administration, inefficient, i. 164, 170, 245, 289, 306; ii. 79, 144, 179.
Adventurers, i. 157, 176.
Agio, ii. 112.
Agitation, pre-Revolutionary, i. 110.
Aggregate Fund, ii. 285, 292, 304, 305.
Aid, sanguine hopes of, i. 287; ii. 103.
Alexander, Wm., ii. 169, 170, 173, 174, 282.
Allegiance, i. 208, 235.
"Alliance," the, ii. 226.
Alma, ii. 260.
Ambassador, the English, i. 164, 183.
"America," the, i. 277; ii. 88, 226.
American Almanac, i. 98.
American character, i. 210, 217.
American history, i. 235.
American Register, ii. 250.
Ames, F., ii. 244.
"Amphitrite," the, i. 165, 171, 174.
Amsterdam, i. 187, 248; ii. 5, 33.
Anarchy, i. 306.
Anburey, T., ii. 144.
Annapolis, ii. 235.
"Anticipations," i. 42, 272, 273, 286; ii. 24, 31, 62, 75, 100, 104, 105, 108, 125, 128, 130, 131, 149, 151.
Appleton, N., ii. 48.
Appleton's Encyclopædia, ii. 162.
Appointments, i. 265, 266.
Appreciation of currency, i. 83, 282, 283; ii. 17, 128.
Arms, scarce or abundant, i. 106, 107, 142. Levied on, ii. 118.
Army, the, committee from, ii. 89. Debt to, i. 272. Description of, i. 306. Disbandment of, ii. 102, 111. Disintegrating, i. 204. Discontent of, i. 303. Distress of, ii. 21, 51, 75, 102, 109. Pay of, i. 301, 303, 305; ii. 63, 75, 91, 101, 104, 105. Mutiny in, i. 272; ii. 75, 90, 103, 113, 235. Unpopular, i. 154; ii. 183. Useless, ii. 59. And the public creditors, ii. 99, 103. The French, supplies for, i. 295, 296, 304.
Arnold, B., i. 146, 233; ii. 223.
Association, the American, i. 23, 104, 108, 115, 142, 188. Articles of, i. 112.
Assumption, ii. 80, 122, 244, 245, 256.
Asylum Company, ii. 263.
Auctions, i. 77.
Avon, ii. 254.
Azores, ii. 223.

BACHE, R., ii. 30.
Bahamas, ii. 1, 14.
Baldwin, J., i. 51.
Baltimore, Congress at, i. 169, 199, 200.
Bancroft, Dr., i. 160.
Bancroft, G., i. 245; ii. 34.
Bank, ii. 21. Proposed in New Hampshire, ii. 30. Of Amsterdam, ii. 112. Of North America, i. 275; ii. 23–35, 157, 158, 164, 178, 183–192, 276. Of Pennsylvania, ii. 22–24, 29, 287. First, of the United States, ii. 261. Second, of the United States, ii. 191, 227.
Bankers of the United States, i. 168, 177, 256, 281, 282; ii. 16, 28.
Banking, ii. 185–189.

Bank-notes, ii. 22, 24, 34, 35, 152, 153, 155, 157, 178. Private, ii. 159. *Versus* State paper, ii. 191.
Bankruptcy, national, i. 87.
Barclay, i. 187; ii. 60.
Barney, Capt., ii. 14.
Bayard, i. 93.
Beall, S., ii. 166.
Beall, T., ii. 245.
Beaumarchais, i. 158, 160-221, *see* Hortales.
Beckwith, ii. 245.
Begging, i. 293, 294; ii. 9, 12, 49, 91, 111.
Bell, Wm., ii. 270.
Berkeley, Dr., i. 119.
Biddle, Chas., i. 97, 120; ii. 135.
Biddle, Jas., ii. 270.
Biddle, N., ii. 173.
Big Tree, ii. 261.
Bill-kiting, i. 282–284; ii. 74, 95, 114, 115.
Bills of credit, i. 18, 20, 21, 22, 26, *see* Currency *and* Paper money.
Bills of exchange, i. 43, 194, 304; ii. 31, 126, 159. Antedated, ii. 8. For Beaumarchais, i. 178; ii. 6, 90. On Congress, i. 295. On the Envoys, i. 173, 216, 247–257, 280–282, 287, 295, 299, 300; ii. 3, 4, 8, 11, 13, 16, 22, 23, 29, 53, 55, 57, 82, 109. For the French army, i. 304; ii. 41. Without funds, i. 249, 252, 296; ii. 7. For Gen. Lee, i. 203–205. On Philadelphia, ii. 152. Protested, ii. 90, 114, 115, 117, 184, 277. On the "Pump," i. 216, 281. On Willink, ii. 113-117, 184. Paid twice, ii. 8.
Bingham, Wm., ii. 17.
Black pins, ii. 136.
Bland, T., ii. 95, 97.
Blankets, i. 106, 127. Impressed, i. 144, 145.
Blockade, i. 169, 170, 240.
Blodgett, ii. 246.
Bolivar, ii. 260.
Bond, J., ii. 303.
Bonvouloir, i. 157.
Bounty, i. 204, 289.
Borrowing provisions of the French, i. 148, 152; ii. 141. Usurious, ii. 114.
Boston, broadside, i. 73. Meetings at, i. 74, 75. Distress at, i. 61, 75, 77, 84.
Braxton, C., i. 129; ii. 166–168.
Brest, ii. 223.
Bristol, i. 3.
Broglie, Prince de, ii. 223.
Bronson, i. 31, 98.
Brown, J., i. 211.
Brown, T., ii. 237.
Bryan, G., i. 147.
Bryan, S., ii. 215.
Budget, ii. 123.
Buenos Ayres, i. 250.
Bull, Col., i. 51.
Bunker Hill, i. 16.
Burnet, Col., ii. 82, 98.
Burr, A., ii. 293.
Butler of S. C., ii. 232.
Butler, J., ii. 257.

CADIZ, i. 250; ii. 4.
Cadwallader, J., i. 199, 230.
Caisse d'Escompte, ii. 112.
Callender, T., ii. 189, 229, 249, 272, 298.
Canada, expedition, i. 107, 194. Plan to reduce, i. 184. Effect of conquest of, i. 156.
Canandaigua, ii. 260, 261.
Canaseraga Creek, ii. 254.
Cannon, i. 206.
Capital, ii. 180, 191.
Capital of the United States, *see* Federal City.
Capitol, ii. 246, 249.
Carey, J., ii. 294.
Carey, M., ii. 190.
Carleton, Sir Guy, i. 107; ii. 156, 277.
Carlisle, Lord, i. 226.
Carmichael, i. 221.
Carrington, E., i. 152; ii. 85, 201.
Carroll, C., ii. 231.
Casenove, ii. 283, 299.
Cash notes, ii. 152.
Castorland, ii. 264.
Cattle, i. 242, 243, 245.
Census, i. 6, 13.
"Centinel," ii. 211, 215–218, 272.
Certificates, i. 272, 273, 279, 286, 287, 304; ii. 20, *see* Loan-office.
Chalmers, G., i. 124.
Chargé, the Prussian, ii. 50.
Charles II., i. 15; ii. 267.
Charleston, ii. 21, 22, *see* Refugees.
Chastellux, Marquis de, i. 78, 240, 303; ii. 222, 274. His translator, i. 79, 231; ii. 150, 163, 223, 275.
Chaumont, Le Ray de, i. 87, 162, 183.
Chesapeake, i. 240.
Chevaux de frise, i. 145.
China, ii. 162, 277.
Choiseul, Marquis de, i. 156.
Church, J. B., ii. 258, 280, 285, 286, 288.
"Cibelle," the, i. 298.
Civil servants, i. 276.
Claiborne, Major, i. 150, 151, 155; ii. 84.
Clark, Lt.-Gov., i. 20.
Clark, D., ii. 52.
Classes, ii. 180.
Clay, H., ii. 198.
Clinton, G., i. 100; ii. 140.
Clinton, Sir H., i. 305.
Clipping, ii. 44, 45.
Cloth, impressed, i. 147, 272.
Cockades of paper money, i. 95.

Coercion of workmen, i. 142.
Coinage, ii. 42–47.
College, the, at Providence, i. 46.
Colonial system, i. 104, 109, 254.
Colony, German, ii. 261. French, ii. 264. Of Unitarians, ii. 264.
Commerce, freedom of, ii. 87. Protection of, ii. 87. Regulation of, ii. 64, 193, 194, 201. State of, ii. 87. As engine, i. 103–132, 159, 198, 200, 201; ii. 72. For supply, i. 103–132, 159, 161, 162, 167, 189, 190, 192, 193, 224, 277. *See* Trade.
Commercial relations, i. 265. Transactions, i. 103, 131; ii. 212, 214–218.
Commissioners, *see* Envoys.
Committees, i. 122.
Committee tyranny, i. 230.
Commonwealth, i. 12.
Commutation of supplies, i. 239.
Compact, the social, i. 88.
Compensation, i. 117–119.
Concord, i. 107.
Confederation, the, i. 93; ii. 64, 194.
Confiscation, i. 8, 28.
Congress, of 1774, i. 15. Continental, i. 25, 28, 41, 93, 198, 199, 202, 210, 258, 260; ii. 95; journal of the, i. 223; factions in, i. 71, 175, 177, 210, 218, 220, 248, 258; ii. 99. The Stamp Act, 14, 108.
Connecticut, i. 18, 19, 29, 31, 39, 40, 127.
Consideration, i. 256.
Constable, Wm., ii. 232, 258.
Constitution, State, ii. 182. The, of 1787, ii. 204, 215, 216. The English, i. 8.
"Conti," i. 43.
Contractors, i. 143; ii. 63, 153–155.
Contracts, i. 237, 288; ii. 61–63, 83, 153, 174, 210, 213.
Convention, Commercial, i. 93; ii. 192–201. Constitutional, i. 93; ii. 192, 200, 203, 249. Price, i. 25, 26, 52–61, 76, 84, 93, 134, 137. At Boston, i. 92. At Concord, i. 74, 75. At East Greenwich, i. 75. At Hartford, i. 53, 76, 84; ii. 64. At New Haven, i. 65, 66, 76. At Philadelphia, i. 84, 137. At Providence, i. 55. At Springfield, i. 60. At Yorktown, i. 59, 129.
Convoy, i. 240; ii. 87.
Conyngham, i. 177.
Cooper, Dr., i. 119, 307.
Co-operation, i. 260, 307.
Cornell, E., ii. 62.
Cornering, i. 231.
Cornwallis, Lord, i. 305, 306, 307.
Correspondence interrupted, i. 165, 169, 202, 203.
Corunna, ii. 14.
Cosby, Gov., i. 19.
Counterfeiting, i. 68, 69, 98; ii. 154, 156.
Coxe, Tench, ii. 200, 241.
Cranch, ii. 281, 284, 287.
Credit, i. 172, 199, 248, 249, 252, 268, 269, 272, 278, 284, 285, 288; ii. 5, 6, 7, 22, 24, 26, 27, 31, 48, 58, 62, 65, 96, 97, 98, 113, 117, 125, 134, 140, 153, 157, 183, 252, 273, 298.
"Crisis," the, i. 30.
Crisis, commercial, ii. 277, 278, 281.
Croghan, ii. 264.
Crooked Lake, ii. 259.
Cruisers, i. 167; ii. 274.
Currency, of Maryland, i. 2, 43. Of Massachusetts, i. 45; ii. 256. Of New York, i. 47. Of Pennsylvania, i. 237, 271, 282, 283; ii. 24; Council to rate, i. 236. Of Rhode Island, i. 46; rate in silver, i. 45, 46. Of the Revolution, ii. 39. Of the States, i. 45. Continental, i. 26, 28, 31, 35, 37, 38–99, 173, 189, 194, 211, 239, 242, 269, 273, 275; ii. 21, 163, 164, 166, 272; amount of, i. 97; derision of, 95; evils of, 78, 80; funded, 98.
Currency doctrines, i. 39, 41–44, 70, 79, 80, 81–83, 88; ii. 24, 26, 188, *see* Paper-money, Bills of credit.
Currency and taxes, i. 14, 88, 97.
Currency legislation, i. 236.
Cushing, Thos., i. 65.
Custis, G., ii. 268, 291.
Cutler, Manasseh, ii. 176, 227.

DALLAS, A. J., ii. 164.
Davies, Col., i. 149, 151, 152, 241, 243, 244; ii. 79.
Dawson, H., i. 20.
Deane, Silas, i. 43, 159–166, 170–186, 193, 207, 212, 213, 217–224, 232–234, 237, 247; ii. 21, 53, 99, 163, 211, 219.
Deane, Simeon, i. 129, 215.
Debt, public, i. 44, 47, 234, 268, 273, 275, 276, 279; ii. 20, 48, 121, 123. Floating, i. 263; ii. 128, 129.
Debts, i. 118.
Decimals, ii. 123.
Defencelessness, i. 106, 107.
De Grasse, i. 303.
DeLancey, Gov., i. 20.
DeLancey, S., i. 93.
Delap, i. 160.
"Delaware," the, i. 207.
Delay, i. 261.
De Noailles, ii. 263.
Denunciations, i. 143.
Depravity, i. 143.
Depreciation, i. 30, 42, 43, 47, 48, 62, 65–96, 180, 200, 203, 228, 231; ii. 25, 106, 163–168, 218–220. Scale of, i. 91, 98, 238; ii. 167, 168. And taxation, i. 79–82, 83, 88, 95; ii. 76.
Deserters, i. 191.

Despatch vessels, i. 176, 193, 199.
Despatches, the stolen, i. 176, 223.
Despondency, i. 258, 259.
D'Estaing, i. 184.
De Veyrac, ii. 38.
Dexter, S., i. 5.
Diary of a French officer, i. 306. Of De Broglie, ii. 223. Of Maclay, ii. 230. Of G. Morris, ii. 300. Of Washington, ii. 203.
Dickinson, J., i. 194; ii. 72, 200.
Dickinson, P., i. 62; ii. 237, 246.
Dictation, ii. 69.
Dictator, i. 297.
Dinner invitation, ii. 222.
Disaffection, i. 203, 228.
Discord, i. 110, 113, 115, 116, 125, 210, *see* Union.
Discount, ii. 32, 35, 114, 158, 164.
Distress, i. 153, 275, 293, 295; ii. 135–148, 179, 180, 181, 195.
Dodging, ii. 259.
Dollar, ii. 36–39, 42, 46, 63.
Dolly, J., ii. 17.
Doniol, i. 177, 185.
Dorchester, Lord, *see* Carleton.
Drafted men, i. 207.
Drayton, W. H., i. 115, 123.
Duane, J., i. 121.
DuBois, A., ii. 44.
Dublin, ii. 278.
Dubourg, Dr., i. 157, 158, 159, 161, 177.
Du Coudray, i. 159, 174.
Dudley, B., ii. 3, 43, 45, 157.
Duer, W., ii. 278.
Dumas, i. 105, 219, 235.
Duponceau, i. 210.
Duportail, i. 209.

Economy, ii. 145.
Ekfield, J., ii. 43.
Eliot, J., i. 61, 84.
Ellery, W., i. 51.
Elliott, A., i. 226.
Elmer, Dr., ii. 232.
Ely, J., ii. 287.
Embargo, i. 92, 132–140, 231, 237, 271, 272; ii. 33, 140, 163, 275.
England, i. 249, 259. King of, *see* George III. Sincerity of, doubted, i. 309; ii. 102.
Engrossing, i. 26, 50, 53, 54, 56–63, 70, 73–75, 77, 134, 228, 231.
Enlistments, short, i. 203. Difficulty of, ii. 135.
Envoys in France, i. 30, 37, 67, 164, 167–171, 173, 176, 185, 186, 202. Quarrels of the, i. 180–186. Salary of the, i. 187. Paid by France, i. 254.
Erie, ii. 255.
Erie Canal, ii. 268.
Escheat, ii. 304.
Exchange, foreign, i. 301, 304; ii. 28, 36, 113, 173. Loss on, i. 304; ii. 16, 41. Pounds sterling in, ii. 47.
Exchequer bills, i. 42, 47.
Excise, i. 13, 19, 21, 23; ii. 174, 233.
Executive, single, i. 202, 203, 260, 261; ii. 213. Independence of the, i. 267.
Expedients, ii. 31.
Expenses of the Colonies, i. 25. Of the United States, i. 31.
Exports, i. 109, 116.
Extortion, i. 143.

Facilities, ii. 170, 173.
Factory materials impressed, i. 146.
Fairmount Park, ii. 227.
"Farmer," the, i. 225.
Farmers-general, i. 164, 166, 170; ii. 168–171.
Farmers' Loan and Trust Co., ii. 262.
Fauches, J., ii. 269.
Fauchet, J., ii. 165, 270.
Favouritism, ii. 74.
Federal City, ii. 121, 175, 228, 230, 235–250, 281, 284.
Finance, public, i. 5; and politics, ii. 79.
Finances of the Revolution, i. 5, 30, 67, 184, 260, 263. State of the, ii. 68, 195.
Findley, W., ii. 191.
Fines, i. 191. Militia, i. 23, 26, 31, 33.
Firewood impressed, i. 145.
Fitzpatrick, i. 126.
Fitzsimmons, T., ii. 166, 251, 252, 262, 289, 292, 293, 294, 296.
"Flammand," the, i. 173.
Flax seed, i. 128.
Fleet, the French, i. 90, 166, 245, 300. The plate, i. 249.
Florence, i. 185.
Florida, i. 250, 310.
Florida Blanca, i. 249, 254; ii. 10.
Flour, i. 229, 230, 239, 241, 242, 244, 278, 304, 308; ii. 3, 16, 163, 274.
Forced circulation, i. 45–99, 236, 237, 269; repealed, 238, 269.
Forced sale, i. 139.
Fort Wilson, i. 232.
Fortifications, i. 194.
Fox, Ebenezer, ii. 135.
Fox, Edward, ii. 247.
France, i. 37. Aid from, unacknowledged, i. 170, 174, 175, 198, 222; ii. 94; acknowledged, i. 200, 248, 275, 288, 291, 293, 294, 299; refused, ii. 49, 56, 89. Alliance with, i. 27, 87, 90, 105, 156, 164, 178, 193, 249. Alliance, who beneficiary of the, i. 91, 297. Complaints by, i. 298. Contract to repay, ii. 49, 56, 57, 91. Dependence on, i. 252, 258, 259, 306; ii. 6, 9, 51, 57, 58, 90, 127, *see* Beg-

ging. Distress in, i. 159. Eager for peace, i. 260. Expenditures in, ii. 215. Finances of, i. 27, 296; ii. 111, 134. King of, *see* Louis XVI. Loans by, i. 158, 167, 170, 171, 178, 291–296, 297; ii. 6, 50, 56, 59, 91, 92, 100, 101, 103, 111. Loan guaranteed by, ii. 8, 57, 130.
Francis, Tench, i. 43.
Francey, i. 178.
Franklin, B., i. 4, 27, 43, 67, 80, 89, 105, 156–259, 292–300; ii. 13, 48–122, 136, 180, 226, 302. Daughter of, ii. 136. Izard and, i. 184. A. Lee and, i. 185. Morris and, i. 213. Recall of, i. 186, 187. Sole minister, i. 184.
Franklin, W. T., ii. 256.
Frauds, i. 130; ii. 108.
Frederick II., ii. 50.
"Freeman's Journal," ii. 96.
Frigates, i. 199, 207. For Spain, i. 255.
Fund, ii. 24.

GADSDEN, i. 115, 223.
Gage, Gen., 106, 107.
Gain, thirst for, ii. 137.
Gallatin, A., ii. 77.
Galloway, J., ii. 144, 146, 228.
Gates, Gen., i. 96, 194, 209.
Gaunt, J. M., ii. 245.
Gautier, A., i. 49.
Genesee Land Co., ii. 253.
Genesee River, ii. 244, 256.
Genesee Trust, ii. 293.
Geneva, N. Y., ii. 255.
Geneva, Switzerland, ii. 221.
Genoa, i. 252.
Geography, ii. 199.
George III., i. 94, 133, 233, 258; ii. 134.
Georgetown, ii. 235, 242.
Georgia, i. 120.
Gerard de Rayneval, i. 8, 162, 169, 221; ii. 144.
Germain, Lord G., ii. 155.
Germantown, i. 232.
Gibeonite office, ii. 48.
Gibraltar, i. 250, 255; ii. 2.
Gillon, Com., i. 298, 300; ii. 9, 12–15, 88.
Gillon, Mrs., ii. 15.
Glover, Col., ii. 139.
Gold, ii. 142.
Goodhugh, ii. 238.
Goodrich, C., ii. 283.
Gorham, N., ii. 253–260, 268.
Gouge, Wm., ii. 34.
Government, the Federal, i. 169, 258. To be grand, ii. 123.
Grain sold, i. 243.
Grand, i. 219, 281; ii. 14, 40, 90, 109–115, *see* Bankers.
Graydon, A., i. 232; ii. 136.
Grayson, Col., ii. 96, 138.
Greene, Gen., i. 43, 67; ii. 66, 81, 83, 84, 86, 147, 152.
Greenleaf, J., ii. 246–249, 252, 264, 281, 283, 284, 295, 304.
Greenway, R., i. 2.
Griffin, ii. 173.
Grimaldi, i. 158.
Gunpowder, i. 6, 107, 122, 125–128.
Gunsmiths, i. 142.

HALF johannes, i. 199.
Half-pay, ii. 69.
Halifax, i. 184.
Hall, ii. 83.
Hamilton, A., i. 29, 42, 83, 93, 99, 259, 260, 261, 274, 289; ii. 21, 24, 25, 38, 66–79, 96, 98, 146, 148, 154–156, 180, 185, 193, 200, 209, 231, 242, 244, 258, 280, 283–286, 288, 302.
Hare, Col., i. 51.
Harper, R. G., ii. 265.
Harriott, T., i. 49.
Harrisburg, ii. 231, 238.
Harrison, Geo., ii. 295.
Harrison, Gov., ii. 83, 140.
Harrison, Jr., & Co., ii. 163.
Havana, i. 254; ii. 2–5, 274.
Hazard, ii. 232.
Head of Elk, i. 302–305.
Hendricks, Col., i. 152, 241.
Henry MSS., ii. 252.
Heyster, Gen., ii. 232.
Higby, ii. 281, 293.
Higginson, Sam., ii. 121.
"Hills," the, ii. 227, 270, 285–288.
Hodge, i. 183.
Holker, i. 229, 230, 231, 304; ii. 42, 163, 165, 168, 278.
Holland Company, ii. 260, 261–263, 293, 300.
Holland, loans in, i. 185, 248–252, 291–293, 297, 300; ii. 8, 12, 49, 57, 58, 66, 90, 111–114, 117. Purchases in, i. 298, *see* Gillon. Trade with, i. 124, 125, 129.
Hollingsworth, i. 2; ii. 293.
Hoops, A., ii. 254.
Hopkins, Capt., i. 206.
Hopkins, S., i. 60.
Hopkinson, F., i. 236.
Horse teams, i. 141.
Horses imported, i. 122. Impressed, i. 148, 151, 152. Cost of, i. 149.
Hortaler & Co., i. 158, 163, 178, 198.
Hospital service, i. 150, 244, 277.
Hospital supplies impressed, i. 150. Wasted, i. 244.
Howe, Gen., i. 194, 203, 211.
Howe, Lord, i. 194.
Howell, ii. 67, 121.
Hudson River, i. 133.

Hughes, J., i. 4.
Hughes of N. C., ii. 120.
Hynson, i. 176.

ILLINOIS and Wabash Co., ii. 251.
Impost, the, i. 274, 285; ii. 48, 54, 57, 97, 121, 192, 196, 198.
Impressment, i. 141–155, 242, 244, 287, 289; ii. 62, 85, 138. Abuse of, i. 146, 147. Effects of, i. 154. Evils of, i. 148, 149. Exemption from, i. 145, 147.
Indents, ii. 123.
Independence, i. 115, 156, 164, 172, 191–197, 210, 211, 219, 254, 260, 267, 285, 307; ii. 112, 117, 136.
"Independent Gazetteer," ii. 217.
Indian title, ii. 260.
Indian treaty, ii. 260, 261.
Indians, ii. 120, 254, 262.
Inexperience, i. 274; ii. 148.
Inglis, ii. 162.
Ink, invisible, i. 163.
Instructions, i. 191.
Interdependence of the colonies, i. 133, 135, 137, 138.
Interest, bills for, i. 167, 173, 247, *see* Bills on the Envoys. Exports for, i. 252.
Intrigues, French, i. 156, 164.
Invoice, i. 171, 172; ii. 109.
Ireland, i. 3.
Iron, i. 106.
Irregularities, i. 242, 244.
Island money, i. 94, 97.
Izard, R., i. 123, 168, 181–187, 213; ii. 232.

JACKSON, Major, i. 298, 300; ii. 12.
Jamaica, ii. 1.
James, R., ii. 292.
Jay, J., i. 21, 164, 166, 171, 227, 233, 250, 254–256; ii. 2, 7, 9, 11, 48, 111, 112, 222.
Jay, Mrs., i. 259, 262; ii. 221, 222.
Jealousy, colonial and State, i. 117, 123, 133; ii. 85, 196, *see* Independence.
Jefferson, T., i. 14, 78, 95, 164, 258, 293; ii. 118, 140, 171, 225, 231, 242, 259, 264.
Johnson of Conn., i. 119; ii. 240.
Johnson, W., i. 305; ii. 81–83.
Johnston, H. T., i. 215.
Jones, Paul, ii. 226–227.
Juniata, ii. 239.
"Junius," ii. 96.
Jurisdiction over water, ii. 193, 197, 201, 202.

KALB, Gen., i. 94, 156, 174; ii. 145.
"King Cong." i. 210.
Kingston, N. Y., ii. 235.
Knox, Gen., ii. 174.

LABOUR, reward of, ii. 71, 180.
Labourers, scarcity of, i. 83; ii. 137, 144.
Lace, ii. 136.
Lafayette, Gen., i. 151, 152; ii. 302.
Lafayette, Marchioness, etc., ii. 23.
"Lafayette," the, i. 298, 300; ii. 15, 61, 94.
"La Gloire," ii. 223.
Lancaster, Penn., i. 211.
Land, i. 80, 218; ii. 121, 190, 233, 251–270. Value of, ii. 265–268.
Landais, Capt., ii. 226.
Langdon, ii. 232.
Laurens, H., i. 185, 222, 225, 247, 250–253, 294, 297.
Laurens, J., i. 130, 171, 186, 259, 294, 295, 297, 298–301, 308; ii. 2, 5, 14, 28, 82, 88.
Law, Mr., ii. 246, 247, 289.
Lawful money, ii. 37.
Lawlessness, ii. 182.
Lawrence, Mrs. J., i. 50.
Lawyers, ii. 180.
Lead, i. 106.
Leaven of Deane and Lee, ii. 99.
Le Couteulx, i. 281; ii. 114, 115, 169, *see* Bankers.
Lee, A., i. 158–169, 174, 175, 177, 180, 181, 183, 185–187, 198, 218, 219, 222, 223, 232, 292; ii. 53, 96, 97, 109, 124, 157, 209, 226.
Lee, Chas., i. 193, 194, 197, 198, 199, 203, 204, 259.
Lee, H., ii. 295.
Lee, R. H., i. 15, 52, 62, 78, 79, 240; ii. 196, 204.
Lee, W., i. 168, 174, 181, 182, 213, 214, 252, 253, 292; ii. 122, 271, 272.
Legal tender, *see* Forced circulation.
Leipsic, ii. 221.
L'Enfant, ii. 228, 229.
Le Normand, ii. 169.
Letter in dictionary, i. 219.
Letters, the Hutchinson, i. 109. The intercepted, i. 233.
Lexington, i. 106.
Liancourt, Duc de, ii. 176, 246, 257, 263, 278.
Liberty, i. 88, 144; ii. 121. Civil, i. 8. Nightmare of, i. 37.
License to export, ii. 125, 126, 128. At Yorktown, i. 309; ii. 52, 85, 86, 128. To transport, i. 135.
"L'Indien," i. 298; ii. 226.
List, the grand, i. 13, 18.
Liverpool, i. 1, 2, 3.
Livingston, Catherine, ii. 221.
Livingston, R., i. 125, 234, 306.
Livingston, Wm., i. 148.
Livingston, Mrs., ii. 180.
Livingston, Walter, ii. 124.

Loan, foreign, i. 83, 84, 164, 168, 169, 172, 173, 253, 270, 281, 288; ii. 195. From the French military chest, i. 303, 307, 308. Public, i. 216; ii. 130. *See* Holland.
Loan office, i. 7, 86; ii. 119. Certificates, i. 68, 81, 83, 91, 102, 288; ii. 53, 54, 96, 105, 231, 232.
Lollar, ii. 190.
London, ii. 278.
"Long Bobs," ii. 151.
Losses, i. 130.
Lossing, B., ii. 229, 278, 287.
Lottery, i. 100–102; ii. 88, 111, 114, 246.
Louis XVI., i. 158, 231, 248, 251, 293, 295, 298; ii. 8, 35, 50, 165, 225–227.
Louisiana, ii. 251.
Lovell, J., i. 66.
Lowell, ii. 224.
"Lucius," ii. 96.
Luxembourg, Prince of, i. 298.
Luxury, ii. 136. War on, i. 112, 129.

MACLAY, W., ii. 209, 211, 230–234, 237, 239–250, 255, 259.
Madison, J., i. 93; ii. 52, 65, 95, 96, 240, 277.
Madrid, i. 187, 250.
Magic, i. 262, 300, 305; ii. 27.
"Magicienne," the, ii. 28, 31.
Magnanimity, ii. 102.
"Magnifique," the, ii. 88, 226.
Mail, i. 289, 290.
Maine, distress in, i. 122, 133.
Malversation, i. 242, 243.
Manheim, i. 209, 211, 213, 220.
Manning, Miss, i. 294.
Marbois, i. 186; ii. 112, 225.
Marshall, C., i. 29, 69, 148; ii. 138.
Marshall, John, i. 308.
Marshall, J. M., ii. 296, 297.
Maryland, i. 43, 239. Loan by, ii. 248, 249.
Mason, i. 258.
Massachusetts, i. 5, 16, 31. Debt and taxes in, ii. 76. Land cession, ii. 253. The plan of revenue, ii. 69.
Massachusetts Historical Society, ii. 46.
Matlack, Col., i. 51.
May, W., ii. 156.
Mazzei, i. 293.
M'Clenalhan, B., ii. 22, 287.
McDougal, i. 21.
McKean, Judge, ii. 287.
Medicine, imported, i. 128, 135, 189.
Merchant, pretended, i. 158, 159–162, 174.
Merchants' Magazine, i. 98.
"Mercure," the, i. 174.
Mexico, Gulf of, i. 250; ii. 1, 2.
Mifflin, i. 224.
Miles, Col., i. 303.
Military service, ii. 148.
Militia, i. 232, 306.
Milligan, ii. 205.
Minott, ii. 244.
Mint, ii. 37, 43–47, 157.
Mississippi, the, i. 250, 255, 256; ii. 9, 11.
Mob, i. 121, 122, 230, 231; ii. 201.
Mock funeral, i. 95.
Money, i. 14. Hard, i. 98, 204, 277, 278, 301, 303. Power of hard, ii. 142, 143.
Money market, ii. 158, 276.
Monopoly, ii. 171, *see* Engrossing.
Montandoin, i. 158.
Montgomery, Gen., ii. 120.
Moody, Capt., i. 26.
Morris, Mr., i. 188.
Morris, Chas., ii. 297.
Morris, Esther, ii. 296.
Morris, Gouverneur, i. 22, 40, 233, 270; ii. 19, 24, 42, 172, 175, 185, 186, 189, 204, 257, 277, 291, 292, 295, 299, 300.
Morris, Henry, ii. 302.
Morris, Lewis, i. 208.
Morris, Maria, ii. 296.
Morris, Robert (1st), i. 1–3.
Morris, Robert (2d), supports the currency, i. 86. Unpopular in the South, i. 97; ii. 52, 60, 81–87, 108. Acts for the continent, i. 169, 199, 200. Whether a whig, i. 188; ii. 273. Charged with toryism, i. 212. Banker, i. 193, 194, 197, 204, 205, 206, 216. His opportunities of gain, i. 193, 194, 205, 206, 217, 227, 304; ii. 18, 150, 167, 275, 276. His views on independence, i. 194–197. Advances by, i. 204, 308. Considered rich, i. 208, 264. False position of, i. 205, 230, 231, 271, 282. Is offered the presidency, i. 206. Has leave of absence, i. 209, 211, 223; ii. 162. And Deane, i. 223; ii. 219. Merchant and statesman, i. 205, 230, 231. His privateers, i. 236; ii. 275. Superintendent of Finance, i. 261. His motives for accepting the office, i. 263, 264, 268, 269. His salary, i. 261. His diary, i. 263, 269, 301; ii. 55, 96, 157, 466. Conditions of accepting, i. 264–267; ii. 8. His commercial relations, i. 266, 267, 268; ii. 30. His "integrity," i. 268; ii. 95, 100, 116, 288. His energy and enterprise, i. 270. His business methods, i. 270; ii. 252, 280. His economies, i. 270, 275, 289; ii. 18, 107. Agent of Pennsylvania, i. 270, 271, 282, 283. Reorganizes the treasury, i. 270. His plans, i. 275; ii. 65. His heterogeneous tasks, i. 276, 278. Agent of the Marine, i. 277; ii. 87. His resources, i. 279, 282; ii. 82. His appeals to the States, i. 284, 287, 289; ii. 50, 58, 65, 75, 105. Calls for information, i. 285, 289. Arouses enmity,

i. 235, 289; ii. 52, 105, 120. Fruitlessness of his efforts, i. 289; ii. 52. Qualifications for Financier, i. 301. Entertains Washington, i. 303; ii. 203. And Washington, ii. 291. His art of multiplying coin, i. 305; ii. 26, 27, *see* Magic. Negotiates bills for the French, i. 304; ii. 41. Issues notes for clothing, i. 291; ii. 49, 55, 89; to pay the army, etc., i. 308; ii. 75, 83, 100, 102–109, 113, 117, 120, 128, 149–161, 170, 173, 178, 229, 275, 282–284, 290, 295, 298. His drafts, ii. 62, 153, 155, 281. Is called to account, ii. 42, 55, 105, 106, 116. His doctrine of banking, ii. 26–28. Proposes a coinage, ii. 42. Prestige of his name, ii. 53. And A. Lee, ii. 53, 54, 65. Is expected to default, ii. 55. His administration raises credit, ii. 56. Influence of his character, ii. 62, 153. His influence, i. 208; ii. 19, 121, 184, 231. His plans for revenue, ii. 69, 70. His views on the lottery, ii. 88. His overdrafts, ii. 89, 111, 112–116, 184. Describes his situation, Jan. 1781, ii. 90. His resignation, ii. 95, 96–98, 103, 110. Conditions of going on, ii. 100, 101. His motives for going on, ii. 102. Goes to Princeton, ii. 104. His Report, ii. 106. He is traduced, ii. 108, 215–218. His administration, ii. 65, 94, 117, 125–132. Sarcasm on it, ii. 112. Is indifferent to France, ii. 118. His views on the Union, ii. 120, 203, 232. His quarterly reports, ii. 125. His commercial operations, ii. 127. How he accomplished his task, ii. 130–132. His Account of his Property, ii. 162, 165, 166, 177, 218, 227, 229, 252, 257, 261, 270, 278–280, 283, 293, 298, 299. He buys an estate in England, ii. 167. His tobacco contract, ii. 168–173. An army contractor, ii. 174. Offers to farm the excise, ii. 174. His speculations in France, ii. 175. His aristocratic notions, ii. 204, 231. Is offered the Secretaryship of the treasury, ii. 204. Is indebted to the United States, ii. 218–220. Sends his sons to Europe, ii. 221. His quarrel with Marbois, ii. 225. His hospitality, ii. 224, 226. On Franklin's death, ii. 226. Is caricatured, ii. 233. Candidate for governor, ii. 233. His retrospect, ii. 218. He "must be a man or a mouse," ii. 269. His wealth, ii. 276. His account books, ii. 279. His watch, ii. 297. Was his country ungrateful, ii. 298. His death and burial-place, ii. 300. His bankruptcy, ii. 302. His will, ii. 303. His estate, ii. 304. Personal description of, ii. 222, 291. His residences, ii. 223, 227, 229, 300. Criticisms on, i. 194, 205, 208, 224, 262, 263; ii. 19–20, 52, 63, 97, 116, 121, 122, 123, 222–224, 242, 257, 292, 298, 301. His opponents, i. 215, 227, 235, 289; ii. 98, 101, 121, 131, 191. Charges against, i. 309; ii. 52, 60, 85, 96, 109, 110, 121, 209–211, 215, 216, 218. His votes, i. 216, 235–237; ii. 189, 190, 230. *See* Bill-kiting, Appreciation, Accounts.

Morris, Mrs., i. 1, 259, 262; ii. 166, 221, 224, 225, 234, 271, 291, 292, 296, 300, 302. On independence, i. 194, 206. Her shoes, ii. 225.

Morris, Robert (3d), ii. 221, 222, 293, 297.

Morris, Thomas (1st), i. 207, 212–215. His accounts, i. 214; ii. 213.

Morris, Thomas (2d), ii. 221, 260, 261, 286, 288.

Morris, William, ii. 176, 290, 291.

Morris, Deane, & Co., ii. 219.

Morris's Folly, ii. 228.

Morris's Reserve, ii. 260.

Morrisville, ii. 238.

OBLIGATIONS, neglect of, i. 172.

Office, refusing, i. 28.

Officers, pay of, i. 96, 199. Memorial of, i. 242. Sent over, i. 163, 170, 175, 217.

Ogden, S., ii. 257, 258.

Ogden, T., ii. 299.

"Olimpe," the, i. 298.

One man power, i. 262.

Orders, neglect of, i. 251.

Orne, A., i. 75.

Osgood, S., ii. 121, 124, 196, 209, 236.

Ostracism, i. 221.

Otis, H. G., i. 224.

Outlook, the, in 1781, i. 263.

Outrages, i. 26; ii. 202.

Overdraft, ii. 17, 89, 111–114, 128.

Ox teams, i. 141.

Oxford, Md., i. 1.

PACKET, the Penn., i. 79, 95, 99, 138, 222, 229, 236; ii. 26, 166.

Paine, T., i. 30, 34, 47, 93, 203, 206, 220, 222–225, 228, 233, 234, 295, 306; ii. 21, 189.

Papers, Laurens's, i. 253.

Paper-money, i. 14; ii. 182, *see* Currency, Bills of Credit.

Paper-mongering, i. 282, 283; ii. 64.

Par, ii. 37–39, 46.

Paris, i. 187.

Parliament, i. 25.

Party, ii. 35, 55, 137, 164, 205, *see* Con-

gress. The Conservative, ii. 182, 183. The Popular, ii. 183.
Paschall, R., ii. 303.
Passy, i. 182, 219.
Patriotism, ii. 137, 138.
Patterson, J., ii. 176.
Peace commission (1778), i. 215; ii. 21; (1782), ii. 110, 112.
Peace expected, i. 256, 258, 259; ii. 57. Negotiations, ii. 11. Propositions, i. 260; ii. 178.
Peddling, i. 77.
Penalties, i. 28.
Penet, i. 157, 158, 175, 293; ii. 61.
Pennell, J., ii. 212.
Penn, Gov., ii. 145, 223.
Penn, Wm., ii. 267.
Pennsylvania, i. 22, 23, 32, 33, 36. Assembly of, i. 237, 238. Constitution of 1776, i. 191. Invasion of, i. 191. Law against Morris, ii. 164. Lawful money of, ii. 164. Morris partial to, i. 271; ii. 52. Parties in, i. 91, 197, 217, 230; ii. 23, 164, 205, 215, 223. And the proprietors, ii. 267. Revolution in, i. 190, 192. Taxes in, ii. 76.
Pennsylvania Company for the Insurance of Lives, ii. 304.
Pennsylvania Historical Society, ii. 279.
Pennsylvania Property Company, ii. 176, 227, 270.
People, the, always right, i. 123. Alienated, i. 154, 239, 258.
Peters, R., i. 213, 301; ii. 96, 271.
Petersburg, i. 240.
Petersen *vs.* Willing, ii. 283.
Phelps, O., ii. 61, 253–260, 264, 266, 268.
Philadelphia, i. 187, 188. Abandoned, i. 199, 200. The Artillery Company of, i. 73. The Committee of (1779), i. 72. Character of the people of, ii. 245. Ladies of, ii. 23. Meeting at, i. 227, 228, 230, 231. Occupation of, i. 167, 209. Panic at, i. 305. Population of, ii. 144. Prison at, ii. 229, 288–292. Rental of, i. 34.
Pickering, T., i. 78, 148; ii. 84, 136, 140, 151, 153, 286.
Pillage, i. 148.
Pilots, i. 184.
Plate, amount of, i. 99.
Pleasants, Shore, & Co., ii. 164.
Pliarne, i. 157.
Pontleroy, i. 156.
Poor, class of, ii. 78.
Popularity, i. 274.
Population of the colonies, ii. 146. Of the Mass. cession, ii. 259.
Portraits, ii. 225.
Portugal, i. 168; ii. 2.
Postage, inability to pay, i. 305; ii. 292.
Post-Office, i. 199; ii. 40, 63.
Powers, delegated, i. 261.
Pownall, T., i. 99; ii. 139.
Pre-emption line, ii. 253, 255, 256.
Price, i. 194.
Price, Dr., i. 260.
Prices, i. 137; ii. 140.
Price tariff, i. 115, 137, 228, 231, 232, *see* Conventions.
Priestley, ii. 264.
Princeton, i. 200.
Princeton College, ii. 17.
Prisoners, Burgoyne, ii. 144.
Privateering, ii. 135–139. Embargo on, i. 133, 135.
Prize cases, ii. 180.
Prize decisions, i. 236.
Proclamation, the King's, i. 114.
Proclamation money, ii. 37.
Profits of colonial trade, i. 83, 104.
Profligacy, i. 208.
Promises, i. 173, 231, 278.
Property, rights of, i. 231.
Prosperity, ii. 256, 274.
Protest, ii. 164.
Providence, i. 17.
"Providence," the, i. 144.
Provisions, i. 148, 154, 229, 241, 271; ii. 140, 141. Magazines of, i. 280.
Prune Street, *see* Philadelphia, prison at.
Pryor, Major, i. 151.
Publicity, i. 289.
Pultney, Sir Wm., ii. 256–259.
Pultney Association, ii. 267.
Punctuality, ii. 32.
Putnam, Gen., i. 51, 52, 200.

QUAKERS, i. 49, 79, 200, 278; ii. 259.
Quebec, i. 184.
Quotas, i. 40.

"RANGER," the, ii. 226.
Ratio of silver to gold, ii. 40, 47.
Rations, ii. 33, 128.
Receipt, *see* Invoice.
Receipts and expenditures, 1781, ii. 16.
Recklessness, i. 106.
Reconciliation, i. 194, 195, 212, 215, 233.
Redemption of paper, i. 83.
Reed, Jos., i. 32, 33, 70, 71, 148, 215, 220, 274; ii. 18, 21, 23, 24, 63, 97, 137, 140, 147, 184.
Reese, J., ii. 259.
Refugees, i. 278, 308; ii. 87, 263.
Remittances, i. 158–164, 167, 173, 178, 203, 247; ii. 6, 11.
Replevin, i. 147.
Report of 1785, i. 283; ii. 4, 125, 206, 208.
Report of 1790, ii. 125, 126, 149, 211.
Report, Hamilton's Mint, ii. 38, 47.
Republic, the French, ii. 165.

Republicanism, i. 262; ii. 231.
Requisitions, i. 9, 28, 32, 33, 37, 239, 272, 273, 275, 279, 280, 285; ii. 31, 52, 55, 57, 67, 104, 117, 194, 196. Excessive, ii. 67, 123.
Rescue from impressment, i. 146.
Resolutions, mock, i. 111.
Responsibility, i. 261, 266; ii. 74.
Retaliation, i. 137.
Revenue, from America, i. 15. Of New York, i. 20. Of Pennsylvania, i. 23. Plan of, ii. 69, 70. Required by the United States, ii. 66.
Review, the American, i. 2.
Revolution, crisis of the, i. 200. Enthusiasm for the, i. 211.
Rhetoric, ii. 137, 190.
Rhode Island, i. 16, 17, 36, 66. And the impost, ii. 65, 69, 97, 193, 194.
Rice exception, the, i. 113, 115.
Ridley, M., ii. 221.
Riot, i. 122, 127, 232; ii. 201, 261.
Rivers, i. 141.
Rivington, i. 233.
Robardeau, i. 227.
"Robert the Cofferer," ii. 215.
Robertson, ii. 44.
Robinson and Price, i. 48.
Rochambeau, Count de, i. 99, 303, 305.
Ross, D., ii. 60, 78.
Ross, G., ii. 220.
Ross, J., i. 183; ii. 17, 166, 218, 219, 292.
Ross, Pleasants, & Co., ii. 171.
Rubsamen, ii. 156.
Ruggles, S., i. 75.
Rum impressed, i. 244.
Rush, B., i. 52; ii. 135, 237.
Rutledge, E., i. 122.
Rutledge, J., i. 116.

SACRIFICE, equality of, ii. 73.
St. Clair Papers, i. 232.
St. Eustatius, i. 128, 129.
Salaries, i. 277; ii. 4, 40, 69, 231.
Salt, i. 50, 54, 76, 106, 126, 127, 132, 134, 136, 137, 140, 153, 203, 243; ii. 64, 201.
Salt-works, i. 207.
San Domingo, ii. 263.
Sands, Comfort, i. 128, 130; ii. 61, 62, 63, 152.
Sansom, W., ii. 228.
Sayre, i. 219.
Schuyler, Gen., i. 107, 278; ii. 20, 237.
Schwab, J. C., i. 20.
Schweighauser, i. 118.
Scott, ii. 251.
Seamen impressed, i. 144.
Searle, Col., i. 293; ii. 14.
Secrecy, need of, ii. 125. Lack of, i. 198, 220, 303.
Secret service, i. 204, 234, 301, 305.
Secret sessions, i. 223.
Sellers, N., ii. 43.
Seneca Lake, ii. 253.
Seton, W., ii. 184.
Sharp shins, ii. 45.
Sheffield, Lord, i. 100, 130; ii. 115.
Shelburne, Lord, i. 309.
Shingle, ii. 96.
Shipments, private, i. 184, 217, 218, 223, 224, 231.
Shippen, J., i. 4.
Ship timber, ii. 1.
Ships for Spain, ii. 9.
Silver, rating of, ii. 63.
Silver *vs.* gold, i. 204.
Silverware, ii. 16.
Simpson, G., ii. 303.
Simpson, H. ii. 278.
Six Nations, ii. 253.
Slave trade, i. 112.
Slaves, ii. 70.
Smilie, ii. 191.
Smith, A., i. 25, 120, 124.
Smith, R., ii. 3.
Smith, W. S., ii. 258, 284.
Social changes, ii. 180.
Social organization, ii. 145.
Soderstrom, R., ii. 258, 294.
Sodus, ii. 262.
South, weakness of the, ii. 81.
South Carolina, i. 24.
"South Carolina," the, i. 298; ii. 12, 14, 15.
Spain, appeals to, i. 168. Alliance with France. i. 250. Loans by, i. 164, 169, 249, 250, 255, 256; ii. 1, 3, 9, 11. Position of, i. 249.
Specie, ii. 170. Comes into circulation, i. 98; ii. 3, 34, 81, 178. False display of, ii. 157. Imported, i. 277, 298-300; ii. 3-5, 17, 40, 96. Loaned to New York, i. 100. Plentiful, i. 99, 100; ii. 34. Requirement, i. 42, 43. Used by the French, ii. 142, 143.
Speculations, ii. 176, 232. Commercial, i. 184, 217, 218, 223, 224, 231.
Spies, English, i. 164, 176, 177, 207, 212, 213.
Springetsbury, i. 303; ii. 227.
Stamp Act, the, i. 4.
State, growth of the American, i. 38.
States, the, accounts of, with the Union, i. 285, 286. Behaviour of, i. 273, 285, 286; ii. 51, 55, 58, 85. Borrowing by, i. 248, 252, 292; ii. 60. Committees sent to, i. 51. Debts of, ii. 122. Reply of, i. 286. Supplies by, i. 285. Small *vs.* large, ii. 204.
State rights, i. 138, 218; ii. 67, 68, 236.
Steam-engine, ii. 176.

Stedman, i. 209.
Steuart, Sir J., ii. 30.
Steuben, Gen., i. 150, 210, 211; ii. 137.
Stiegel, Baron, i. 211.
Stormont, Lord, *see* Ambassador.
Story, T., i. 158, 166, 167, 198.
Subsistence, i. 142.
Subsistence, notes, ii. 110, 152, 157.
Suffolk, Lord, i. 207.
Sullivan, Gen., i. 145, 262; ii. 254.
Sullivan, W., ii. 291.
Supineness, English, i. 209. American, i. 286.
Supplies, ii. 22, 94. Specific, i. 19, 239-246, 258, 271, 278, 280, 282-284, 296, 302, 304, 307; ii. 71, 79, 126, 206. Left in the West Indies, i. 171, 172; ii. 88. Magazines of, i. 260, 296. Monopolized, i. 171. Quality of, i. 166, 174, 175; ii. 15, 89. Sale of, ii. 89, 127.
Subsidies, *see* France, loans by. Drawn by Washington, i. 297.
Susquehanna, improvement of the, ii. 239.
Swanwick, J., ii. 44, 154, 157, 158, 162.
Swanzey, ii. 292.
Swords, silver-mounted, i. 295.

TALBOT and Allen, ii. 283, 293.
Talon, ii. 263.
Tarleton, Gen., i. 150.
"Tartar," the, i. 201.
Tax, auction, i. 20. Collectors, i. 82, 240, 241, 244, 245. Export, ii. 3, 169. Import, i. 15, 20; ii. 64, 169, 198. Income, i. 13. In kind, i. 29, 240. Land, i. 13; ii. 251. On non-associators, i. 23, 191. Old man's, i. 29. Poll, i. 12, 13, 19. Property, i. 13, 19. On rents, i. 34, 306. On sales, i. 34, 125. Sinking Fund, i. 18, 19. Stamp, i. 14, 19, 20. On Suffolk County, etc., ii. 77.
Taxes, i. 81, 92, 173, 234, 272, 274, 275, 284, 285-287; ii. 2, 18, 34, 59, 62, 66, 67, 92, 99, 101, 103, 114, 126, 129, 137, 150, 152, 154. Ability to pay, ii. 58, 71, 72, 76, 103, 137-140. Arrears of, i. 34; ii. 131. And contracts, ii. 85. Excuses for not paying, ii. 72, 75. Protective, ii. 178, 199, 230, 231. State *vs.* federal, ii. 71.
Taxation, i. 6, 11-34, 41, 56, 60, 62, 65, 72, 172, 273, 289; ii. 6, 21, 64-80, 104, 196. Dogmas of, i. 18, 29. Hardship of, i. 33. Inequality of, i. 29. And representation, i. 17. And slave-owners, i. 84. Why unproductive, i. 32.
Tea, i. 49, 50, 54, 110, 112, 115, 125, 126, 127; ii. 136.
Ten Alley, ii. 278.
Tenants, i. 236.
Tennessee Company, ii. 252.
Tenor, new, i. 85.
Terrorization, i. 120, 121, *see* Forced circulation.
Theatricals, ii. 189.
"Three-eighty-one Trust," ii. 303-305.
Tilghman, Tench, ii. 116, 158, 160, 277.
Tobacco, i. 129, 163, 165, 167, 197, 239, 309; ii. 52, 85, 86, 113-115, 128, 150, 158, 164, 166-173, 268, 276, 277.
Tom's River, i. 207.
Tools impressed, i. 151, 153.
Tories, i. 8, 26, 28, 49, 52, 62, 65, 69, 75, 79, 121, 142, 232, 235; ii. 138, 179, 189, 190.
Tower of London, i. 251, 281, 294; ii. 11.
Tracy, ii. 180.
Trade, balance of, ii. 191, 196. Colonial, i. 105. With the enemy, i. 99, 132. Good or bad, ii. 40, 74, 88. Of New York, i. 99. Notions about, i. 104, 193, 254. Protection of, i. 193. Of the United States and Great Britain, i. 130, 254. Of the United States and France, i. 235. Violating the Association, i. 120, 124, 126, 128.
Trading company, i. 207, 226.
Transportation, i. 92, 141, 142-144, 242, 243, 278, 301, 308; ii. 35, 140. Rates, i. 141.
Treasury, philosophy of a, i. 35.
Treasury, the, i. 5, 6. Board of, i. 34, 51; ii. 22, 46, 196. Book-keeping, ii. 109. Commissioners of, ii. 119. Reorganization of, ii. 123, 124. State of, i. 307. System of, ii. 107.
Trenton, i. 200; ii. 236, 250.
Troops, number of, ii. 147, 148. Quotas of, i. 190. Quality of, ii. 148.
Trout springs, ii. 227, 270.
Trumbull, Gov., i. 35.
Trumbull, J., i. 293; ii. 14.
"Trumbull," the, i. 281; ii. 3, 4.
Tryon, Gov., i. 20; ii. 146.
Turnbull, Marmie, & Co., ii. 163.
Turner, O., ii. 257.
Tuscany, i. 293.

UNION, i. 29, 41, 92, 108, 116-119, 196, 285, 286, 292; ii. 67, 70, 120, 138, 183, 194, 199, 200, 207, 244.
Unit of account, ii. 38.

VALLEY FORGE, i. 7, 209; ii. 148.
Value, i. 237.
Van Berkel, i. 253.
Varnum, J., ii. 17.
Vergennes, Count de, i. 87, 88, 91, 158, 198, 259, 295, 297-299; ii. 8, 49, 92.
Vessels impressed, i. 143-145.
Violence, i. 120.

Virginia, i. 24, 33, 36. Accounts of with the Union, ii. 79. Arms imported by, i. 175, 180. "A Farmer of," i. 79. Law on trade, ii. 201. And Maryland, ii. 192–199, 240. Papers, i. 149, 155, 240; ii. 79, 84. Taxes in, ii. 57, 78. Yazoo company, ii. 251, 259.

WADSWORTH, Col., ii. 62, 174, 232, 257, 260, 268.
Wagon service, i. 146–150.
Wagons, broken, i. 151, 153.
Walker, ii. 243.
Waln, ii. 157, 162.
"Walsingham," i. 80; ii. 25.
War, the Seven Years', i. 3; ii. 145. Of 1812, ii. 268. Commercial, i. 62, 104, 112, 130. The Board of, ii. 22, 97. Of the Revolution, to be short, i. 41; expected end of, i. 71, 258; offensive, i. 109; cost of, i. 270, 287; ii. 50, 132–134; cost of, to France, i. 295, 296; weariness of, i. 85, 148, 154, 258, 307; ii. 57; English view of the, i. 160; the strength of the United States for, ii. 145–147. Between France and England, i. 201, 207. Between England and Holland, i. 252, 253.
Ward, A., i. 261.
Wardens of Philadelphia, i. 26, 189.
"Warren," the, i. 144.
Washington, G., i. 7, 26, 36, 70, 74, 130, 133, 147, 148, 153, 200, 215, 218, 234, 239, 241, 258, 259, 266, 297, 301, 303, 305; ii. 21, 23, 99, 148, 203, 228, 221, 260, 268, 269, 291, 302. Influence on Washington City, ii. 243, 249, 250.
Washington, Mrs., ii. 234, 291.
Washington City, *see* Federal City.
Waste, i. 240–244, 275.
Watkins, ii. 252.
Wayne, Gen., i. 148.
Webb & Co., ii. 167.
Webster, D., ii. 198.
Webster, P., i. 28, 30, 42, 43, 83, 86, 98, 154, 260; ii. 139, 178, 180, 181, 191.
Weeden, i. 13.
Wentworth, P., i. 100, 207, 208, 218, 233; ii. 273.
Wertz, Major, i. 94.
Western boundary, i. 250.
Westham, i. 241.
West India planters, i. 113.
Wharton *vs.* Willing *et al.*, ii. 164.
Wheeler, S., ii. 43.
Whigism, ii. 136.
Whigs, ii. 179.
White, Bp., i. 3; ii. 297.
White, Mary, *see* Mrs. R. Morris.
White, T., i. 3; ii. 296.
White Marsh, i. 1.
Wilcox, M., ii. 44.
Wilkinson, Gen., i. 199.
William III., i. 108.
Williams *or* Williamson, C., ii. 259.
Williams, J., i. 181, 183, 185, 212; ii. 169.
Willing, C., i. 3.
Willing, T. (1st), i. 3.
Willing, T. (2d), i. 188, 211; ii. 30, 162, 219.
Willing and Morris, i. 192, 194, 205, 207, 209, 212, 215, 223, 225–227; ii. 162, 167, 184, 209, 211, 213, 218, 219, 271, 272, 275.
Willings, the, i. 3.
Willink, ii. 113, 115, 262.
Wilson, J., i. 232; ii. 96.
Wise, Sarah, i. 2.
Women in the fields, ii. 143.
Wood, ii. 176.
Woodbury, L., i. 98.
Workmen, impressed, i. 142, 151.
Wounded suffer, i. 150, 244.
Wright, ii. 37.
Wyoming, ii. 255, 263.

YELLOW fever, ii. 290.
Yorktown, Penn., i. 25, 167, 210, 215.
Yorktown, Va., i. 34, 242; ii. 31. Campaign, i. 149, 151, 153, 241, 244, 301–309; ii. 5, 94, 142, 150, 151. Forces at, i. 306, 307.
Young, Arthur, i. 27; ii. 133.
Young, C., ii. 291, 294.
Yrujo, Marquis de, ii. 286.

ZEAL, i. 300. Penalty of, i. 155, 205, 218; ii. 86.

www.ingramcontent.com/pod-product-compliance
Lightning Source LLC
LaVergne TN
LVHW050929080826
845145LV00001B/267

* 9 7 8 1 8 9 3 1 2 2 9 8 7 *